The Aftermath of Road Accidents

D1431059

Accidents on the road are so commonplace in our lives today it's easy to believe that there are plenty of support systems in place for the victims. Death and injuries on the road are construed primarily as medico-legal phenomena, reinforced both by the way accidents are described and by issues of insurance and compensation for damage and personal injury. But there are many profound psychological and social consequences that remain underestimated.

Margaret Mitchell has compiled this collection from leading researchers to examine this neglected area for the unseen victims: the families who have to cope with bereavement or a disabled relative, the driver who has killed but is medically injured.

The Aftermath of Road Accidents will be of great value to psychologists, psychiatrists and other health professionals and will serve as a useful reference for those in the legal profession, voluntary associations and those with personal experience of road accidents needing advice about where to seek further help.

Margaret Mitchell is reader in psychology at Glasgow Caledonian University and director of research at Glasgow Caledonian University Police Research Unit.

The Aftermath of Road Accidents

Psychological, social and legal consequences of an everyday trauma

Edited by Margaret Mitchell

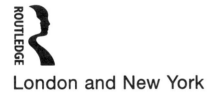

London and New York

First published 1997
by Routledge
11 New Fetter Lane, London EC4P 4EE

Simultaneously published in the USA and Canada
by Routledge
29 West 35th Street, New York, NY 10001

Typeset in Times by J&L Composition Ltd, Filey, North Yorkshire
Printed and bound in Great Britain by
Mackays of Chatham PLC, Chatham, Kent

British Library Cataloguing in Publication Data
A catalogue record for this book is available from the British Library

Library of Congress Cataloging in Publication Data
The Aftermath of road accidents: psychological, social and legal
  perspectives/edited by Margaret Mitchell.
      p.   cm.
    Includes bibliographical references and index.
    1. Traffic accidents—Great Britain—Psychological aspects.
  2. Traffic accidents—Social aspects—Great Britain.   3. Liability
  for traffic accidents—Great Britain.   I. Mitchell, Margaret, 1955–   .
  HE5614.5.G7A65   1997
  363.12'5'0941—dc20   96–8386

ISBN 0–415–13052–2 (hbk)
ISBN 0–415–13053–0 (pbk)

This is for my mother
Katharine Logan Scott Mitchell
a spirited survivor of very serious injuries
with love

Contents

Part II Legal consequences

Part III Social consequences, support and intervention

Figures

Tables

Contributors

Dr Margaret Mitchell is reader in psychology at Glasgow Caledonian University, Scotland and honorary press officer for the British Psychological Society. She is director of research at Glasgow Caledonian University Police Research Unit. Employment at the Workers' Compensation Board of British Columbia stimulated her interest in the psychological impact of sudden injury, and in the social and psychological predictors of recovery. She became interested in the psychological consequences of road accidents through her research on police officers dealing with sudden death; her research on the consequences of the Lockerbie disaster of 1988 provided her with an enduring interest in the sequelae of major life events. An active research interest within the police service is the development of professional decision making and the effect of experience, especially of traumatic incidents, on judgement.

Dr Gwen Adshead trained in forensic psychiatry at St George's Hospital, London. She became interested in post-traumatic disorders, and studied the efficacy of an intervention to reduce psychological morbidity. This was helpful when she became involved in managing the psychological sequelae of the Clapham rail disaster in 1988. She then worked as principal clinician at the Traumatic Stress Clinic at the Institute of Psychiatry, Maudsley Hospital, when it opened in 1992, producing a report about the provision of psychological support following disaster for the UK Department of Health. She currently works as a therapist with perpetrators and survivors of child abuse, and is carrying out research into childhood risk factors for PTSD.

Dr Michelle Atchison completed her training in psychiatry in 1991. She was a lecturer in psychiatry with the University of Adelaide before commencing studies for a Ph.D. Her thesis, in collaboration with Professor Alexander McFarlane, investigates the concept of acute stress disorder and its importance in the development of later psychiatric disorder, especially post traumatic stress disorder. Her other research interests include Type A behaviour and the psychological effects of morbid obesity. She is currently working in private practice with a clinical focus on survivors of trauma.

Dr Edward B. Blanchard received his Ph.D. in clinical psychology from Stanford University in 1969. He has previously held faculty positions at the University of Georgia, University of Mississippi Medical Center and University of Tennessee Center for Health Sciences. Since 1977 he has been a Professor in the Department of Psychology at the State University of New York at Albany. In 1990 he was named Distinguished Professor of Psychology. He began research on PTSD with Vietnam veterans with Dr Lawrence Kolb and the Albany VAMC. His work on road accidents started in 1990 at the Centre for Stress and Anxiety Disorders in collaboration with Dr Hickling.

Dr Jeremy Broughton is a research fellow of the Transport Research Laboratory in England. He trained as a mathematician, and has worked in the field of road safety for the last eleven years, studying statistics related to: the effects of compulsory seat belt legislation; the level of alcohol-related road accidents; long-term casualty trends; the relative accident rating of different car models; and the effects for road safety of adopting Central European Time. He was Secretary of the PROMETHEUS Safety Group and, as part of this work, carried out several studies to assess the consequences of the advanced systems currently being developed to assist car drivers.

Bridget Bryant is a medical sociologist working at the Department of Psychiatry, Oxford University. Her recent interests have been in the social and psychological factors associated with long-term outcome in patients with organic disease and with medical symptoms not explained by organic disease, and in various groups of road accident survivors. She is currently working with Dr Richard Mayou on a longitudinal study of a cohort of 1,500 road accident survivors admitted to the John Radcliffe Hospital, Oxford, over a twelve month period.

Rachel Canterbury is lecturer in psychology at the Institute of Psychiatry, University of London. She is honorary clinical psychologist at the Maudsley Hospital, London, where she works for the adult trauma service. Her research interests include the psychological impact of trauma on individuals and their families.

Giuseppe Di Stefano obtained his bachelor's degree in clinical psychology at the University of Freiburg, Switzerland. His interest in the psychological implications of diseases developed when examining coping processes in patients with rheumatic pain, after which he took part in multidisciplinary studies examining the medical, neuropsychological and psychological sequelae of whiplash injuries. He is working as clinical neuropsychologist in the Bethesda Clinic of Epilepsy and Neurorehabilitation in Tschugg (Switzerland) where he is engaged in rehabilitation work with brain injured patients, as well as clinical research.

Dr Angela Hetherington is senior lecturer in occupational psychology at Leicester Business School, De Montfort University, England. She is a member of the International Society of Traumatic Stress Studies (ISTSS), and the International Association of Trauma Counsellors. She has been a member of a number of delegations invited by the International Law Enforcement Stress Association to visit China and the Far East to discuss the management of disaster-related stress and trauma in police and the military. Her research on traffic officers within the police is described in this volume.

Dr Edward J. Hickling received his Psy.D. in clinical psychology from the University of Denver, School of Professional Psychology, in 1982. He worked as director of training and as a consultation liaison psychologist at the Veterans' Administration Medical Centre in Albany until 1987, when he left to enter full-time private practice. In addition to his practice in clinical psychology, he has taught and holds faculty appointments at several colleges and at the Albany Medical College. His earlier research on PTSD included the assessment and treatment of Vietnam veterans. Since 1990 he has completed research on road accident survivors with Dr Blanchard at the Centre for Stress and Anxiety Disorders.

Dr Michael Hobbs is a consultant psychotherapist with Oxfordshire's Mental Health Services and honorary senior clinical lecturer in psychotherapy at the Oxford University. He has worked in a consultative capacity with Oxfordshire ambulance and fire services. His clinical work with survivors of road accidents generated the interest in preventative psychological interventions which led to the research described in this volume.

Professor David J. de L. Horne is Associate Professor and Reader in Medical Psychology at the University of Melbourne. He trained in clinical psychology at the Institute of Psychiatry in London, working as clinical psychologist at Guy's Hospital, London, before moving to Australia. At the University of Melbourne he established courses in psychology for medical, dental and physiotherapy students. Professor Horne is also senior clinical psychologist at the Royal Melbourne Hospital; it is through his clinical work that he became involved in the assessment and treatment of survivors of road accidents.

Dr Glennys Howarth is lecturer in sociology at the University of Sussex. Before that she held the T.H. Marshall Research Fellowship in the Department of Sociology at the London School of Economics, where she studied the role of coroners in England in relation to sudden death. She is author of *Last Rites: The Work of the Modern Funeral Director* and is co-editor of *Mortality*, an interdisciplinary journal of death studies.

Sue Jeavons is a clinical psychologist currently working as a lecturer at La Trobe University, Bendigo, Australia, and in private practice. She obtained her clinical qualification at the University of Edinburgh and is currently completing doctoral studies at the University of Melbourne. Her interest in the area of road trauma started with work in a hospital rehabilitation unit and she has continued with research in the area. Sue Jeavons is a foundation member and past president of the Road Trauma Support Team in Bendigo.

Dr Sally Lloyd-Bostock is senior research fellow in psychology and law at the Centre for Socio-Legal Studies, Oxford University, where she is responsible for the research programme in psychology in law. She has degrees in both psychology and law from Oxford University, and is a fellow of the British Psychological Society and a fellow of Wolfson College. She has conducted extensive research into psychological aspects of civil legal disputes and legal decision making, and is a co-author of *Compensation and Support for Illness and Injury*, the major British study of compensation systems, including personal injury claims under the tort system. Her current research is on complaints to hospitals and medical negligence claims.

Dr Warren R. Loos received his Ph.D. in clinical community psychology from the University of Nebraska-Lincoln in 1988. After completing post-doctoral training in behavioural medicine, he served as staff psychologist at the Stratton VA Medical Center, Albany, New York, with clinical administrative responsibilities for the center's inpatient chemical dependency unit, and the psychiatric crisis team. Here his interest in the assessment and treatment of PTSD began. Since 1993, he has been in full-time private practice with Dr Hickling, and, in collaboration with the Centre for Stress and Anxiety Disorders, continues his interest in the research and treatment of trauma. He is Assistant Professor of Clinical Psychology at the Albany Medical School.

Professor Alexander McFarlane was appointed the Foundation Professor of Community and Rehabilitation Psychiatry at the University of Adelaide in 1990. He has conducted a series of investigations examining psychophysiological aspects of post-traumatic stress disorder, in which he has a considerable interest, and is currently conducting a study with Dr Michelle Atchison that looks at the immediate reactions to motor vehicle accidents and their role in predicting long-term psychiatric morbidity. In addition, he has an active interest in the categorisation, description and measurement of disability in both psychiatric and physical illness.

Dr Richard Mayou is clinical reader in Psychiatry at Oxford University. He is one of the three authors of the *Oxford Textbook of Psychiatry* and has had a long standing interest in psychiatric aspects of physical disorders and physical symptoms. He was founder Chairman of the Liaison Group of the Royal College of Psychiatrists. Dr Mayou's activities have included research on the psychological characteristics and quality of life in patients with myocardial infarction, heart failure and non-cardiac chest pain. He has a particular interest in the psychiatric and psychological consequences of road traffic accidents.

Alan Munro is an Inspector in Strathclyde Police, Scotland. Since 1992 he has been based at their Training Centre where he is responsible for aspects of training probationary constables, including the investigation and reporting of incidents of sudden death. He is working with Dr Mitchell on a Home Office Police Research Group project which is examining how probationary constables learn how to cope with incidents where a death has occurred.

Michael Napier is senior partner of Irwin Mitchell, Sheffield, and President of the Association of Personal Injury Lawyers. He is Visiting Professor and Chairman of the Centre of Advanced Litigation at Nottingham Law School. He is co-author with Kay Wheat of *Recovering Damages for Psychiatric Injury.*

Dr Bogdan P. Radanov is Associate Professor of Psychiatry at the University of Berne. Following studies in human medicine, he trained in psychiatry, neurology and neuropsychology at the Universities of Zurich and Berne. He has been head of the psychiatric consultation and liaison service at the University General Hospital in Berne since 1981, and deputy chairman (and head of the consultation liaison service) of the Department of Psychiatry, outpatient service, at the University of Berne since 1995. Dr Radanov also has teaching affiliations with the faculty of medicine, psychology and dentistry at the university.

Professor Derek Rutter is Professor of Health Psychology at the University of Kent at Canterbury. He has published widely on social psychological processes in health outcomes, most recently on breast cancer screening, pregnancy and motorcycling. His books include *Social psychological approaches to health* (with Lyn Quine and David Chesham, Harvester Wheatsheaf) and *Social Psychology and Health: European Perspectives* (with Lyn Quine, Avebury, 1994).

Dr Matthias Sturzenegger is Associate Professor of Neurology at the University of Berne. He studied medicine with postgraduate training in pathology, medicine, neurosurgery and neurology. For the past ten years he has been attending physician at the Department of Neurology, University of Berne. Applied Psychology, University of Kent, Canterbury.

Ann Taylor received her training in clinical psychology from the University at Albany in 1992. She has worked at the Centre for Stress and Anxiety Disorders on several projects. Her involvement with PTSD research began with an extension of the psychophysiological assessment study of Vietnam veterans. Her work with road accidents started in 1990 with the first assessment study, with her main contribution being psychophysiological assessment and data analysis.

Kay Wheat is a solicitor and a senior lecturer at Nottingham Law School, Nottingham Trent University. She is co-author with Michael Napier of *Recovering Damages for Psychiatric Injury.*

Dr Lindsay Wilson is senior lecturer at the Department of Psychology, University of Stirling, Scotland. For the past eight years he has conducted neuropsychological research on traumatic head injury with colleagues at the Institute of Neurological Sciences in Glasgow, with a primary focus on neuro-imaging. His work has been published as numerous papers and chapters. He is currently on the editorial boards of three scientific journals, including the *Journal of Neurology, Neurosurgery and Psychiatry.*

Dr James Youngjohn is a Diplomate of the American Board of Clinical Neuropsychology and the American Board of Professional Psychology. He is past director of the Neuropsychological Testing Laboratory at the National Rehabilitation Hospital in Washington, DC, as well as past director of the Neuropsychological Research for Memory Assessment Clinics, Inc. Presently he is an Adjunct Professor of Psychology at Arizona State University, where he participates in clinical training of doctoral students. He maintains an active practice in Scottsdale, Arizona. His areas of research interest and expertise include memory disorders, brain injury, chronic pain syndromes, and forensic issues.

Professor William Yule is Professor of Applied Child Psychology at the Institute of Psychiatry, University of London. He is on the board of the *International Society for Traumatic Stress Studies,* and on the editorial boards of the *Journal of Traumatic Stress* and the new electronic journal, *Traumatology.* Since 1993 he has been adviser to UNICEF on its psychological programme for war-affected children in former Yugoslavia, and is technical director of a major programme to develop services for war affected children in Mostar in Bosnia. He has developed links with researchers in countries of the former Soviet Union and is exploring how best to foster good practice there.

Acknowledgements

I would like to thank all the contributors most sincerely for their interest and enthusiasm, which endured my nagging for their contributions, my questions on details in their excellent texts, and my demands for the occasional missing reference. Hopefully, they will be well pleased with the end product. Gwen Adshead's conference in London in February 1994 'Psycho-Social Aspects of Disaster: Planning for the Future', was a major starting point for the volume. I was fortunate to meet Ed Hickling at David Horne's small working group on road accident trauma at the Conference on Applied Psychology in Madrid in July 1994. My thanks also to Ulrich Malt who, regrettably, was unable to contribute but who told me about Sandy McFarlane's new work with Michelle Atchison. The other contributors are all people whom I believe have an extremely valuable contribution to make to our understanding of this topic, and in many cases, whose work I have long known and admired. Finally, Michelle Cowan and Louise Lawson at Glasgow Caledonian University deserve many, many thanks; as do Vivien Ward, Jon Reed and Ian Critchley at Routledge.

Introduction and background

Chapter 1

Death and injury on the road

Margaret Mitchell

In January 1896 the first motorised vehicle appeared on the streets in Britain. This volume marks some of the human consequences of that technology. In August 1896 a pedestrian was killed by a car travelling at four miles an hour, so becoming the first of Britain's 430,000 road accident fatalities. Throughout this volume the continuing and extreme loss of life, and damage to peoples' lives caused by cars and other motorised traffic, is expressed in different graphic ways. Although statistics vary and are, in general, following a downward trend, every year in Britain, over three-and-a-half thousand people are killed in road accidents, and well over a quarter of a million people are injured, around 50,000 of which injuries are classified as 'serious'.

Numbers are important. To understand the human issues and the scope of the problem, I wanted to place the work reported in this volume within an informed context of statistics, and I am very grateful to Jeremy Broughton of the Transport Research Laboratory in England for his contribution. Concern expressed early in this century about the rising number of road deaths led to statistics first being collected in Britain in 1909; and this collection of data has continued in various forms since then. The numbers can be understood and categorised in many different ways: for example, by the type of vehicle, or type of injury, or the age group of the victim or accident survivor. It is evident that interventions such as better road engineering, the use of seat belts, and treating very seriously the problem of drinking and driving have had a significant positive impact.

These statistics, however, do not reflect the lifelong effects on survivors and their families in coping with orthopaedic and neurological injury, or bereavement. Some recent projects conducted by the Road Transport Laboratory do, however, address some of these issues. Nor are the statistics yet designed to reflect the psychological sequelae and damage to quality of life which can result with or without actual physical injury. One aspect of the phenomenon is quite certain, however: there are plenty of data to work with, although it is collected by different organisations and in quite different forms. Perhaps some advancement in our understanding of the magnitude of the problems associated with road accidents could be achieved simply by co-ordinating the various sources of data from, for instance, the insurance industry, police records, and hospital or GP records. Only by seeing these existing data together and articulated can we understand their implications. Dr Lindsay Wilson points to the relative difficulties of examining the neurological consequences of road accidents, due to the tradition, even in the research literature, of not categorising injuries according to cause. Nevertheless, that this present volume exists attests to the increasing interest in the damage specifically caused by road accidents, as distinct from accidents in general.

It may be that the purposes of the distinct public bodies with an interest in road accidents, and the way they collate information, have unintentionally obfuscated the seriousness of the problem. Deaths and injuries on the road primarily are construed as medical–legal phenomena, and so are embedded within medical and legal discourses. The medical discourse which considers the number and severity of *physical* injuries is reinforced by the way road accidents are accounted by government Department of Transport statistics and in police reports; and the legal discourse is reinforced by issues of insurance and compensation for damage and personal injury. The social and psychological consequences of road accidents, and the fact that the incidence and seriousness of these consequences are often underestimated, makes this an extremely important area for critical examination by psychologists.

Considering that road accidents are the source of so many deaths and so many other serious and not so serious injuries, they are treated in a very odd way. In Britain, road traffic bulletins are broadcast every morning which provide information about accidents on the main roadways, along with other information about major road repairs and other impediments on the road. The information is delivered in a bright and friendly manner, most often by a woman, and it is accompanied by cheerful music. The bulletins advise drivers to avoid particular areas because of an accident, and that emergency vehicles have been called to the scene and are blocking the road. The purpose of the bulletins is to keep traffic moving, and to prevent further accidents due to congestion. It is a strikingly odd way to present information which may represent that a person, or more than one person, may have been killed or seriously injured. A proportion of the people we hear about (represented by the accident reports) will go on to develop affective and cognitive problems associated with the accident, and may develop excessive worry about the safety of travelling in a car.

It is not frivolous, but illuminating to reflect on what we would think if some other aspect of our everyday technology caused this much harm to people: if the central heating system, for example, with which many of us heat our homes killed ten people each day (this figure is based on 1994 road fatality rates), this method of warming ourselves would be banned. To draw a closer comparison in the sphere of communication, if ten people a day were killed using the telephone (and over 500 a day had been injured), we would not use telephones. Reflect also on our reaction if we were advised on the radio about gunfights occurring at various places around the country, and we knew that every day ten people were shot and killed – of course, we simply would not tolerate it. Conceptualising the car as a potential lethal weapon is further illustrated by the annual statistics on assault on police officers in one British police force. In a period of one year, 13 per cent of the incidents of assault in which police officers were physically injured were due to a vehicle being driven at them (Mitchell 1995, unpublished report to the Home Department of the Scottish Office). Many more such incidents occur in which the officer, though not injured, is deeply shocked by a car, often a stolen vehicle, ramming the police car or being driven repeatedly at it.

That the toll of road deaths and injuries is incorporated into our day-to-day expectations makes road accidents of the greatest interest psychologically, from very many points of view. It would appear that our lives are so bound up with the motor vehicle that any resultant harm is dealt with in a way which is quite different from how we deal with other potentially destructive elements. However, the focus of this volume is not the 'psychology of the car' so to speak, rather it is on the aftermath of accidents on the road for which this extraordinary social context provides the backdrop.

In this volume, a range of perspectives is presented which will assist our thinking about the human consequences of road accidents within three interrelated domains: the psychological and psychiatric effects on the survivor; the legal context within which the physical and psychological damage caused by a road accident is organised and adjudicated; and finally, the interventions which have been attempted to manage the emotional impact of this sudden life event. Statistical and epidemiological information is provided as a background against which to understand the main theoretical models. Each contributor, where appropriate, provides a review of the relevant literature in that particular domain and within which their own research or expertise is placed. In this way, each of the areas is represented broadly and is also illustrated by contemporary work. The diversity of ways in which psychological theory and perspectives can inform an understanding of the potentially traumatic experience of a road accident, and its legal and medical sequelae, is presented.

Another important reason for this collection is the disproportionate attention (in terms of frequency) that is paid to the sequelae of larger-scale disasters, compared with the everyday trauma of a road accident. Several edited volumes are devoted to post-traumatic stress reactions, such as the *Handbook* edited by Wilson and Raphael (1993), or to conceptual and theoretical approaches to the sequelae of life events, such as Fisher and Reason (1988), or to bereavement (Dickenson and Johnson 1993; Stroebe et al. 1993). In addition, there are various volumes providing practical advice on appropriate intervention and management following various personal crises (Parry 1990), or disaster (Scott and Stradling 1992). McCann and Pearlman (1990) in their volume on adult survivors of trauma, discuss armed conflict, genocide, crime and torture as sources of trauma, but not road traffic accident. Stroebe et al.'s (1993) seminal *Handbook of Bereavement* gives no special consideration to the topic of bereavement through road traffic accident, undoubtedly reflecting the lack of published work in this area. The relative lack of attention to road accidents is thrown into further relief by the large amount of work that is valuable from both practical and theoretical perspectives on the effects on survivors of civilian disasters, such as the King's Cross Fire, the Clapham Rail Crash, and the sinking of the *Marchioness* pleasure boat. Feinstein (1993) argues that the trauma associated with more commonplace events such as road accidents is probably dismissed for no reason other than that they are relatively frequent and interest is 'dwarfed by the drama of major disasters'.

Norris (1992) surveyed the incidence of traumatic experiences in adults in four cities in the US, and concluded that the combined frequency and severity of road accident trauma made it stand out 'from the pack' of other significant stressors:

> This event was less frequent than some (robbery, tragic death) and less traumatising than some (sexual or physical assault), but when both the frequency and severity data were considered together, it emerged as perhaps the single most significant event among those studied here. At a lifetime frequency of 23% and a PTSD rate of 12% of that, this event alone would yield 28 seriously distressed persons for every 1,000 adults in the United States. This is an interesting observation given how seldom this event has been studied relative to crime, disasters and bereavement.

A road accident may indeed be a potent source of post-traumatic stress reactions, and it is a life event which shares some aspects of the shocking and the unusual and many aspects of the common and everyday. Psychological reactions to a road accident are complex (see Chapter 4 for the discussion of patterns of acute reactions by Atchison and McFarlane) and the perspectives and research presented in this volume emphasise the range of possible reactions and outcomes. Clearly not all people who have been involved in a road accident develop post-trauma symptoms, although some do. There are many other questions that can only be answered by longitudinal observation of samples of all road accident survivors. What is the incidence of post-trauma symptoms such as intrusive thoughts after a road accident? Also, why is it that some people quite simply do not develop such symptoms, while others develop chronic and disabling anxiety and phobic reactions? In examining recovery after road accident, to what degree does improvement occur spontaneously over time, with or without intervention?

The section of the book concerning psychological and psychiatric consequences begins with a review by Richard Mayou. In his contribution, he reminds us that there is still debate on the nature of post-traumatic stress disorder (PTSD) and that potential reactions to road accidents encompass a range of emotional disorders, similar to those observed in association with any physical injury or illness. Mayou, with Bridget Bryant and other colleagues at Oxford University, has studied the sequelae of road accidents for many years, conducting one of the few longitudinal investigations of outcome in an unselected Accident and Emergency population. New work by Michelle Atchison and Sandy McFarlane at the University of Adelaide reports on the first stage of a longitudinal analysis of a non-selected population of road accident survivors. Their findings are based on interviews with road accident survivors in hospital, and argue for the existence of quite distinct categories of acute response patterns to road accident. This requires us to question many assumptions that are explicitly stated, or are implicit in the literature on the response to significant stressors and to bereavement, and which presently guides much of our thinking in research and practice. The ability of such immediate reactions to predict longer-term outcome will be of the greatest interest to us. This contribution and others in the volume, such as by Hickling and colleagues at Albany, provide rich data on individual responses to a single stressor.

Rachel Canterbury and Bill Yule's work on post-trauma responses in children following road accident is presented within the context of other work on trauma and children, most notably Yule's research on children involved in the *Jupiter* sinking (1992). Two issues struck me as of the greatest interest. Previously and typically, children have not been asked directly about their own emotional reactions; rather, the testimony of parents and teachers has been used as an index of the child's affective state. The validity of this as a measure of disturbance may be questionable in view of the response of some parents to the researcher's request for access to the child for interview purposes. It is understandable that parents will want to protect their child from what they construe as an upsetting reminder of the incident (the interview), and some therefore did not allow access. Many aspects of this chapter are instructive, not only in terms of the likely reactions of children, but also in terms of how researchers can approach work with children. For parents to believe that interviewing children about their experiences will upset them is understandable, but that too is a subject to be studied. Much more work on children's reactions to road trauma needs to be undertaken, working sensitively with caring and protective parents.

The multiple murders at a school in Dunblane, Scotland in March 1996, in which the killing of sixteen 5 and 6 year olds and their teacher was observed by other children in the class, underlines the need to understand the potential reactions of children in this age group and to work very carefully with parents and teachers who will, themselves, be severely emotionally upset. Adshead (1994) has argued for the development of an infrastructure, based on the considerable corpus of information that we have accumulated on the impact of trauma, which can be mobilised when necessary to respond to such devastating occurrences. This issue with reference to the management of road trauma is discussed further by Adshead.

It is almost a cliché that a person who has been involved in a minor road accident, particularly one in which the car was hit from behind, wears a large white supportive neck collar. The image of a collar of this type is used in cartoons and is intended to signify a person who is claiming compensation for an injury which may be of minor severity, or indeed may be imaginary. 'Whiplash' is an injury which has for long been associated with litigious action on the part of the survivor. The exacting longitudinal investigation over a two-year period carried out by Radanov and his colleagues at the University of Berne, and reported in this volume and elsewhere, provides an informed perspective with which to understand this type of injury. The exquisite detail of the data which have been collected on each individual in this study provides a fascinating and comprehensive evaluation of the range of factors considered to be relevant to prognosis.

Lindsay Wilson at Stirling reports on the particular types of brain injury caused by the sudden breaking or stopping involved in a car accident. Modern neuro-imaging techniques allow lesions to be identified, and have improved the understanding of the neuropsychological significance of different patterns of diffuse and focal injuries. Again as a consequence of the legal context within which road accidents are understood, the issue of whether behavioural changes resulting from head injury are 'real' in the sense of organic, or whether they are 'imagined', is something which has troubled researchers and practitioners. This contribution clarifies some of the debate surrounding the reason for the apparent personality and behavioural changes which can result from road accident injury. James Youngjohn is a private practitioner working in a very different legal context from that in Britain. His contribution presents a controversial and interesting perspective on 'post-concussion syndrome' which is, again, of direct relevance to clarifying the issues of typical symptoms following head injury in a road accident and the degree to which their source can be attributed to organic pathology. Youngjohn's work supports the view that the symptoms associated with post-concussion syndrome are the consequence of seeking compensation, rather than organic damage. If this is the case, it should not be surprising that the different legal and insurance contexts influence behaviour.

My own work on recovery from physical injury specifically considered the social context of recovery, finding many explanations by treating physicians of 'slow' recovery to be in terms of seeking compensation or malingering (Mitchell 1991a). It has long been a matter of interest to me that Miller's (1961, 1966) propositions on 'compensation neurosis' have endured for well over thirty years. That the work continues to be cited is perhaps even more surprising in view of the lack of empirical evidence that accident survivors are, in general, motivated by financial gain or work avoidance (Harris et al. 1984; Mayou 1996). Dr Youngjohn's work provides a robust contribution to the debate. To some, that a person's life has become disordered following a road accident may be of more significance than the reasons for that disorder, whether they be physical, social or psychological. The legal context of road accidents and the way in which compensation is adjudicated demands such distinctions, and Youngjohn's contribution provides an apposite bridge between the section of the volume on psychological and psychiatric consequences and the next section on legal consequences.

The first contact which road accident survivors have with the legal context into which they are inevitably thrust, is their interactions with the police at the accident scene. Angela Hetherington and Alan Munro's chapter on the role of the police service *vis à vis* road accident survivors and victims' families presents interesting data from Hetherington's research on post-trauma reactions in police officers. Some of the work I have conducted with Alan Munro on how police officers manage the often competing roles at the scene of a sudden death is also reported. The appearance of the police at the scene of an accident is the start of a legal process which can be lengthy and unforgiving. Also within the context of the police service, but not reported in this volume, is work by Mitchell et al. (1996b) on scenes-of-crime officers. These are police officers or civilians who photograph an accident scene for evidential purposes. As part of interviews which we conducted on a range of aspects of their work, we asked whether there were particular images which had remained with them of the various scenes they had photographed. In the sample of 45, nine said there was nothing they could think of, but of the remaining 36, six recalled a particular fatal road accident (others recalled murder scenes, forensic work at Lockerbie and other situations which would be considered outside 'normal' experience) and were able to recall it in great detail up to ten years afterwards. Impact of Event scores were also substantially elevated. This work is mentioned here to emphasise the number of people working around road accidents who are deeply affected by them.

Kay Wheat and Michael Napier discuss the legal concepts which are relevant to claiming for psychiatric injury, and, in particular, post-traumatic stress disorder, following a road traffic accident. They emphasise that the legal requirements set down are aimed more at controlling the potential number of claims following road accidents and other traumatising incidents, than at reflecting the likelihood and incidence of psychiatric damage. This is based on the fear that, if such restrictions were not in place, the system would become overloaded with claims. This chapter also presents the many interesting common-sense and lay psychological notions regarding the conditions under which a person is likely to develop post-traumatic reactions (e.g. to do with proximity to the incident, or the relationship to a survivor or victim). These are embodied in the legal requirements which a plaintiff must satisfy in order to claim. In the same way that physical injury must be assessed and disability demonstrated, the accident survivor must also persuade that his or her emotional or cognitive difficulties are directly attributable to the accident. Napier has argued here and elsewhere that such a system can produce many more and additional difficulties for the plaintiff. This contribution and that by Sally Lloyd-Bostock point to the complexity of the process of claiming and the sheer length of time which it takes for personal injury cases to be resolved. Perceptions of the attribution of cause and blame underpins much of Lloyd-Bostock's chapter: that there is a close relationship between perceptions of fault and claiming compensation is not clear, and many other social factors and other considerations enter into decisions about whether to claim.

Throughout I have used the commonly understood term which describes the source of death and injury on the road – an 'accident'. Glennys Howarth's analysis of the discourse of the coroner's court in England forces us to question why we speak of road accidents as events to which blame (rather than cause) cannot be attributed. This is particularly surprising when a road death is caused by a drunk person driving a car, or by a person not qualified to drive. Why is it that the judicial system treats a person who kills or injures using a knife so differently, and what is the impact of this on bereaved families? Howarth makes us look at a fundamental issue which has motivated this collection: why death on the road is thought of as an accident. From her extensive research on the coroner's system, Howarth describes the surprise and anger on the part of family members who attend the coroner's court who leave feeling that no one has been made accountable for the killing. Howarth's contribution brings into sharp focus the way death on the road is socially constructed. This background explains why bereaved family members actively engage in self-help groups or in community-based volunteer groups, a subject discussed by Jeavons in the fifth section of the book on interventions and support for road accident survivors and victims' families.

Perhaps emotional reactions in survivors of road accidents are not expected to the same degree as in survivors of larger-scale civilian disasters. Mike Hobbs at Oxford, and Gwen Adshead, while she was at the Institute of Psychiatry in London, separately conducted very similar controlled trials of early intervention with an Accident and Emergency sample. Their account of the impact of such a measure is thought-provoking in terms of what therapeutic or even social function such interventions might serve. Prophylactic approaches which can be delivered simply and easily soon after the incident, if they have an impact on subsequent wellbeing, would be the preferred modality in view of the frequency of road accidents.

From the perspective of the practising clinician, the contributions by Hickling, Loos, Blanchard and Taylor from the US, and David Horne in Australia provide insight into the individual responses to road accidents and into the sorts of interventions found to be effective. The contribution by Hickling et al. is of particular interest in that it describes psychotherapeutic intervention which is 'embedded' within their large-scale longitudinal research project (the findings of which this group of researchers have published extensively). Again the detail of the case study information attests to the complexity of response. While it appears that some treatment modalities (e.g. relaxation) are of use in most instances, highly individualised responses require highly individualised treatment modalities. This model is presented, as is the psychometric data on twelve accident survivors with PTSD collected independently over the period of treatment. The case study presented by Horne provides a graphic illustration of the degree to which an accident survivor's quality of life and enjoyment of life can be severely compromised by a road accident. He proposes that the initial referral he received from the woman's general practitioner is typical of the helplessness which some general practitioners may feel when confronted with chronic psychological difficulties after a road accident. This case study also reflects the suffering of a road accident survivor for whom the simple passage of time has been ineffective in reducing her symptoms, and for whom the interventions previously offered have not been helpful.

Bridget Bryant's contribution presents the experience of the individual and the many ways in which a road accident can have far-reaching effects on the person's everyday life. Using data gathered from interviews with road accident survivors in the Oxford series (see Chapter 3), it is evident that even in cases of relatively minor physical injury a survivor can experience disruption in work, social and leisure pursuits. The serious effect that driving avoidance can have on everyday life is emphasised again, underlining the degree to which every aspect of our lives is bound up with car driving. Perhaps as a result of the failure of health services and the justice system to manage the effects of road accidents, many survivors and victims' families will join or form self-help groups. Sue Jeavons's contribution on self-help and voluntary organisations describes the development and function of one particular support group in Australia – the Road Trauma Support Team – and the function of such groups in general. In Britain and elsewhere, organisations such as CRUSE and the Victim Support Scheme assist people who have been bereaved through road accident. Within the context of the topic of this volume, some groups have road death as their specific focus: RoadPeace, Mothers Against Drunk

Drivers (MADD) and Keep Death Off the Roads. All these groups have emerged either as a consequence of personal bereavement through a road death, or through a concern about the damaging effects of cars on the environment – or both. The psychological function of such groups for the members individually and collectively is examined, as is the way in which the membership and activities of such groups or organisations can assist coping. Gwen Adshead concludes this section on interventions with the implications for the psychological care of road accident of findings from her survey of how English Health Authorities would provide psychological support in the event of civilian disaster. Typically, few accident survivors are seen by clinical psychologists and psychiatrists, and often only after their emotional difficulties have become chronic. In the main, general practitioners – who may not be well prepared to deal with psychological distress – and families provide the support for accident survivors. Finally, the disproportionate numbers of young men who are killed or very seriously injured in motorcycle accidents made me decide to include a chapter which considers not the *consequences* of road accidents but ways in which they can be prevented. Thus Derek Rutter's thoughtful work on safety on motorcycles completes the volume.

In compiling this volume, my aim was to produce an energetic collection of what researchers and practitioners wanted to say about the human consequences of road accidents. There may be other perspectives which could have been included: for example, work on the psychological sequelae of coping with the serious *physical* injuries most usually associated with road accident is lacking. Considerable research currently exists on how families look after a person who has been brain injured in an accident (e.g. McKinlay et al. 1981); similarly, any work on individual, and family, coping with facial disfigurement, limb amputation and spinal cord injury resulting from road accident is not represented. There is an implicit notion in many medical texts on physical rehabilitation that a severe injury somehow 'swamps' the psychological impact; and the rhetoric of such works includes concepts of 'adjustment' and 'motivation'. In other words, the interaction between the severity of a physical injury and psychological sequelae may be confused because of the traditional dominance in medicine of the physical. Both practice and understanding are changing as the psychological sequelae of serious physical injury are increasingly understood.

The relationship between severity of injury and subsequent psychological status is an area of great practical interest since the approach of medical practitioners may be informed by their assumptions about coping, and what is an appropriate response. Research continues: for example, Turnbull et al. (1994) has found that in veterans of the Falklands conflict, PTSD is less frequent in those who have sustained physical injury, when compared with those who have not. O'Brien and Hughes (1991) found that wounded veterans of the same conflict were more likely to fulfil criteria for

PTSD than those who had not been injured; this is similar to findings by Orner et al. (1993). Existing longitudinal work (e.g. Mayou, and Blanchard and colleagues) notes that the relationship between injury severity and subsequent psychological disorder is variable. Overall, the morbidity and damage to the quality of life which can result from quite moderate injury in an accident, or indeed as a result of an accident with no resultant injury, is of the greatest interest and is an area which requires meta-analysis of existing data. Over and above research data, there is information on the consequences of road accidents held by different organisations, which has been collected for different purposes. Only some of these data have already been analysed.

Other research questions include how medical practitioners in the community manage the consequences of road accidents. The argument has been put forward throughout this volume that general (family) medical practitioners in the main deal with the subsequent difficulties experienced by road accident survivors, and with families bereaved by road death. Another interesting inquiry would be to interview general practitioners on their management of such patients – a method which was used in investigating how the Lockerbie general practitioners understood and assisted the community during the three years following the disaster in 1988 (Mitchell 1993). These interviews were aimed at understanding the models of recovery which the doctors had used in treating their patients. The same type of informal counselling and pharmaceutical interventions which the general practitioners considered helpful for people recovering from this disaster may well mimic the approach they take with people recovering from the trauma of a road accident.

Howarth's chapter on the coroner's system provides an insight into the experience of bereaved families caught up in the justice system. This reflects a theme implicit throughout the book: how killing on the road is managed by the justice system and the obvious questions this raises about the ability of bereaved relatives to cope. It is an area ripe for further psychological exploration within an interdisciplinary context. A further particular area of interest is the experience of people who, themselves, kill on the roads without sustaining injury themselves, which is frequently the case in pedestrian fatalities. I am unaware of any work in this area, and it appears that it may have been almost entirely ignored, mostly because the medical context (often the driver is not physically injured) and the legal context (often they are construed as blameworthy) overwhelms such considerations.

Although a chapter on the work of the police in relation to road accidents has been included, the work of the Fire Service and the Ambulance Service are obvious and regrettable omissions. Responding to road accidents is multidisciplinary response at the scene: the impact of this aspect of their work on emergency service workers and, in turn, the impact on survivors of the way this work is done, are aspects of interest. Adshead's chapter points to the substantial contact which Accident and Emergency staff have with survivors and survivors' families. An investigation of how road accident survivors are dealt with and supported within this setting would assist the planning of service provision and perhaps lead to a greater integration of services for survivors.

Over thirty years ago Nader wrote his famous critique of the car, *Unsafe at Any Speed*. Although many of the design faults he talked about have been corrected, it is arguable that the car remains unsafe at any speed. Individual car ownership is a potent symbol of freedom of choice, but public attitudes are changing. Perhaps the various perspectives and evidence reflecting the robust interest in the impact of the car on quality of life which are provided in this volume may contribute, usefully, to the debate. The collection is intended for psychologists, psychiatrists, medical and legal practitioners, and others who manage the psychological, social, medical and legal consequences of road accidents. It will also serve as a reference for voluntary organisations, and perhaps for those with personal or family experience of road accidents. From a variety of theoretical and practical perspectives a coherent approach to understanding the impact of road accidents and managing their sequelae needs to be found. Compared with ten or even five years ago, substantial longitudinal work has already been undertaken, and this needs to be continued and co-ordinated. It is hoped that this volume will be a step towards that goal in consolidating and developing a network of interested and committed researchers and practitioners throughout the world.

Note: The term 'survivor' is used to denote a person who has been involved in a road accident and who may also have been physically injured; 'victim' is used to denote a person who is killed. 'Road accident' is used rather than 'motor vehicle accident' (MVA) or 'road traffic accident' (RTA).

Chapter 2

Road accident statistics

Jeremy Broughton

The first official road accident statistics for Great Britain were collected in 1909, in response to contemporary concerns about the increase in motorised traffic. In this chapter the development of British road accident statistics over the intervening years is reviewed, summarising the major legislative changes that have influenced this development. Current statistics are then discussed in more detail, to provide a setting for the volume, and the chapter concludes with some comparable statistics from other countries.

THE HISTORY OF THE CURRENT NATIONAL ACCIDENT REPORTING SYSTEM

The early history of the British system for collecting road accident statistics has recently been uncovered by Dr Brenda White of the University of Glasgow's Department of Economic History. The following account draws heavily on chapters that she contributed to the 1991 and 1992 editions of *Road Accidents Great Britain* (published annually by HMSO for the Department of Transport). Incidentally, one indication of the extent of public interest in road safety in this country is the fact that this report, based on the official accident statistics, has been published since 1951, and about one thousand copies are sold each year. Until recently, relatively few other countries published such a report.

The origin of the present system can be traced to a request in 1909 that the Home Office should issue an annual 'Return of Street Accidents' to the House of Commons. Until 1928, only the numbers of fatal and non-fatal accidents were collected, broken down by the vehicle 'to which accident is attributed' (pedal cycle accidents were not included until 1914). The question of attribution or 'accident causation' is now recognised as being rather more complex, but the fatal accident data shown (Figure 2.1) provide a fascinating insight into the changing pattern of road transport during the first quarter of the twentieth century.

The first moves towards a more sophisticated collection of accident data

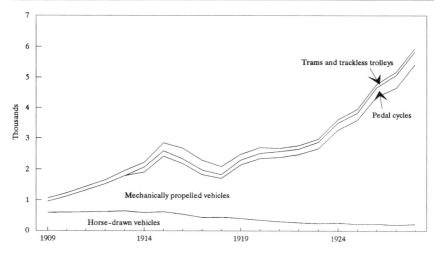

Figure 2.1 Fatal accidents in Great Britain, 1909–1928, by 'vehicle to which accident is attributed'

came in 1926, under the auspices of the National Safety First Association (the forerunner of the present Royal Society for the Prevention of Accidents, ROSPA). A Royal Commission recommended in 1929 that the Ministry of Transport should collect detailed data for fatal accidents and, after protracted negotiations, the Ministry organised the first national collection of data in 1933. This was repeated in 1935, and in 1937 the system was extended to cover all accidents involving personal injury.

Only basic information was collected during the Second World War; indeed, the recording of non-fatal accidents was suspended in the early war years. Road accidents attracted little attention immediately after the war, not least because petrol rationing suppressed the level of traffic, but a new national system was established on 1 January 1949. Police officers recorded information about any accident 'involving personal injury occurring on the public highway (including footways) in which a road vehicle is involved and which becomes known to the police within 30 days of its occurrence', using a standard reporting form known as the 'Stats19 form'. Completed forms were forwarded to the Ministry of Transport and stored at the Road Research Laboratory (now Transport Research Laboratory).

With periodic amendments, and changes to take advantage of developments in computing technologies, the system continues to this day. The forty-three police forces in England and Wales and the eight forces in Scotland are responsible for collecting data within their own areas, under the supervision of the national Standing Committee on Road Accident Statistics. Each force collects a common set of accident data, although some collect additional data under local arrangements. The data are used locally to guide road safety activities, for example designing remedial measures at road junctions with poor accident records. They are also forwarded to the Department of Transport, where they help to determine national road safety policy and are widely used in the research that influences these policies. Northern Ireland is not part of the Stats19 system. The Royal Ulster Constabulary (RUC) collects accident data using a generally similar form, but the RUC retains these data.

The Stats19 form is designed to be completed at the scene of the accident, or very soon after. Consequently, it contains only a minimum of clinical information: casualties are recorded as being killed, seriously injured or slightly injured. Only when a casualty dies within 30 days from injuries sustained in the accident would this information be amended. Thus the severity coding represents a police officer's 'on-the-spot' judgement of the casualty's state, rather than an official medical opinion. When the Stats19 system was being revised in 1978, it was planned to receive such medical data from the Department of Health, but this never materialised. Instead, specific research projects (for a recent example, see Simpson 1996) have collected such data for samples of accidents, and used them to augment the police accident reports for more detailed analyses of the injury consequences and costs of road accidents.

Three further qualifications need to be made about the Stats19 system. It deals only with personal injury accidents, that is, accidents in which at least one person is injured. Hence, vehicle 'damage-only' accidents are excluded from the system. There is very little information about the ratio of damage-only to injury accidents, but it is thought that there are approximately ten damage-only accidents for each accident resulting in injury. Second, and self-evidently, it deals only with accidents reported to the police. There is no legal requirement to report each injury accident to the police: in particular, those involved in an accident can continue their journeys without contacting the police provided that the drivers involved exchange the necessary details. The level of underreporting has been studied extensively, and has been found to vary with type of accidents. At one extreme, effectively all fatal accidents are reported; at the other, as few as one quarter of those accidents where the only casualty is a pedal cyclist with slight injuries, are reported to the police and so enter the accident database. Fortunately, the level of underreporting appears to be stable in this country from year to year, although some foreign accident reporting systems have experienced significant fluctuations caused, for example, by changed police reporting procedures or local government reorganisation. The importance of this stability is that changes over time should be shown correctly: if the *reported* number of accidents falls by so many per cent between one year and the next, the *actual* number also falls by that percentage. Finally, and of particular relevance to the subject of this book, the system collects no information about the immediate or long term psychological consequences of an accident.

LONG-TERM TRENDS

One advantage of the long and relatively stable history of the Stats19 system is that accident totals can be traced over many years. Figure 2.2 brings together the available data to show how the number of people killed and injured on British roads has fluctuated since 1909. The rapid increase in the number of deaths in the decade following the First World War is striking; the main cause was probably the rapid growth of motor traffic, mainly involving motorists with little driving experience. The early years of the Second World War saw another dramatic increase, arising from the unfamiliar conditions of the blackout and the appearance on the roads of large numbers of inexperienced drivers involved in the war effort. The increase was reversed in 1942, and it was only in the 1950s that the number of deaths began to rise once more in response, as in the 1920s, to the traffic growth that accompanied economic growth. The number has generally fallen since 1966, until in 1993 the number had returned to a level last seen in the early 1920s. While the number of people injured has also tended to fall since 1966, the fall has been less rapid and the number remains at the level last seen in the late 1950s. Within this total, the number of seriously injured has fallen in line with the number of deaths, so someone injured in a road accident today is, on average, less severely injured than someone injured thirty years ago.

The volume of road traffic and number of journeys by road have expanded enormously over these years. In 1949, for example, motor vehicles travelled about 46.5 thousand million (i.e. billion) kilometres (traffic volume is measured by the total distance travelled by motor vehicles in vehicle-kilometres); this figure had risen almost ninefold by

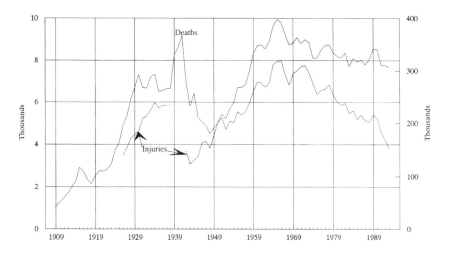

Figure 2.2 Road deaths (left scale) and injuries (right scale) in Great Britain

1993 to 410.2 thousand million kilometres. Over the same period, the number of licensed motor vehicles rose from just over four million to just over twenty-five million, more than six times as many. The falling numbers of deaths and injuries over the past three decades represent a major success in coping with the problems of motorised transport.

A turning point was reached in road safety in the mid-1960s (Figure 2.2), and this has led some people to hunt for the panacea administered at that time which halted the earlier rises and prepared the way for the subsequent reductions. A more likely explanation is provided by the pattern of national traffic growth, as will now be discussed.

It is natural to expect the national accident total to be related to the national traffic volume: broadly, more traffic at any one time is likely to lead to more opportunities for conflict and hence to more accidents. The first step in investigating this relationship is to calculate annual accident and casualty rates, that is, the number of accidents and casualties per million vehicle-kilometres travelled. The annual traffic volume is available from 1949, and four rates have been calculated for the period 1949–93: the number of people killed per million veh-km (*the fatality rate*); the number of people killed or seriously injured per million veh-km (*the KSI rate*); the number of people injured per million veh-km (*the casualty rate*); and the number of injury accidents per million veh-km (*the accident rate*).

In order to bring out the similarities of the four series, each has been expressed relative to its mean value over the first decade (Figure 2.3). Dividing the original series data by traffic volume has eliminated most of the irregularities, leaving generally exponential graphs: the turning point of 1966 has now disappeared, suggesting that the changes in the mid-1960s

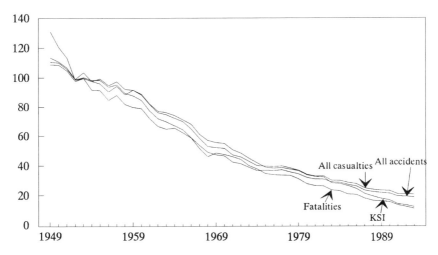

Figure 2.3 Annual casualty and accident rate in Great Britain (100 = 1949–58 mean)

are indeed related to the pattern of traffic growth. To compare how close the casualty and accident data graphs (Figure 2.3) are to the exponential form, the logarithm of the four rates are presented (Figure 2.4). Simple statistical models represent the four rates very effectively; the fatality model fits very well, and the fit is only slightly worse for the other three. In more detail:

1 The 'fatality rate' fell by 4.5 per cent per annum until about 1980, since when it has fallen more steeply, by 6.4 per cent per annum.
2 The 'killed or seriously injured (KSI) rate' fell by 4.1 per cent per annum until about 1984, since when it has fallen more steeply, by 7.5 per cent per annum.

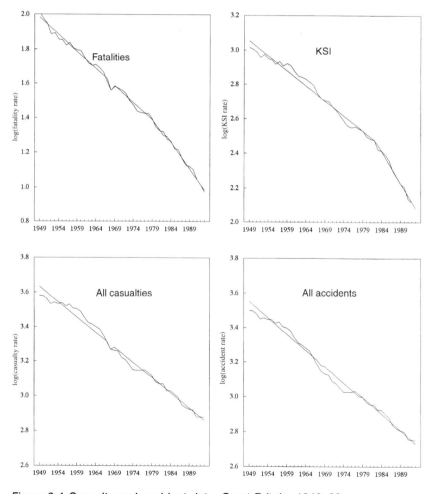

Figure 2.4 Casualty and accident data, Great Britain, 1949–93

3 The 'all casualties and all accidents' rates fell throughout by 4.0 per cent and 4.2 per cent per annum respectively, with no indication of a change in the early 1980s.

4 The 'non-fatal rates' have deviated systematically about the fitted lines, being below up to 1955 and between 1967 and 1977, and above between 1955 and 1965. This ceased after 1977, which may indicate that the earlier deviations were related to variations in accident reporting procedures which have since been eliminated.

Thus the downturn of the graphs shown in Figure 2.2 in the mid-1960s is explained by the difference between the rate of traffic growth and the rate of decline of the casualty rates. Traffic grew by more than the critical value of 4.5 per cent per annum throughout the earlier period (Figure 2.5), so casualties increased. Subsequently, the traffic growth rate was less than 4.5 per cent and casualties fell. When the rate again exceeded 4.5 per cent for a short period in the 1980s, casualties grew once more; by this time, however, the rate of decline of deaths and serious casualties had risen (items (1) and (2) above), so these series continued to fall. Traffic growth has been the main factor influencing the overall casualty trends over these years: when traffic has grown strongly, there have been more casualties; when traffic growth has been weak, there have been fewer.

The consistency of the falls in the casualty and accident rates over almost half a century is remarkable. Most aspects of road traffic have changed markedly during this period, yet the rates have continued to decline by an almost constant proportion each year. Moreover, this pattern is also found in the accident statistics of other industrialised countries, such as Germany and the USA. This suggests that there might be some underlying 'law', of

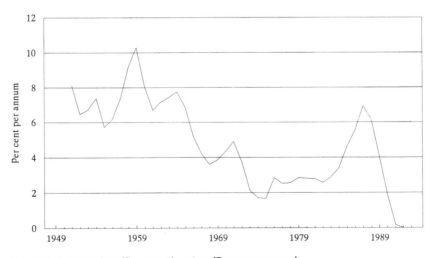

Figure 2.5 Annual traffic growth rates (5-year average)

the sort widely found in the physical sciences. Perhaps the most plausible explanation draws a parallel with findings from studies of industrial processes, where the rate of failures (e.g. defective goods manufactured) normally declines exponentially over time. From this perspective, accidents and casualties are the failures of the national road transport system, and the rate of failure would be expected to decline exponentially as the nation learns collectively to cope with the problems of motorised transport. The decline is then the result of a combination of national factors, such as improved standards of vehicle design, and the increasing personal experience of modern road conditions.

Whatever the underlying causes, the changing rates are not deterministic, that is, it was not inevitable that rates would continue to fall; they are the result of the considerable efforts that have been made to improve road safety (summarised below) and of the steady development of the road transport system. If this system were to change radically in the next few years, it would clearly be unwise to expect these rates to continue to fall. However, continuation does not imply stasis, and the maintenance of current standards will not be sufficient; for example, vehicle standards have risen over the years, and they must continue to rise if the casualty rates are to continue to fall as fast in future as they have since 1949.

SPECIFIC ROAD SAFETY MEASURES

Developments in road safety fall into three categories: those which affect personal behaviour; the construction and maintenance of vehicles; and the road environment. Some can be clearly identified and their effects analysed, such as compulsory seat belt wearing. Other developments, such as the increasing provision of pavements and street lighting, occur gradually and are difficult, if not impossible, to evaluate. The many developments for which national and local government are responsible are relatively easy to catalogue, and the most important of these are summarised in the following paragraphs. Other developments are less easy to summarise but have probably made important contributions, such as the many improvements in vehicle design and engineering (often prompted by national or international regulation). There have also been advances in road design techniques which have been applied to both new and existing roads: for example, to separate out conflicting streams of traffic and reduce the scope for vehicles coming into conflict.

Less visible and even more difficult to measure has been the steady increase in the knowledge and experience available to the typical member of the public to help him or her to travel in safety. The interpretation of the steadily declining casualty rates as the outcome of a learning process suggests that this factor has made a significant but unmeasurable contribution to the declining casualty total. There has been considerable research into the beneficial effects of learning for the individual: for example, Maycock et al. (1991) showed the dramatic reduction in an individual driver's accident liability as they become more experienced, independent of the effects of ageing. These separate results have not been 'fitted together', however, to understand the consequences at the national scale.

The first national measures aimed at improving road safety were introduced in 1930, when third-party insurance and tests for some driving licences were made compulsory; however, the 20 mph speed limit for cars and cycles was abolished. The first Highway Code was published in the following year. In 1934 a speed limit of 30 mph in built-up areas was introduced, as were some basic regulations covering vehicle equipment. The driving test for cars was introduced in 1936.

There were few new measures until 1959, but thereafter they began to appear at an increasing rate. Annual testing of cars and vans over 10 years old (the 'MOT test') began in 1959, aimed at removing the risks associated with unroadworthy vehicles. A trial national speed limit of 70 mph was introduced in 1964, together with a 'Drink/Drive' publicity campaign, and from 1966 new cars had to be fitted with front seat belts. In the following year it became illegal to drive with over 80 mg of alcohol per 100 ml of blood (it had previously been illegal to drive while under the influence of alcohol, but there had been few successful prosecutions under the old law). In 1969 the MOT test was extended to cover vehicles over 3 years old. Safety helmets were made compulsory for motorcyclists in 1973, and a temporary 50 mph speed limit was introduced as a result of fuel shortages.

Licensing arrangements for learner motorcyclists were tightened in 1982, and 1983 saw the introduction of compulsory seat belt wearing for front-seat occupants of cars and vans and evidential breath-testing for alcohol (only blood or urine tests previously). The Secretary of State for Transport set a target of reducing the number of road accident casualties by one-third by the year 2000 (relative to the 1981–85 average) in 1987, and all new cars had to be fitted with rear seat belts or child restraints. Children were required to use these rear restraints from 1989, and the regulations were extended to adults in 1991. The 'High Risk Offender' scheme for the more severe drink/drivers was developed in 1990, and the first 20 mph zones were introduced the following year.

Unless it is widely observed by the travelling public, even the most well-intentioned measure will be ineffective, and there are wide variations in the extent to which traffic laws are obeyed in this country. Speed limits provide a salutary example: although the role of excess speed in causing or aggravating accidents is widely understood, large numbers of British drivers routinely break speed limits. A survey of speeds in 1993 at sites with free-flowing traffic found the results shown in Table 2.1.

In contrast, compulsory seat belt wearing has been highly effective, in terms both of public compliance and of the casualty reductions achieved. In

Table 2.1 Survey of vehicle speed

	Motorway	Dual carriageways	Single carriageway/ A roads
Per cent of cars exceeding speed limit	56	40	7
Per cent exceeding limit by at least 10 mph	18	10	1

the decade before the law took effect, there had been extensive publicity aimed at raising the wearing rate by voluntary means; there were also several well-publicised attempts to pass a seat belt law through Parliament. The wearing rate rose from about 30 per cent to just under 40 per cent over this period. Within three months of the law taking effect, however, the rate had risen to 95 per cent – despite public announcements by the police that no prosecutions would be brought during this introductory period. This rate has since been largely maintained, more by persuasion and personal choice than by enforcement; there have been periodic publicity campaigns but relatively few prosecutions (e.g. about eight thousand convictions in 1988 out of a total of 1.57 million convictions for motoring offences). In the first year of the new law's operation, compulsory seat belt wearing led to about 370 fewer people being killed and 24,000 fewer being injured (Broughton, 1990). Most types of injury were reduced, but two increased: fractures of the sternum and strained necks (Rutherford et al. 1986).

Drink/driving provides an example of the successful combination of publicity and legislation backed up by police enforcement. The number of fatal accidents involving illegal alcohol levels is estimated to have fallen from 1,000 in 1984 to 470 in 1993, while the total number of drink/drive accidents fell from 17,330 to 9,500. Over this period there has been extensive publicity warning of the dangers of drink/driving – indeed, the Department of Transport Christmas drink/drive publicity campaign now appears to be a fixed part of the Christmas celebrations. The police also breath-test an increasing number of riders and drivers involved in accidents: 11 per cent in 1984, compared with 28 per cent in 1993. This reflects an increased emphasis on enforcement with a successful deterrent effect, rather than any growth in drink/driving; 3.2 per cent of accident-involved riders and drivers failed a breath test in 1984, compared with 1.8 per cent in 1993.

WHO IS INJURED?

Accident data can be analysed in many ways. The results presented below focus on casualty rates by age, sex and mode of transport. Figure 2.6 shows

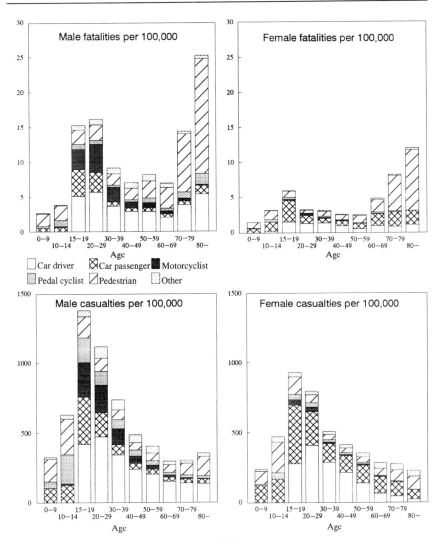

Figure 2.6 Fatality and casualty rates, 1993

how the number of casualties per 100,000 population varied in 1993 by age and sex. The data are stacked, so the height of each bar denotes the overall casualty rate for that group. Thus, of each 100,000 young men aged 15–19 in 1993, 1,380 were injured in road accidents and sixteen died. The overall rates peak for the 17–19 age group, then fall progressively for the middle-aged: fatality – but not casualty – rates rise strongly among the elderly.

These results take no account of exposure: there are, for instance, far fewer motorcyclists than car drivers, so the figure does not bring out the particular risks of motorcycling (see Chapter 19). On the other hand, it does show how the balance of risks faced by the typical British traveller varies as he or she grows older. Young adults tend to be killed and injured in cars, young men on motorcycles as well, but the balance shifts to the pedestrian mode after 60. Fatality rates for women are about two-fifths as high as for men, but the fraction rises to about three-quarters for casualty rates.

One useful way of summarising this detailed information is to consider the likelihood of a typical person being killed or injured by a certain age. For simplicity, the calculation assumes that casualty rates will remain constant in future years, and Figure 2.7 shows the probability of being killed or injured by the age of 10, 15, 20, etc. (some of those who are injured may be injured more than once during their lives). Thus, at 1993 rates, 7.4 men per thousand will be killed in road accidents before they are 80, and three women per thousand will be killed: 376 men per thousand

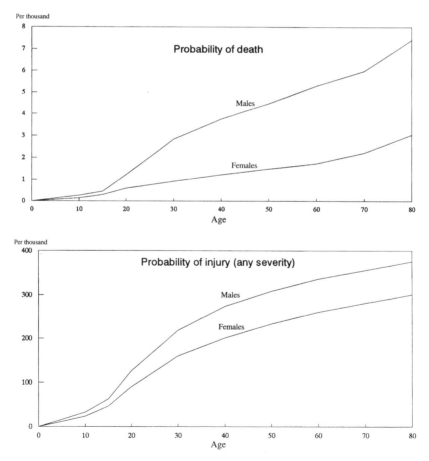

Figure 2.7 Probability of being killed or injured in a road accident by a certain age

will be injured, as will 301 women per thousand. The calculations can be repeated for earlier years, when casualty rates were higher, and the corresponding figures are consequently rather higher. Equally, if rates continue to fall as they have in the past, the figures will in future be rather lower.

While road accidents account for only a small minority of deaths (e.g. 1.1 per cent of male deaths and 0.4 per cent of female deaths in 1992), they account for a major proportion of *accidental* deaths (45 per cent for males and 27 per cent for females). This is especially true for the young: the peak occurs in the 17–19 age group, where 79 per cent and 77 per cent of accidental male and female deaths occur in road accidents. That young people are also injured far more frequently than older people has great implications for families, in that they must provide care for the individual for a long time and in terms of the individual's subsequent quality of life.

The average age of those killed in road accidents is low compared with most other causes of death, so the loss of life expectancy is proportionately greater. When someone dies prematurely (relative to actuarial expectation) through accident or illness there is a loss of life expectancy, that is, they have not lived as long as expected; the younger they die, the greater the loss. It has been calculated that in 1990 road accidents accounted for 1.3 per cent of male deaths and 0.5 per cent of female deaths, but 4.3 per cent and 1.7 per cent respectively of lost life expectancy.

SOME INTERNATIONAL COMPARISONS

This chapter concludes with some current road accident statistics from other countries, to set the British statistics in context. The countries included are broadly comparable with Great Britain, being relatively motorised and prosperous. Countries such as India face road safety problems which differ greatly from those found in this country – for example, a wide mix of traffic, overcrowding of vehicles, poor planning and design, and lack of associated resources – so such countries are not included in the comparison.

The data presented below come from the International Road Traffic and Accident Database (IRTAD) sponsored by the OECD. They are collected by national authorities in the various countries and then passed to IRTAD, so depend entirely on national definitions and methods of collection. This complicates international comparisons, as definitions can vary widely. Most countries follow the British example and include as a road death anyone who died within 30 days of an accident; at the other extreme, the Japanese follow a '1 day rule', and their fatality numbers have to be increased by 30 per cent to bring them into line with the '30 day rule'. The position is much worse with casualties, as most countries adopt a rather vague but high severity threshold, and their statistics therefore do not include many casualties that should be included according to the British definition. Problems also arise from legal differences and varying reporting standards.

In view of these (and other) difficulties, the simplest approach is to compare the number of deaths per 100,000 population, corrected to the 30-day definition. Figure 2.8 presents these rates for the fifteen member states of the European Union, together with nine others. The countries are presented in order of declining fatality rate, and it can be seen that the British rate in 1993 was virtually the lowest of any motorised country. According to this measure, the level of road safety in Great Britain is matched only in Norway. Moreover, this is no temporary phenomenon: in 1988, for example, the four countries with the lowest fatality rates were Norway (9.0), Great Britain (9.1), the Netherlands (9.3) and Sweden (9.6). Figure 2.9 shows that the British record is less impressive in one respect, in that the pedestrian fatality rate is relatively high. Conversely, the fatality rate for vehicle occupants is definitely lower in Great Britain than in Norway. Several non-European countries are included in Figures 2.8 and 2.9, from which it can be seen that fatality rates in the USA, Canada and Australia are somewhat higher than the best European rates, although this may partly be explained by their relatively high levels of vehicle ownership and use.

Many factors are likely to influence accident rates. Geography is important: a largely rural country such as France would be expected, *ceteris paribus*, to have a higher fatality rate than a largely urban country such as the Netherlands, because accidents on rural roads are likely to involve high speeds and consequently greater risks of death. The ranking in Figure 2.8

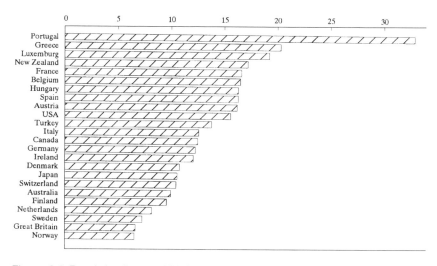

Figure 2.8 Road deaths per 100,000 population, 1993

suggests that the length of a country's experience of coping with the problems of motorised transport is also important. In this context, it is worth noting that the current ranking of Germany is rather worse than the ranking of West Germany used to be, since unification allowed large numbers of East Germans – familiar with driving old-fashioned cars such as Trabants – to purchase and drive powerful modern cars. Accident rates in the east of Germany remain clearly higher than in the west.

Finally, Figure 2.10 shows the rate of deaths per 100 million vehicle-kilometres travelled. Only half of the countries included in the earlier comparison publish figures for the national traffic volume, so only these countries can be represented in the figure. The significance of this comparison arises from the earlier examination of the evolution of this fatality rate over the long term, and the rate is again found to be lower in Great Britain than in other countries.

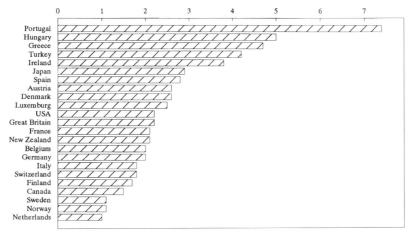

Figure 2.9 Pedestrian deaths per 100,000 population, 1993

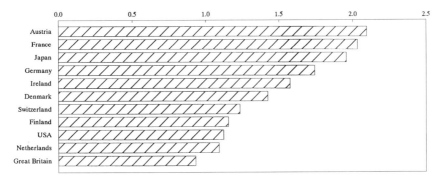

Figure 2.10 Road deaths per 100 million vehicle-km, 1993

CONCLUSION

This chapter has described in outline the development of road safety in Great Britain during the twentieth century, and has shown that the current position compares favourably with other countries in Europe as well as motorised countries in other continents. Nonetheless, 3,621 people were killed in 1995 on British roads (3,650 in 1994 and over 3,800 in 1993), so there is still substantial scope for further progress. Most of the more obvious and effective national measures have already been taken, such as the introduction of compulsory seat belt wearing. Thus, building on past progress to maintain the downward casualty trends will continue to present many challenges in the future.

Part I

Psychological and psychiatric consequences

Chapter 3

The psychiatry of road traffic accidents

Richard Mayou

Although road traffic accidents are the leading cause of death in those aged under 40 years in developed countries and a major cause of morbidity, there has, until recently, been very little interest in their psychological and psychiatric consequences. This book is evidence of a change in interest and attitudes, which is resulting in increasing research and in opportunities for changes in clinical practice. This chapter begins with a critical review of the nature of the available evidence and then considers the various types of psychiatric complication. The final sections cover the special issue of compensation and consider the implications for clinical care, road safety and for the law.

Current evidence is sparse, and there are many unresolved issues about the extent and nature of psychiatric morbidity and the implications for the design of effective psychological intervention and its delivery to large numbers of people. Even so, it is now very clear that psychological and psychiatric complications are considerable and associated with very substantial adverse effects on quality of life. Changes in hospital and primary care of accident survivors should be vital immediate priorities for medicine and should not be delayed pending further research.

THE NATURE OF THE EVIDENCE

Evidence can be drawn from many sources (Table 3.1) even though there have been very few satisfactory studies concentrating on representative samples of road accident survivors. While information on general effects of physical illness, on other trauma and on a variety of selected subgroups of road accident survivors is informative, it is essential to be aware of the limitations of such evidence and to be cautious about generalisations from inadequate data. The findings must be considered in the light of what is known about psychiatric responses to trauma and to physical illness in general.

Table 3.1 Sources of evidence

- General evidence on reactions to life events and physical disorders
- Research on accidents in general (mixed groups, head injury, concussion)
- Prospective and other studies of road accidents (psychological outcome and disability)
- Research on Post Traumatic Stress Disorder
- Studies of whiplash neck injury
- Medicolegal series
- General clinical experience

General evidence on life events and physical illness

There has been a great deal of carefully designed research on the general psychiatric consequences of life events and on numerous forms of physical disorder (Mayou and Sharpe 1995). The general nature, course and determinants of anxiety and depression are clear. In addition, it is evident that particular types of physical illnesses have specific psychiatric consequences. For instance, functional somatic symptoms, such as chest pain and palpitations, are frequent after a heart attack and phobic anxiety often occurs during cancer chemotherapy. The consequences of road traffic accidents should be considered in this broader context. There are three main aspects: emotional distress as seen after all illness; cognitive problems attributable to head injury and brain damage; and the specific effects of what is often a frightening trauma.

Trauma in general

Recent trauma research has focused on specific post-traumatic symptoms. It is apparent that there are very considerable differences in the immediate and longer-term responses to different types of trauma. Many accounts relate to extremely severe experiences either acute (such as rape) or long-continued (such as prolonged maltreatment as a prisoner of war). Most road accidents are experienced as being less threatening, both because the trauma may be very brief and because only a minority of accidents are life threatening. Even so, a minority of accidents involve prolonged and very frightening experiences, for example being trapped, being in severe pain, and then suffering prolonged and intensive care.

The very considerable research on trauma is relevant to understanding road accidents, but it is essential to keep in mind that there are continuing uncertainties about the validity of the condition *post-traumatic stress disorder* (PTSD), and about the relationship between post-traumatic symptoms and other psychiatric comorbidity. In successive editions of the *Diagnostic and Statistical Manual of Mental Disorders* (DSM) the nature of the stressor criteria has changed considerably. The original DSM-III

(American Psychiatric Association 1980) version largely excluded road accident injury, whereas the DSM-IV (American Psychiatric Association 1994) revision is rather more broad, apart from a concentration on physical types of injury. There are uncertainties about the symptom criteria, particularly the treatment of numbing symptoms. It may well be that the numbing / re-experiencing syndrome should be separated from the phobic avoidance and perhaps from general anxiety symptoms (Foa et al. 1995). The precise definition has a substantial effect on estimates of prevalence and also on the way in which comorbidity with other major psychiatric disorder is viewed (Andreasen 1995).

Although trauma research has been largely concerned with post-traumatic symptoms, substantial comorbidity of other psychiatric disorder has always been noted. Patterns of comorbidity appear to differ with the type of trauma. We should be aware that anxiety and depressive disorders may not only be more frequent but may also be more disabling than PTSD.

Road traffic accidents

Table 3.1 lists sources of evidence about psychiatric complications of road traffic accidents. Unfortunately, there have been very few studies of representative patient groups using prospective designs and proven quantitative measures. Much of the evidence relates either to highly selected groups (especially whiplash neck injury and those involved in compensation proceedings) or to accident survivors in general in which no distinction is made between road accident and other types of injury. Although epidemiological studies suggest that road and other accidents are amongst the most common causes of post-traumatic symptoms, they have received very little attention compared to combat, disasters and assault.

Case reports and descriptions of highly selective samples are of interest in indicating the range of complications, but it is important to avoid drawing general conclusions. Even hospital attenders are unrepresentative in that many of those with minor injury do not seek medical help at all, or attend their primary care doctors rather than hospital emergency departments. For example, hospital attenders with whiplash neck injury may be very different from the total population of those who suffer whiplash symptoms, many of whom either do not consult their family doctors or do so at a later stage. There is clearly a need for prospective studies of road accident injury using methods proven in research on the consequences of other medical disorders, such as heart disease and cancer. Such research should be based on representative samples, use a range of proven measures and can be expected to show many similarities with the psychological impact of other physical conditions and also the specific consequences of trauma in terms of post-traumatic symptoms.

Inevitably, psychological research has concentrated on adult occupants of motor vehicles and motor cyclists. We know much less about the consequences of road accident injury for pedestrians, cyclists and those in public service vehicles or for children (see Chapter 5). Clinical experience suggests that although there are substantial demographic and other differences between these groups (Tunbridge et al. 1988), the patterns of psychiatric complications may be similar. This appears to be confirmed by the initial findings of our own current study of over 1,100 consecutive attenders at an emergency department following a road accident. It is also important to consider those who are involved in road accidents (as participants or bystanders) but are uninjured; clinical experience of talking to uninjured friends and relatives and of preparing medical reports suggests that psychological complications can be significant.

There have been several accounts of disability following road traffic accidents. Most studies, and especially the earlier ones, have used rather simple measures of adverse effects on quality of life (Bull 1985; Tunbridge et al. 1988; Report of the Transport and Road Research Laboratory Department of Transport 1986; Report of the Transport and Road Research Laboratory Department of Transport 1980). We find such disability is often considerable and not always closely related to physical impairment. There is much individual variation in response, and effects on the quality of each domain of life need to be assessed separately. Failure to assess disability in its widest sense has undoubtedly led to a very substantial underestimate of the individual impact and cost of road accidents.

Medico-legal experience

It is unfortunate that clinical and legal views have been strongly influenced by scepticism deriving from experience with the very small proportion of accident survivors involved in disputed compensation litigation. These conspicuous examples have had an excessive influence on the ways in which road accident survivors in general are viewed, and this is especially so in relation to whiplash neck injury (Mayou 1995).

The importance of pre-accident psychiatric disorder

Although any road user may suffer accidental injury, accidents are not random and a variety of medical and psychiatric factors predispose to accident, and thereby to injury (Table 3.2). Some medical causes (such as myocardial infarction or strokes) are unpredictable, but a number of chronic conditions, such as diabetes (Stevens et al. 1989) and epilepsy, place responsibility on individuals either to admit that they are unfit to drive at all or to take special precautions to ensure they are fit and safe.

The psychological and behavioural factors which make up 'accident proneness' are difficult to identify precisely but include personality traits

Table 3.2 Some medical and psychological causes of road accidents

- Medical:
  Cardiac disorders
  Cerebrovascular disorders
  Epilepsy
  Hyperglycaemia

- Psychiatric:
  Schizophrenia
  Mood disorder
  Organic mental disorder
  Anxiety disorders
  Deliberate self-harm
  Risk taking

- Drug side effects

- Personality and behavioural characteristics

and excessive and inappropriate drinking and drug taking. In addition, all types of major psychiatric disorder are more common in those suffering road accidents than in the general population, with a marked excess of personality disorder and substance abuse (Brewer et al. 1994). Alcohol and drug abuse are especially associated with more severe accidents. Affective disorder, schizophrenia and dementia (O'Neill et al. 1992) are occasional direct causes of road accident both directly and because of the side-effects of prescribed psychotropic drugs (Edwards 1995). Suicide is believed to be uncommon but risk-taking suicidal behaviour is a cause of considerable concern. Sleepiness and sleep disorders are a common cause of accidents (Horne and Reyner 1995).

THE PSYCHIATRIC CONSEQUENCES OF ROAD ACCIDENTS

In understanding the psychiatric consequences of any physical disorder, it is necessary to distinguish between *concurrent unrelated* psychiatric problems and those *precipitated* or *exacerbated* by disorder. Since those suffering road traffic accidents are more psychiatrically disturbed and psychologically vulnerable than the general population, one expects, following accidents, to find both substantial continuing and concurrent psychiatric disorder and relatively high rates of new psychiatric problems.

The main psychiatric consequences are listed in Table 3.3. The following account is mainly based on our own Oxford research on: a representative sample of 188 multiple injury and whiplash patients (Mayou et al. 1993; Mayou and Bryant 1994); a prospective study of acute problems; and a current study of over 1,100 consecutive road accident survivor hospital attenders. A further important source is a prospective study of PTSD

Table 3.3 Psychiatric problems following road accident injury

- Organic mental disorder
- Acute stress disorder and reaction
- Emotional distress:
  Anxiety and depression
- Post-traumatic syndromes:
  Post-traumatic stress disorder (DSM-III-R)
  Phobic travel anxiety
- Alcohol and substance abuse

reported from New York State by Blanchard and his colleagues (Blanchard et al. 1995a; Blanchard et al. 1994b). Supporting evidence comes from several other smaller series which have been studied in less detail (Blanchard et al. 1995b; Sturzenegger et al. 1993; Bryant and Harvey 1995; Brom et al. 1993; Kuch et al. 1994).

Cognitive (organic) disorder

Major head injury is relatively uncommon but may well have devastating neuropsychiatric consequences, including cognitive impairment, mood disorders and changes in personality. The care of younger people with serious brain damage poses very serious problems for families and for psychiatric services. A considerably greater number of survivors suffer minor head injury associated with relatively short periods of unconsciousness and amnesia. It seems probable that the significance of 'minor' head injury has been underestimated and can be of considerable clinical importance. Concussional symptoms are common following head injury. Their course and aetiology have been controversial, but it is likely that there is interaction of physical and psychological factors which varies over time (Jacobson 1995; Watson et al. 1995).

Acute stress disorder

There is a general public acceptance that 'emotional shock' is to be expected after a road accident; indeed, emergency department staff describe survivors as usually being surprisingly calm about their experiences and injuries. Systematic evidence is scarce. Theoretical discussion has focused particularly on the role of dissociation as interfer ing with information processing and increasing the likelihood of re-experiencing phenomena (Foa et al. 1995; Horowitz et al. 1979). The rather few reports following a variety of types of trauma indicate that intrusion, arousal, avoidance and dissociation or numbing are all conspicuous. The association between these immediate phenomena and longer term psychiatric outcome are uncertain (Foa et al. 1995).

Table 3.4 Acute psychiatric syndromes

DSMIV Acute Stress Disorder
1 *Traumatic event* which involved or threatened death or serious injury; or a threat to the physical integrity of oneself or others *and* intense fear, helplessness; or horror.
2 At least three dissociative symptoms during or immediately after the event, together with at least one re-expressing symptom, avoidance arousal.
3 Symptoms for a minimum of two days and maximum of four weeks.

ICD10 Acute Stress Reaction
1 Exceptional mental or physical stressor.
2 Anxiety or dissociative symptoms.
3 Immediate onset and diminish after not more than eight hours.

Criteria for acute stress disorder are included in ICD-10 (World Health Organisation 1992) and DSM-IV (American Psychiatric Association 1994) but there has been almost no research and little clinical experience of their use for any form of trauma. Table 3.4 shows that the two sets of criteria are distinctly different in terms of their symptom criteria and the duration of the syndrome. Apart from issues of definition, it is unclear that it is useful to separate immediate responses to a particular type of stressful experience from adjustment disorder and other syndromes which are seen as following other forms of life event. However, if the categories are seen as provisional and intended to provoke interest and research, they will be useful in focusing on distress which is common in clinical practice.

Clinical impression can be misleading. In a recent study we rated almost one-fifth of subjects as appearing dazed or numbed on the day after a road accident. However, most of these patients completed self-report scales with responses indicating considerable stress. Research suggests that the commonest early symptoms are avoidance, intrusive thoughts, denial, numbing and dissociation as part of a complicated clinical picture; there is much individual variation and there may be marked changes in the hours and days after trauma. Even so, the majority of survivors are phlegmatic following a minor or major road accident.

While it is difficult to make comparisons with other types of trauma, it is clear that road accident survivors are markedly less distressed than those suffering rape or criminal assault in which distressing intrusive memories and other psychiatric symptoms are more frequent and indeed usual (Foa et al. 1995). However, around a fifth of subjects describe severe acute distress, which may be characterised by agitation and mood disturbance, intrusive memories, numbing, denial or association, or a changing mixture of all these elements. It remains uncertain to what extent this acute syndrome is associated with the severity of injuries and to what extent the nature of the accident or pre-morbid characteristics. However one categorises the acute reactions, early distress is associated with a greatly increased likelihood of later post-traumatic or other psychiatric disturbance.

It is of considerable clinical importance to determine which features of early distress predict later psychiatric problems since most injured road accident survivors are seen only briefly in emergency departments or by doctors elsewhere and have no organised follow up.

Emotional disorder

The course, determinants and characteristics of anxiety and depression are similar for all types of major physical disorder. All cause acute emotional distress in a high proportion of subjects in the early days and up to a quarter describe persistent mood and anxiety disorders. Continuing psychiatric complications are most likely in those who are psychologically vulnerable, in those who have difficult social circumstances, and where there is evidence of continuing or relapsing physical problems.

We have found emotional disorder to be more common than population expectation throughout the year after being injured in a road accident, a finding which is consistent with the rather limited other evidence. The clinical features and the correlates are very similar to those described for other physical conditions. Persistent and severe distress is associated with evidence of previous psychological vulnerability and poor psychological adjustment, severe initial distress and with continuing medical problems and disability (Mayou et al. 1993). Continuing anxiety and depression can be expected to be most frequent in those suffering major injury with persistent disability, yet we found little difference between one form of minor injury, whiplash, and those suffering multiple injuries (Mayou et al. 1993). It is clearly not uncommon for medically trivial injuries to precipitate severe psychological problems.

Post-traumatic syndromes

Post-traumatic stress disorder (PTSD) is less frequent, and possibly less severe, than described following cases of major assault and disasters. Nonetheless, it is common, and epidemiological surveys of general populations suggests that road traffic accidents may be one of the commonest, or even *the* commonest cause of the syndrome in the general population. Norris (1992) in her survey of adults in four US cities concluded:

> If one event stood out from the pack, it was motor vehicle crash. This event was less frequent than some (robbery, tragic death) and less traumatizing than some (sexual or physical assault), but when both the frequency and severity data were considered together, it emerged as perhaps the single most significant event among those studied here. At a

lifetime frequency of 23% and a PTSD rate of 12% of that, this event alone would yield 28 seriously distressed persons for every 1,000 adults in the United States. This is an interesting observation given how seldom this event has been studied relative to crime, disasters and bereavement.

Discussion and clinical and legal interest has centred upon DSM-defined post-traumatic stress disorder. While avoidance is an important feature of the definition, the prominence of phobic anxiety about travel (which satisfies criteria for specific phobia) makes it sensible to describe PTSD and phobic anxiety separately.

POST-TRAUMATIC STRESS DISORDER

The original DSM-IIIR (American Psychiatric Association 1987) definition of post-traumatic stress disorder took little account of road traffic accidents; indeed, it largely excluded them as being within the realm of normal stress. DSM-III and DSM-IV have varied the stressor criterion and it is now relatively broad, with a particular focus on physical trauma (Andreasen 1995). The problems of the precise definition of the stressor criterion suggests that it might have been better to omit it altogether and to base the syndrome definition entirely on the symptoms. Indeed, it is in many ways tautologous to include both the *stressor criterion* and *symptom criteria*, which clearly relate to a previous upsetting event. The occurrence of post-traumatic symptoms have been recognised over many years and there have been a number of case reports and small series studies. It is only very recently that more systematic research has consistently shown that a range of post-traumatic symptoms are common following both major and minor injuries. Blanchard and his colleagues (1995a) have usefully reviewed the published studies and have noted a wide variation in reported prevalence of post-traumatic stress disorder. We have found post-traumatic stress disorder to occur in about 10 per cent of those with major injury (Mayou et al. 1993).

Post-traumatic stress disorder after a road traffic accident is much less common immediately after the incident than has been reported following some other forms of major trauma, such as rape. It is probable that even when it does occur after a road accident, the symptoms are usually less intense and less disabling. While the rates of PTSD in the early months are relatively modest, the *persistence* of PTSD at a year or later is striking, and

Table 3.5 Predictors of PTSD

- Not conscious.
- Immediate intrusive memories.
- Blame others for the accident.
- Pre-morbid psychopathology.

the rates are somewhat closer to those observed after more severe trauma. Though it is probable that determinants and predictors of PTSD are similar to those that have been discussed in relation to other types of trauma, evidence is somewhat conflicting. Some of the suggested predictors are listed in Table 3.5.

TRAVEL ANXIETY

Effects on attitudes to travel and anxiety about travel are amongst the most common and important consequences of road accidents (Table 3.6). Many survivors describe themselves as being more cautious and being more alert to the behaviour of other road users. There is a tendency to change to driving a safer vehicle. While these changes may all be seen as welcome and sensible, other consequences are less appropriate.

Table 3.6 Social consequences

- Financial problems
- Work
- Limitation of travel
- Impaired leisure and social activities
- Effects on family life
- Litigation and compensation proceedings
- Consequences for carers

A minority substantially reduce their travel, and indeed may stop driving altogether and make strenuous efforts to avoid being a passenger. Although much of the concern about travel clinically is of only moderate severity, up to 20 per cent of survivors describe significant effects on everyday behaviour as drivers or passengers, and some suffer from diagnosable phobic anxiety. Avoidance, in the form of travel anxiety, is a particularly prominent feature and is often associated with considerable limitation of travel. It would seem that the inevitable re-exposure to traffic makes avoidance so much more prominent than that following other forms of trauma. Anxiety is especially associated with travel in situations similar to that of the accident. Survivors can generalise from being a driver to being a passenger or even to other forms of transport. Occasionally there is considerable concern about travel by others, especially children and close relatives (Mayou and Bryant 1994; see Chapter 15). A large postal survey of accident survivors five years after a road accident shows that driving problems can be remarkably persistent (Mayou et al. 1991).

ALCOHOL

Alcohol problems are frequent amongst those suffering road accident, and it might be expected that accident and injury would have a salutary effect.

The evidence suggests otherwise. Both in the short term and in the longer term, most of those with drinking problems continue to drink excessively. We found little evidence of changes in drinking habit, or of drinking in relation to driving (Mayou and Bryant 1995). Where changes occurred more often, this was associated with drinking less for financial reasons, or drinking more because of emotional distress. Changes in alcohol consumption, and especially in relation to driving, seemed to be rather more common in those who do not have a problem with drinking and are generally more careful.

OTHER PSYCHOLOGICAL PROBLEMS

The most conspicuous feature is *anger*. This includes the anger of those who feel innocent towards those who are responsible, anger about the lack of recognition by others of their undeserved suffering, and anger about the legal system. Sometimes the result can be to regard recovery as a challenge, and an opportunity to demonstrate to others that in spite of everything the survivor will get back to a normal life. Perhaps more often, anger is less constructive and interferes with normal recovery, and harms relationships with family, friends and others involved. It seems probable that greater recognition by others of accident survivors' suffering and misfortune, and especially by the administration and compensation processes, would be very valuable.

Other problems include worry about disfigurement caused by prominent scarring or by limb deformity; a further real worry is the prospect for many of those who have bony injuries that there is not only a prospect of permanent impairment but also the possibility of later arthritis or other serious physical complications.

EFFECTS ON QUALITY OF LIFE

Physical symptoms of impairment inevitably affect disability and quality of everyday life. Psychological factors also contribute to the extent of changes and the whole range of domains of quality of life. Severe injury and some minor injuries may have many effects on all areas listed in Table 3.7. We find much individual variation, but the effect of minor and major injuries on the person's overall quality of life may be considerable. Any adequate clinical assessment must be concerned not only with impairment of function, but also with the effect this has on everyday activities and interests which are important to that person. Estimates of the costs of road accidents need to take proper notice of full social effects (Tunbridge et al. 1990).

Description of the psychiatric and psychological consequences of having a road traffic accident need to be seen in the wider context of changes in quality of life. It is inevitable that those suffering temporary or permanent

Table 3.7 Effects on travel

Driving
    Giving up car or motorcycle
    Changes to safer vehicle
    More cautious
    Phobic travel anxiety
    Limitation of extent of travel
    Specific anxiety about place of accident and similar situations
    Avoidance

Passenger
    Avoidance of travel
    Phobic anxiety

disability and having to undergo unpleasant and painful treatment should report effects on everyday activities. However, it is clear that, as with all physical illness, psychological factors are also important determinants of quality of life outcome. In the Oxford series, patients reported effects on work, leisure, social life, family life and financial status, and these were only partly related to measures of physical progress or impairment. It is important to be aware of the ways in which disability that might be considered medically relatively 'trivial' or 'minor' can have substantial effects on a patient's way of life. It is also apparent that travel anxiety can have far-reaching consequences for the survivor and their family.

LONG-TERM OUTCOME

A postal five-year follow-up of a large cohort of road accident survivors (Mayou et al. 1991) and a five-year self-report study of the Oxford cohort described above, demonstrated that PTSD and travel anxiety can be persistent (Table 3.8). This results in continuing significant effects on everyday life for 10 to 20 per cent of respondents. It is our clear impression that while road accidents are immediately less distressing than many other forms of trauma and associated with less severe intrusive memories, their continuing impact on everyday life is considerable, so that, in the long term, morbidity may be comparable to that reported following rape and other initially more distressing traumas.

CHILDREN

Most published research concerns adult road accident survivors, although clinical experience and reports of post-traumatic symptoms in children following other forms of trauma suggest that children too are at risk of significant psychiatric complications (see Chapter 5). In our recent postal study at around five months after an accident, we found clinically significant psychological and behavioural symptoms as a consequence of the

Table 3.8 Long-term outcome

- Cognitive disorder
- Anxiety and depression
- Persistent travel anxiety as driver; as passenger
- PTSD
- Concern about disfigurement
- Concern about future disability
- Dissatisfaction / anger

Table 3.9 Psychological consequences in children

- Worry about travel
- Intrusive thoughts
- Behavioural changes
- Psychological symptoms
- Parental concern and protection

accident in almost half the sample of children. These included post-traumatic symptoms (intrusive memories and travel anxiety), but also a range of non-specific changes in mood and behaviour (Table 3.9). Parental concern and overprotection were common and may have explained some of the changes. What is perhaps most noteworthy is the finding that despite the severity of some of the psychiatric complications, and the impact on family life, none of the respondents had had any form of medical or social help.

COMPENSATION NEUROSIS

A high proportion of those injured in serious road accidents who believe they are innocent seek compensation for injury. 'Compensation neurosis' continues to be seen in medico-legal contexts as a common clinical complication after an accident. Research evidence has cast very considerable doubts on widely held traditional views about this syndrome, although they remain influential amongst doctors and lawyers (Mayou 1995). There is no substantial evidence that the prospect of compensation is a major determinant of any aspect of outcome following road accident injury, even though a small proportion of patients involved in disputed litigation may simulate or exaggerate their difficulties (see Chapter 11).

Our own six-year follow-up of ninety-six accident survivors seeking compensation found rather few differences between claimants and non-claimants, although we noted very considerable anger and dissatisfaction with compensation processes (Mayou 1995). Few were involved in disputes about the extent of the disabilities and it was notable that awards were relatively modest, and seemed to take little account of severe psychological and social complications and the associated impact on the quality of the person's life (see Chapter 10). We identified no more than one or two as presenting a clinical picture in any way consistent with descriptions of compensation neurosis, or in whom exaggeration might have been an element. There was no obvious difference in outcome between those seeking compensation and those not pursuing it, and there were very few disputes about the extent of disability and loss. Follow-up suggests that symptoms do *not* improve on settlement. Our impression is that a considerable proportion of accident survivors decide not to claim or are reluctant to pursue claims vigorously in order to avoid the frustrations and difficulties of dealing with the law and would prefer to get on with returning to a normal life. An important factor in deciding to seek compensation is the anger felt by innocent victims at the lack of recognition of their suffering by those responsible, by legal processes and others. For many, sympathetic recognition of their suffering was seen as more important than any financial reward. Lack of evidence for 'compensation neurosis' should not obscure the undoubted importance of financial hardship, the frustrations with the legal process, and the prospect of receiving some compensation as social determinants of outcome, amongst many other variables (Mayou 1996).

WHIPLASH NECK INJURY

'Whiplash' has attracted much more attention than any other form of road accident injury because of its medico-legal implications, and because of a widely held belief that persistent physical symptoms may have psychological rather than social causes. Simulation and exaggeration have been seen as prominent. Despite the ferocity of the arguments about the role of psychological aetiology, there have been few attempts to look at the course, outcome or aetiology using quantitative measures. The overwhelming proportion of current evidence fails to support historical views, and substantial reviews have concluded that the aetiology of persistent somatic symptoms is basically physical. It would be reasonable to see psychological and social variables having an influence, as they do in reaction to any other type of physical disorder.

A small number of studies have described psychiatric outcome (Mayou and Radanov 1996). In the Oxford study the psychiatric outcome at three months and one year was very similar to that described by accident survivors with multiple injuries; with a higher prevalence of anxiety and depression in the general population and frequent post-traumatic symptoms, both phobic anxiety and PTSD. It is notable that even when symptoms might have been seen as rather slight, they were frequently of a nature to significantly affect everyday activities, and that disability associated with psychiatric problems, especially travel anxiety, was common.

Neither a Swiss study (see Chapter 6) nor the Oxford study have found significant evidence that psychological factors are determinants of physical symptoms, although they indicate that psychological factors are much more substantial determinants of associated social impairment. It is evident that, although whiplash neck injury is seen as medically minor, it can often result in persistent physical symptoms and limitation, which are a nuisance in themselves and can interfere with highly valued activities. The psychological consequences, and especially those of travel anxiety, have also been ignored but are important since the adverse effects on quality of life resulting from physical impairment and from travel anxiety can be very considerable.

The widely held belief that whiplash patients are neurotic and motivated by desire for compensation is erroneous and has been harmful. Psychosocial factors play the same role as they do in other physical illnesses and there are particularly close comparisons with the consequences of back pain and other musculo-skeletal injury. As with road accident injury in general, it is important not to draw general conclusions from experience with a highly selected group who may exaggerate or fabricate symptoms and disability.

CONCLUSION

The psychiatry of road traffic accident injury in many ways is just one example of the psychiatry of any significant physical disorder, although it differs with respect to post-traumatic symptoms. While the intrusive thoughts associated with a diagnosis of PTSD have attracted overwhelming attention, the phobic anxiety associated with travelling as a driver or passenger probably has a greater impact on everyday life.

The problems of the definition of PTSD, and the attempts to differentiate it from other psychiatric comorbidity, pose continuing theoretical difficulties. Whatever the validity of an arbitrarily defined syndrome, it does appear that intrusive thoughts and memories, and phobic anxiety, do have somewhat different determinants to anxiety and depression. The emphasis in this chapter has been on the psychiatry of road traffic accident *injury*, although there is reason to believe that those involved in frightening accidents who are not injured may also suffer psychiatric consequences, including travel anxiety and PTSD. It seems probable that close relatives of those who have been injured may themselves become more nervous about travel.

Whatever the uncertainties about the psychiatric consequences of road accidents and their determinants, there is no doubt that they pose a significant clinical problem. It would seem likely that problems are best identified during convalescence rather than immediately following an accident. Immediate reactions may be some guide to risk, but it is more appropriate to concentrate on early recognition and then on providing

Table 3.10 Implications for psychological care following a road accident

- Advice about driving for those in medical or psychiatric high-risk groups.
- Care in prescription of drugs with CNS side effects.
- Routine advice to RTA victims: road safety, return to driving.
- Extra help for high-risk subjects: interventions of post-traumatic symptoms.
- Early intervention for other psychological and social complications.
- Specialist care for psychological and behavioural consequences of head injury.
- Management of alcohol and substance abuse.
- Assessment and management of 'accident neurosis'.
- Support for relatives and for others involved in care.
- Assessment for legal proceedings.

individually formulated help to meet particular needs (see Table 3.10). The problem for clinical services is how to provide such help to large numbers of people, especially when a high proportion of patients are not systematically followed up after injury (see Chapter 13). The long-term answer would seem to be a matter of awareness of a need to recognise problems, on the part of specialist and primary care doctors and others involved in treating road accident survivors. It also perhaps depends on a greater public awareness that difficulties in travel and other common consequences of involvement in a road accident are common, but are medically treatable.

Chapter 4

Clinical patterns of acute psychological response to trauma

Michelle Atchison and Alexander McFarlane

Litigation and compensation issues have long obscured the systematic investigation of the effects of road accidents. The definition of post-traumatic stress disorder (PTSD) in the third edition of the diagnostic and statistical manual of the American Psychiatric Association was an important breakthrough, as it recognised the importance of distinct traumatic events which involved death and threat to life and limb as causes of psychiatric disorder. The subsequent history requires little elaboration.

Increasingly there have been many attempts to characterise better both the prevalence of experiences which might cause PTSD as well as the relative risk of PTSD arising after different types of traumatic events (Norris 1992; Kessler et al. in press). Correspondingly, the definition of the events that lead to PTSD have not been changed, with DSM-IV (American Psychiatric Association 1994) proposing that such events should involve actual physical injury or threat to an individual's integrity. The study of the epidemiology of this disorder has provided a substantial justification for the proliferating interest in the disorder and has done much to counter the many influences that have minimised the acceptance and significance and prevalence of traumatic stressors (van der Kolk and McFarlane 1996). While there is little doubt that many people experience the threat and distress of these events without being disabled or developing long-term psychological symptoms, Norris (1992) in a study of 1,000 adults in southern USA found 69 per cent of the sample had experienced a traumatic stressor in their lives. Road accidents represented the most adverse combination of frequency and impact, highlighting the importance of a road accident as a cause of PTSD. However, as Mayou (this volume) describes, PTSD is only one of the psychological consequences of road accidents. Major depressive disorders, panic disorder and substance abuse are also important outcomes.

In this context, there has been increasing focus on the acute responses to trauma and how they predict longer-term reaction. As well, DSM-IV and ICD-10 have, for the first time, included categories of 'pathological acute responses' to traumatic stress situations. Many road accident survivors are admitted to hospital, which emphasises the importance of understanding acute, as well as longer-term reactions. If the acute patterns of distress which particularly predict the long-term outcomes could be defined, this means that it would be possible to focus acute preventative interventions. This raises a series of questions which this chapter will aim to investigate.

First, what is the phenomenology of patterns of acute psychological response to trauma? The majority of descriptions of acute stress responses at time of trauma are retrospective reconstructions a while after the event. Patterns of acute psychological response to trauma were detailed by Lindemann (1944) although he focused on patterns of grief in people who had lost a relative or friend. Malt and Olafsen (1992) described the cognitive, emotional and behavioural responses of a group of 109 accident survivors, including a number of interesting but brief vignettes. Few other published accounts focused on clinical descriptions until Shalev et al. (1993) described the early psychological responses of the survivors of a horrific bus accident in Israel. This study was of particular interest because it demonstrated the fluidity of the early reactions. It also demonstrated that intrusions were common in most survivors but were of little predictive value for later psychopathology. Malt et al.'s (1993) study of Scandinavian train drivers involved in on-the-track accidents supported this observation by demonstrating that in those subjects who developed PTSD, symptoms such as avoidance and hyperarousal were not immediate responses to the accident; they tended rather to develop during the days following the accident. These studies provide no comment, however, on whether any of the subjects would have been diagnosed as suffering from an acute stress disorder.

A substantial limitation for research in the area of phenomenology is the lack of instruments for describing acute psychological responses. Commonly used instruments for assessing depression and anxiety do not capture the immediacy of these acute reactions. Recent developments of the Stanford Acute Stress Reaction Questionnaire (Cardena et al. 1991) has added to the area. The questionnaire, however makes assumptions about patterns of response, focusing on the axes of anxiety and dissociation.

Second, a fundamental question concerns the relevance of acute psychological responses to the development of later psychopathology. Military medicine has formed the basis for many opinions concerning vulnerability to PTSD, with assumptions that PTSD sufferers must have had personality defects that conferred vulnerability – the 'only cowards develop PTSD' view. Other vulnerability factors such as social support (Solomon et al. 1987) and post-trauma events (Solomon et al. 1988) have been more recently explored. A consistent finding has been that the more 'traumatic' the event, the greater the likelihood of developing PTSD (Foy et al. 1987; Green et al. 1990b; Norris 1992). However, the means by which a traumatic situation confers vulnerability to PTSD is still poorly understood. The DSM-IV category of Brief Psychotic Disorder acknowledges the development of psychotic illness after traumatic events. Mayou et al. (1993) described different patterns of acute emotional distress in 188 road accident survivors. Different patterns of response conferred vulnerability to different psychiatric outcomes. PTSD was predicted by 'horrific' intrusive memories soon after the accident, while development of mood disorders was predicted by pre-accident psychiatric illness and high neuroticism scores in the Eysenck Personality Inventory.

This chapter describes the acute pattern of reaction in road accident survivors. Clinical interviews were carried out two and ten days after the accident, and on the day following admission (i.e. 12 to 36 hours after the accident). Study participants were part of a larger prospective study of consecutive road accident survivors admitted for at least one night to the Royal Adelaide Hospital in South Australia. This is the hospital that deals with major trauma for the state of 1.2 million people. Those who sustained a head injury with loss of consciousness greater than fifteen minutes, or who were too physically unwell from their injuries to co-operate, were excluded. The sample consists of 81 males (67 per cent) and 39 females (33 per cent): mean age was 31.8 years (SD 14.3). Accident types were car (67 per cent), motorbike (19 per cent), push bike (6 per cent) and pedestrian (8 per cent). Damage to vehicles was severe in 64 per cent of the accidents. Injury Severity Scores (ISS) (Baker et al. 1974) were minor (<6) in 60 per cent of cases, moderate (6–13) in 33 per cent and major (>14) in 7 per cent of cases.

Over the course of 120 interviews, the clinical impression of the first author, a psychiatrist who conducted all the interviews, was that four broad categories of psychological response to accident exist, according to the person's general level of anxiety and their anxiety while describing the event, and the quality of their memory for the event. It became clear that the term 'intrusive thoughts' was inadequate to describe the distressing thoughts of the accident experienced by the survivor, and that the phenomenology of the acute cognitions and affective recollections has been over-simplified by the current diagnostic criteria.

ABSENCE OF DISTRESS, GOOD RECALL

The first group was characterised by minimal anxiety either at rest or when describing the accident. The accident and its consequences were described in a very matter-of-fact way. When discussing previous traumatic events it was clear that people in this group dealt with these experiences by not dwelling on them, and that even in the immediate aftermath they dealt with what were potentially life-threatening circumstances by 'getting on with life'.

Subject 1 was a 24-year-old single man with a strong interest in motorcycle racing. He described a history of conduct disorder as a teenager but had settled into a job selling and racing motorcycles. He had had numerous previous accidents without psychological sequelae. While on a 'fun run' with 150 other motorcycles another motorcycle slid into him, pushing him on to a parked car where he sustained a compound fracture of his left patella and a fractured metacarpal. On interview he described being in terrible pain at the accident scene and feeling anxious, but improving as soon as the ambulance arrived. In hospital he dealt well with the medical procedures and when interviewed the next day saw the accident as 'just another one to get over'. He denied subjective anxiety and objectively was calm and co-operative. He presented as a man who did not dwell on psychological issues and had little capacity to introspect on his emotions. He dealt with problems by working on them in practical ways and he was co-operative with staff over procedures.

Subject 2 was a 23-year-old single man who was completing a university degree in sciences. He described a happy early life with no previous traumatic experiences. While walking across a busy city street he was hit with no warning by a car, sustaining a simple fracture of his right tibia and fibula. He remembered lying on the ground and believing he was not injured, but his leg buckling underneath him at an angle when he tried to stand up. He described screaming with pain 'to release energy' and feeling intense relief at the sight of the ambulance. On the way to the hospital he 'chatted' with the ambulance staff about the accident, and on interview the next day described the event in an offhand way. There was no evidence of anxiety objectively or subjectively, and he spoke in an intellectualised manner about what his 'mind's response' was to the accident. He spoke of 'just fixing up the leg, then I'll be back in life'.

Wortman and Silver (1989) point out that our society, and the research literature, has strong assumptions about how individuals deal with events. While Wortman and Silver focused largely on responses to grief and loss, similar assumptions are made about individuals' responses to traumatic events. There is a general assumption that distress is normal, and that the absence of distress is a marker of pathology, usually that the individual is not 'properly working through' the experience. These assumptions are generally made by professionals who have experience dealing with psychological issues. From the first author's experience on trauma wards, most staff do acknowledge that minimal distress can be a normal and adaptive response, but will view overly distressed patients as 'abnormal'. The range of responses has also been demonstrated in studies of disaster and combat veterans where, even in situations of extraordinary threat, some individuals experience a minimal sense of vulnerability and have no significant distress response. This emphasises the importance of epidemiological research in the investigation of the effects of trauma, and that hypotheses about aetiology and formulations about phenomenology should not be based solely on clinical samples.

Findings from the present study also challenge the commonly held belief amongst trauma workers that intrusive thoughts are a 'normal' and universal response to traumatic events. Malt and Olafsen (1992) reported on a sample of 109 accidentally injured adults and found that 15 per cent reported no intrusive thoughts of their accident, and only a minority were thought to be in a 'denial-numbness phase'. In their study, intrusive thoughts were commonly associated with pre-accident pathology and the development of new psychiatric illness after the accident. These results again emphasise the need to look beyond clinical samples when describing normal patterns of acute response to trauma, where intrusive thoughts may be a marker of vulnerability to psychiatric illness.

HYPERMNESIA WITHOUT AFFECT

The second group was characterised by an intensely clear memory of the accident which was conveyed with no associated affect. They differed from the previous group in that their memories had a vivid 'burnt-in' quality with recollections in all sensory modalities. Despite the intensity of their memories, they were recalled with no subjective or objective anxiety, or distress.

Subject 3 was a 21-year-old woman who was hit on the driver's side by another car while travelling through an intersection. She sustained severe facial lacerations and soft tissue injuries to her neck, arms and abdomen. On interview the next day she described feeling 'just fine' and went on to describe the accident in intricate detail, right down to the number of times she yelled out 'I'm hurt' to witnesses after the accident. She described what bystanders had been wearing, and what conversations she had with each of them. Her account of the accident was given with no evident distress, and on questioning she said she felt quite calm.

Subject 4 was a 21-year-old man who had lost control of his car while driving on a country road. His car hit a tree and he sustained a compound fracture of his right humerus. He described the accident in clear detail, including getting himself out of the car and lying against it to wait for help. He described the smell of petrol and the sounds of birds in the trees nearby in minute detail. He remembered feeling 'calm and indifferent' and believing that his arm was only sore, but that it couldn't have been broken. In interview, he described this event in detail, but with no associated distress or concern. He said that it was 'as though it had happened to someone else'.

Dissociation during a traumatic event is believed to be a risk factor for PTSD (Spiegel et al. 1988). This is usually seen in terms of dissociation causing a fragmented memory of the event that is then poorly integrated into existing cognitive schema, and re-experienced in the form of intrusive thoughts, dreams or flashbacks (van der Kolk and van der Hart 1989). In this group, however, dissociative experiences were described but the memory of the accident was intense and was not experienced as intrusions or flashbacks. This raises questions about the nature of dissociation and its effects on memory traces. There seemed to be evidence in this group that the memory was disconnected from appropriate affect. The memories also differed from usual traumatic memories or intrusive recollections in that they occurred in all sensory modalities. The nature of these intense memories may lead to a better understanding of flashbacks which have a vivid quality encompassing many sensory modalities but are accompanied by anxiety.

INTENSE INTRUSION

A third group was characterised by minimal anxiety but strong intrusive thoughts and dreams of the accident.

Subject 5 was a 26-year-old single man. The brakes on his car failed as he was driving a number of friends down a steep road. He tried to swerve the car off the road and ran head on into a tree, sustaining a fractured right ankle and left radius, with a degloving injury and tendon damage to his arm. He remembered people running to give him help, having blood all over his arm and his foot being stuck in the crumpled metal of the car. He was given nitrous oxide to breath while he was cut out of the car and was quickly operated on when he arrived at the hospital. On interview the next day he described a brief episode of anxiety earlier that day, 'when the shock hit', but he felt that was now behind him, saying that he felt lucky to have survived. He described strong intrusive thoughts of the accident, especially of hitting the tree. He had been unable to sleep the previous night because of intrusions in the form of a strong visual image of his body being flung forward, but he described this without subjective anxiety, seeming, instead, to be intrigued by his 'mind's tricks'.

Subject 6 was a 28-year-old single woman who was the front-seat passenger of a car that rolled on a country road as it was overtaking another car. She sustained a fracture of her left tibia, bilateral periorbital haematoma and marked microvascular damage over her face. After the car had come to a stop she was still in her seat, but with one leg out of the passenger window. She remembered being aware of the sound of someone screaming, and then realising it was her own voice. In interview the next day she described mildly disturbed sleep and concentration, and said she was more angry about the effect her injuries would have on her ability to work, than anxious. She clearly described dissociation after the accident, feeling as though the memory of the event was 'like watching it on the movies'. She felt she had 'blanked out' the worst bits of the accident but denied consciously avoiding thoughts of it. She did, however, describe very strong intrusive thoughts of the accident but was not distressed by them, viewing them as her mind 'replaying' the event.

Subject 7 was a 56-year-old widow who was the front-seat passenger of a car hit on the driver's side by another car in an intersection; she sustained a compound fracture of her thumb and 'seatbelt' bruising. She remembered being thrown under the dashboard. At the accident scene she felt 'terrified' and was worried she had sustained more serious injuries. This anxiety quickly settled in hospital and by the time of the interview she denied anxiety. She described poor sleep the previous night and strong intrusive thoughts, especially about the sound of the crash at impact. These thoughts came unbidden, but were also triggered by loud noises (especially metallic noises) in the ward. She denied avoiding thinking about the accident.

Horowitz's model of the stress response after a traumatic event is characterised by the oscillation between periods of intrusive re-experiences and – in an attempt to escape these psychologically painful experiences – avoidance behaviours (Horowitz 1976). Another aspect of this model is that re-experiencing a traumatic event is associated with hyperarousal, which itself encourages more intrusive recollections (Easterbrook 1959).

Survivors in this group show that intrusive re-experiencing of the event is not necessarily coupled with either heightened arousal or avoidance behaviours. It would seem more likely, and clinically valid, that avoidance behaviours may begin to emerge in those people whose intrusive recollections do not extinguish with time after the traumatic event. If intrusive thoughts are not always coupled with heightened arousal, this raises the possibility that disturbances of arousal may run a parallel, and perhaps independent, course. Factors other than the intensity of intrusive recollections may determine disordered arousal: for example, trait anxiety, neuro-hormonal response at the time of the traumatic event or prior traumatic experiences. Of interest in this group, is that memories of the accident occurred in only one or two sensory modalities. It was unusual to encounter survivors who had intrusive thoughts of a 'complete' nature.

OVERT DISTRESS

The last group was characterised by persisting anxiety, intrusive recollections and 'cognitive reworking' of the event. They tended to dwell consciously on the accident and its possible consequences. Avoidance strategies were uncommon.

Subject 8 was a 42-year-old married man who had just found work after an extended period of unemployment. He was knocked off his motorbike by a car during a lunch break from work, sustaining a compound fracture of his right tibia and fibula. He described being 'in a hell of a shock' and feeling panicked as he waited for help. Thoughts of being again unemployed and how he would pay his ambulance or hospital bills began as he was lying on the roadway. He was concerned that because he was taking antibiotics they would show up as a positive alcohol reading. In interview the next day he was still very distressed with numerous worries about the future. Staff had been unable to reassure him. Far from avoiding thoughts of the accident, he described purposely going over and over the accident in his mind to determine what he had done wrong. He had slept poorly the previous night, found it difficult to concentrate and was easily distractible.

Subject 9 was a 21-year-old man whose brakes failed as he was approaching a main road. The car ran out into traffic and he was hit on the driver's side by a truck. The bonnet of the truck was pushed through his car's windscreen. His legs were crushed, sustaining a left fractured patella and a right fractured malleolus. He described intense pain and was worried that his legs were damaged beyond repair. On interview the next day he described feeling anxious and 'on edge'. He denied intrusive recollections, but said that he was purposely going over the accident in his mind to see if he could have changed anything. He described a very chaotic early life with physical abuse from both parents and time in jail for stealing. He had left home at 14 and generally felt that life had been a series of trials for him. Interestingly, his reworking of the accident revolved around having done something to have caused it, and whether he would be punished. These cognitions had obvious parallels in his developmental history.

Subject 10 was a 42-year-old married man who had an ongoing post-traumatic stress disorder from an accident eight years previously when he was involved in a fire in a prison. He was hit from behind by a car while driving a motorcycle. The motorcycle flipped and landed on top of him, causing simple fractures of his right tibia and fibula. He described being intensely frightened during the accident and fearing that he might die. While waiting for the ambulance he felt himself hyperventilating and purposely tried to slow his breathing. In interview the next day he described feeling very anxious, having difficulty concentrating and generally feeling 'on edge'. He had strong intrusive recollections and was also consciously going over the accident in his mind. He felt that if he 'understood' the accident he would be able to get back on a motorcycle again. He denied avoidance strategies.

This group was more atypical of a pathological 'acute stress reaction' as they viewed themselves subjectively as distressed and unable to function. They felt they had been adversely affected by their accident and viewed their psychological symptoms as outside their normal range of experiences. There was also a strong sense that they felt psychologically overwhelmed by their experience and were either unable to call on coping strategies or fell back on old, and perhaps inappropriate, ways of coping.

Two points of interest arose from this group. First, dissociative experiences at the time of the accident in this group, and in groups one ('absence of distress, good recall') and three ('intense intrusion'), were uncommon. In the post-accident phase, dissociative experiences were most commonly associated with intense pain or nitrous oxide administration. Although much research has suggested that dissociation at the time of the traumatic event has a pathological effect, this study raises issues that require greater clarification. In particular, both the 'timing' of dissociative experiences, and whether there are particular pathological dissociative experiences have not been adequately addressed. Malt and Olafsen (1992) looked at derealisation as a marker of dissociative experiences in their accident group. Fifteen per cent of the sample described derealisation, in all but one of the sample lasting seconds and usually occurring in the minutes after the accident. Derealisation was found to be a poor predictor of later 'post-traumatic mental disorders'. Waller (1994) suggested that dissociative experiences do not fall along a continuum, but can be grouped into non-pathological and pathological experiences. The same may be true of dissociation during or immediately after a road accident, with only certain experiences conferring vulnerability to later psychopathology. In the first author's experience, for example, dissociation at times of intense pain after an accident seemed to have a protective, rather than pathological effect.

Second, another point of interest was the common phenomenon of 'cognitive reworking' or consciously going over and over the accident. This contrasted with intrusive thoughts which were differentiated by being an involuntary process. In the semi-structured interview it was easy to differentiate between intrusive recollections that came unbidden or were triggered by reminders, and cognitive reworking of the accident. The first author noted, however, that it was common for subjects to answer positively on the intrusion items of the Impact of Events Scale (IES) when, in fact, they were describing conscious cognitive reworking. This raises questions about the validity of these items. Given the widespread use of the IES in trauma research, this has implications for the results of many studies and for our conceptualisations of 'intrusive recollections'. The role of conscious reworking of the trauma in persistent hyperarousal also warrants further investigation.

DISCUSSION

Four patterns of acute psychological response appeared to emerge. This highlights the protean nature of response to the acute threat and injury following road accidents. Above all, PTSD, particularly in its acute forms, is not a static state. It is a disorder that progresses and changes with the passage of time. Although the immediate precipitant of the disorder is known, PTSD as a full syndrome does not begin at the time of the trauma. In fact, in the DSM-IV, there is an explicit statement that symptoms must be present for at least one month. Thus according to current formulations, the disorder that occurs following exposure to a trauma is by necessity a prolonged response, that may or may not have its immediate antecedents at the time of the trauma, but is nonetheless conceived of as separate from the acute response to trauma.

PTSD only develops in a proportion of individuals who are exposed to traumatic events and may involve a complex set of antecedents as well as a cascade of biobehavioural changes. Thus realistic models for the development of PTSD must account for a modification of a range of biological systems. One of the critical questions about PTSD is how the acute response to what is often a single stressor of brief duration merges into the constellation of PTSD symptoms. The majority of individuals who experience a traumatic event will immediately have at least some intrusive and distressing recollections of this event. However, only a subgroup of individuals subsequently develop symptoms of avoidance, hyperarousal and intrusive memories. Based on the longitudinal progression of the way these symptoms emerge in the immediate aftermath of a trauma, it has been suggested that the intrusive and distressing recollections and not the direct experience of the traumatic event, actually drive the biological and psychological dimensions of PTSD. Thus the traumatic event, while being necessary for the induction of PTSD is not a sufficient explanation for the emergence of the syndrome.

The group not distressed after their accident challenges our views of the 'normal working through' of a traumatic event. The role of dissociation during a traumatic event, and, in particular, the question of whether there are only certain 'noxious' dissociative experiences, requires clarification. The effect of dissociation on memory traces appears to be more complicated than previously acknowledged. Avoidance behaviours are shown to be quite uncommon in the acute phase. The role of hyperarousal, and, in particular, whether this runs a course independent of intrusions, requires clarification. It is clear that the term 'intrusive thoughts' is inadequate to describe the distressing thoughts of the accident that many experienced, and the phenomenology of acute cognitions and affective recollections has been overly simplified by current diagnostic criteria.

Chapter 5

The effects on children of road accidents

Rachel Canterbury and William Yule

Road traffic accidents are a major cause of death and injury in children. In 1994, over 45,000 children in Britain under the age of 16 were injured in road accidents, of whom approximately 7,200 were seriously injured and 300 died (Department of Transport, 1994). Although continuing improvements in road and vehicle safety have played a vital role in reducing the frequency of road accidents and the severity of injuries sustained, attention also needs to be given to the consequences of such accidents. Medical services are readily available to those who have been physically injured but consideration is rarely given to the emotional needs of children involved in such accidents.

It is now well documented that children react to life-threatening stressors with various forms of distress, including depression, anxiety, fears and bereavement reactions as well as post-traumatic stress disorder (PTSD). Without treatment, such disorders can persist for a considerable time. However, the psychological impact of road accidents on children has received scant attention in the literature. The authors' clinical experience clearly indicates that some children suffer severe post-traumatic stress reactions following a road accident. This view is supported by studies of adult road accident survivors (Brom et al. 1993; Mayou et al. 1993; Blanchard et al. 1995). In this context, the authors undertook to further investigate the psychological sequelae in child survivors of road accidents (Canterbury et al. 1993). This chapter will describe the findings of their study as well as discussing possible risk factors associated with more severe emotional reactions.

THE EMOTIONAL IMPACT OF TRAUMA IN CHILDREN

It has long been recognised that children, like adults, react to stressful events, but until the last decade it had largely been assumed that such reactions were temporary adjustment reactions. However, many researchers did not ask children about their symptoms but instead relied on the reports of parents and teachers. As a result, individual psychopathology was overlooked and levels of distress greatly underestimated. By interviewing children directly and using appropriate standardised measures, it is now clear that children and adolescents can develop adult-like PTSD following exposure to a wide variety of traumatic events (for reviews see Yule 1991, 1993; Saylor 1993; Gordon and Wraith 1993; Pynoos and Nader 1993).

While the construct of PTSD as operationalised in DSM-IV (American Psychiatric Association 1994) and ICD-10 (World Health Organisation 1992) is of value in guiding clinicians, it does not fully reflect the complex reactions of children. As well as the tripartite grouping of symptoms which characterise PTSD – re-experiencing the traumatic event, avoidance of stimuli associated with the trauma, and increased arousal – children and adolescents commonly describe a range of other reactions. Although there are few published studies on the effects of trauma on pre-school children, there is some evidence that pre-school children show much more regressive behaviour as well as more anti-social, aggressive and destructive behaviour. There are also many anecdotal accounts of pre-school children showing repetitive drawing and play involving themes about the trauma they experienced. More recently, it has become apparent that very young children are able to give graphic accounts of their experiences and also to report their levels of distress, provided they are given a means of doing so that is appropriate to their age (Sullivan et al. 1991; Misch et al. 1993). For example, Misch et al. found that children with limited language ability were able to describe their experience of a particular trauma through play, using a model representing the trauma scene.

In older children, sleep disturbance is very common. As well as difficulties in getting off to sleep and being woken by nightmares, children also report fears of the dark and the fear of being alone. Separation difficulties are frequent, even among teenagers. Many children become more irritable and angry, feel a sense of aloneness and find it difficult to talk to parents and peers. Others report memory problems and difficulties in concentration which interfere with school work and other activities. A sense of foreshortened future leads some children to feel that they should live each day to the full and not plan ahead. For others, priorities change. Many experience guilt about escaping when others died, about thinking they should have done more to help others, or about believing that their actions endangered others. A significant number become very anxious, although the appearance of panic attacks is sometimes considerably delayed. Some children will have been bereaved and, given the traumatic circumstances surrounding the death, pathological grief reactions may also contribute to the presenting picture (Yule 1991; Pynoos and Nader 1993). Adolescent survivors in particular report high rates of depression, some becoming clinically depressed. Premature movement towards independence and risk-taking behaviour have also been reported (Yule 1991; Pynoos and Nader 1993).

There is still a need to investigate the prevalence of post-trauma symptoms at different ages, and for careful descriptive studies of representative groups of traumatised children studied over periods of time to establish the natural history of the disorder in this age group. Nevertheless, a number of general conclusions can be drawn. By and large, the more threatened a child feels during a traumatic event, the greater the risk of developing PTSD (Pynoos and Eth 1986; Pynoos et al. 1987; Pynoos and Nader 1988; Yule et al. 1990). The subjective appraisal of threat is as important as the objective risk (Williams et al. 1992). On the whole, girls react with greater levels of distress than boys (Gibbs 1989; Yule 1992) and less able children are more affected than bright children. School work can be badly affected and children can be thrown off the normal educational trajectory if they fail to achieve well in crucial examinations (Tsui et al., unpublished report).

ASSOCIATED FACTORS IN ROAD ACCIDENTS INVOLVING CHILDREN

Injury

Department of Transport (1994) data indicate that, of the total number of accidents involving children, approximately 45 per cent were pedestrians, 35 per cent were passengers in cars and 20 per cent were cyclists. Of the total, 17 per cent sustained injuries that were serious or fatal. Pedestrian accidents carry the greatest risk of serious injury or death, accounting for approximately 60 per cent of children killed or seriously injured. This particular risk to pedestrians has been reported by other authors (Jaworowski 1992; Wheatley and Cass 1989; Illingworth 1979).

Illingworth (1979) described the pattern of accidents and injuries in 227 consecutive children who attended at the Accident and Emergency Department at the Children's Hospital in Sheffield following road accidents (about 12 per cent of all new attendees). Of these, approximately three-quarters were pedestrians, with roughly equal numbers of passengers and cyclists. Injuries were graded using a five point scale, '1' representing very minor injuries and '5' indicating potentially life-threatening conditions. Injuries graded 4 or 5 required admission to hospital. Of the total sample, 37 per cent had injuries in grades 4 or 5 (three of which were fatal). Serious head injury occurred in nearly 30 per cent of children and accounted for the majority of hospital admissions (total 38 per cent). Illingworth compared the pattern of injuries in this sample with data from two previous studies, one of skateboard injuries and the other of playground equipment injuries. In these groups the proportion of injuries graded 4 or 5 was considerably less (10.7 per cent and 7.5 per cent respectively). Serious head injuries were found in less than 1 per cent of skateboard accidents and only 6 per cent of playground accidents. Admission rates were also much lower (4 per cent and 10 per cent respectively).

Although comparisons are complicated by the use of different measures of injury severity and changes in the patterns of road accidents and injury over time, it appears that the majority of children involved in road accidents suffer injuries that are mild to moderate in severity. Head injuries are common and account for a sizeable proportion of admissions. Compared with some other common causes of accidental injury, road accidents carry a greater risk of severe or fatal injury with pedestrian accidents accounting for a sizeable proportion of this group.

Individual and family factors

The relationship between such factors and post-accident psychopathology has yet to be fully explored. Jaworowski (1992) summarises some of the literature examining personality and behavioural disposition to accidental injury in children including road accidents. Impulsivity and deficits in concentration and co-ordination have been reported as risk factors. In addition, three forms of family disruption or disadvantage – crowding, family problems and placement in local authority care – have also been found to be associated with traffic injuries in children (Pless et al. 1989). Jaworowski comments on the difficulty in accurately assessing the child's level of functioning before the accident, what vulnerabilities existed and how they were manifested.

Emotional impact of road accidents in children

There are no reported studies on children involved in road accidents which examine the prevalence of psychological symptoms. In light of this, the authors compared a group of children who had survived a road accident with a group attending a hospital fracture clinic on a number of measures of psychopathology. The fracture clinic group was included in order to control for the possible effects of hospital attendance. Subjects in both groups were traced through the Accident and Emergency Department patient register at King's College Hospital, London. Questionnaires, together with a covering letter, were sent by post to the children's parents. All the children were between 8 and 16 years of age at the time of their accident and were contacted between eight and fifteen months post-accident. Children who had experienced head injuries necessitating admission to hospital were excluded from the study in order to reduce the possible confounding effects of brain injury.

Each child was asked to complete the following self-report measures: The Impact of Events Scale (IES) (Horowitz et al. 1979); the Birleson Depression Inventory (Birleson 1981); the Revised Children's Manifest

Anxiety Scale (RCMAS) (Reynolds and Richmond 1978); and the Fear Survey Schedule for Children–Revised (FSSC–R) (Ollendick et al. 1991), which contains items relating to a wide variety of possible fears. The first three measures had previously been reported as useful in screening post-traumatic stress reactions in adolescents (Yule and Udwin 1991).

Twenty-eight children – sixteen girls and twelve boys – who had survived road accidents completed and returned questionnaires, a response rate of 33 per cent. Eighteen were pedestrians, eight were cyclists, one jumped off a moving bus and one was a passenger on a bus. The response rate among children attending the hospital fracture clinic was lower, only twenty-four children (20 per cent) returned questionnaires. This group comprised ten girls and fourteen boys. Fifteen had sustained injuries as a result of a fall and nine as a result of sport or leisure activity. The difference between the mean age at the time of the accident of the road accident group and the other injury group was not significant (13 years and 12.2. years respectively). However, the time between accident and screening was significantly shorter for the road accident group (a mean of 10.7 months) compared with the fracture clinic group (12.5. months).

The injuries sustained by the children in both groups were coded for severity by the Accident and Emergency Department consultant using the Abbreviated Injury Scale (AIS) (Association for the Advancement of Automotive Medicine 1990) for individual injuries, and using Injury Severity Scores (ISS) (Baker et al. 1974) for multiple injuries. Both groups of children were assessed as having sustained minor, non-life-threatening injuries, all having been treated as out-patients and returned home the same day. It is interesting to note that none of the study sample had more severe injuries, and, in the light of Illingworth's (1979) findings, it is likely that many of the more severely injured children had head injuries and were therefore excluded from the study.

Although the injuries were judged of similar severity, the road accident group obtained significantly higher scores on the IES than the fracture clinic group – indicating an emotional impact of a road accident over and above that associated with an accidental injury necessitating hospital attendance. The distress, however, did not extend to increased levels of anxiety, depression and fears, with the exception of one item on the FSSC–R: 'Going in the car or bus'. Significant gender differences were found on measures of anxiety, depression and fears, girls obtaining higher scores, which replicated other work (Yule 1992).

In order to anchor scores obtained on the IES with DSM III-R criteria for diagnosis of PTSD, three children from both the road accident and fracture clinic groups were later interviewed in accordance with DSM III-R criteria and using the Child Post-Traumatic Stress Reaction Index (PTSRI) (Frederick and Pynoos 1988) which provides an indication of the severity of the disorder. Higher scores on the IES were found to be associated with higher levels of depression and anxiety, a greater number of symptoms of PTSD and a higher score on the PTSRI. Only one girl interviewed fulfilled DSM III-R criteria for PTSD. She was a road accident survivor with an IES score of 50, placing her in the top 25 per cent of scores in the road accident group. Her score of 39 on the PTSRI is at the upper limit of the band indicating PTSD of moderate severity.

This study confirms that PTSD does occur in some survivors of relatively minor road accidents, although given the rather poor response rate (32.6 per cent), and the small number of children interviewed, estimating prevalence is difficult. It is, therefore, useful to draw upon previous findings. Yule has described the emotional impact on child survivors of the cruise ship *Jupiter* which sank in Piraeus harbour in 1988 (Yule and Udwin 1991; Yule 1992). Four hundred British school children and their teacher were on board. One teacher, one child and two seamen assisting in the rescue died. Approximately 50 per cent of a sample of survivors met diagnostic criteria for PTSD (with a mean IES score of 36.44).

Given that six children within the road accident group had IES scores of 36 or above and that one of these children was found to meet diagnostic criteria, the best estimate of prevalence of PTSD is 1–6 out of the study sample (3.6 per cent to 21.4 per cent) or 1–6 out of the total 92 road accident survivors contacted (1.1 per cent to 6.5 per cent), giving a possible range 1 per cent to 21 per cent. Even the most conservative estimate of 1 per cent implies large numbers of children presenting with emotional difficulties that may go unrecognised. This does not include children with more serious injuries or head injuries. Furthermore, it is significant that contact with a number of parents indicated that they had chosen not to participate in the study as they felt that their child had been upset by the accident and the questionnaires would serve as an unwelcome reminder. This may also have been true for other parents of the more severely affected children.

Stallard and Law (1993) report on the psychological impact and value of debriefing in a group of seven children involved in a minibus accident. All the children sustained only minor physical injuries and, with the exception of one girl who was admitted overnight, were treated and discharged home the same day. Stallard and Law screened the children six months after the accident using the battery of self-report measures recommended by Yule and Udwin (1991). The children then participated in two sessions of group debriefing. The measures were repeated three months later and five children responded. They compared the results of the initial screen with scores obtained by survivors of the cruise ship *Jupiter* (Yule and Udwin 1991). There were no significant differences between the minibus survivors when assessed at six months before debriefing and survivors of the *Jupiter* disaster at five months who had already undergone debriefing. However, following the intervention, assessment of the minibus survivors demonstrated significant reductions on all measures. Although only one child was formally interviewed, Stallard and Law conclude that, on the basis of group discussion and questionnaire results, all seven survivors would probably have fulfilled DSM-III-R criteria for PTSD.

Stallard and Law note that as well as significant post-trauma symptomatology, the children also reported being distressed in relation to the way they were treated in hospital and subsequently by the media and the school. As their injuries were relatively minor, they had to wait for some time at the hospital before receiving medical treatment and were particularly distressed when one girl was removed from the group to a separate cubicle. The children reported that they were collected from the hospital in a minibus not unlike the one in which they had crashed and that they arrived back at the school to be confronted by the local press. Both were seen as causes of unnecessary anxiety. Many said that their school work was affected but that this was regarded unsympathetically by teachers. It is also reported that the school singled out two children as heroes and awarded them certificates of merit. This was resented by all the survivors.

The wider emotional implications of accidents involving children were examined by Heptinstall in association with the Child Accident Prevention Trust (Heptinstall 1996). Questionnaires designed by the first author were distributed to the parents of children who had attended Accident and Emergency Departments at hospitals in three different localities following any form of accidental injury. Parents were asked about the child's and their own immediate reactions to the accident, the longer-term effect of the accident on the child and the impact on the family as a whole. In addition, parents were asked to comment on the support that they received or would have liked. Children over the age of 8 were asked to give their own account of what happened and how they felt afterwards. They were also asked to complete the Impact of Events Scale. The questionnaires were distributed approximately four to six months after the accident.

It is not possible to discuss this comprehensive study in detail; however, a number of its findings are particularly pertinent. In relation to post-traumatic symptoms, scores obtained on the IES were strikingly high among children who had been involved in road accidents when compared to other forms of accidental injury. Of the total number of 273 children who completed the scale, twenty-five (9 per cent) scored above 36 while nearly 60 per cent scored less than 10, with 30 per cent reporting a total absence of symptoms. Out of the total sample, twenty children had been involved in a road accident of whom half scored more than 36 on the IES (mean 38, range 18–64). As indicated above, scores greater than 36 have been found to be associated with significant post-traumatic symptomatology. Falls from heights also resulted in high scores on the IES. Most children who reported high levels of distress had minor head injuries or fractures, but very few were admitted to hospital.

Although not directly measured, parents were asked to comment on their own distress following the accident. Many reported feelings of guilt, anxiety and depression. Some also observed increased distress in the siblings of the child involved. It is also noteworthy that some parents were surprised by the level of their child's distress as revealed by the child's comments on the questionnaires. It appeared that none of the children or parents had received emotional support other than the initial reassurance provided by Accident and Emergency staff. While many were very positive about this support, some parents also commented that further support both for themselves and their children would have been of benefit. Most parents of children involved in road accidents said that they were aware of their child's distress but did not know what psychological help would involve or how to go about finding it.

The CAPT report (Heptinstall 1996) emphasises the need for increased awareness among parents, medical personnel, teachers and other professionals, of the emotional impact of accidents on children and families. Parents also need to be informed of psychological and other services available to assist them and their children.

The results of these studies are summarised in Table 5.1 (adapted from Stallard and Law 1993). Scores obtained from the minibus survivors at six months and road accident survivors at a mean of over ten months (Canterbury et al. 1993) are compared with survivors of the cruise ship *Jupiter* at five months (Yule and Udwin 1991) and a sample of secondary school girls who had not been exposed (Yule and Udwin 1991). Of course the IES cannot be given to control children who have not experienced a traumatic event. Instead, Table 5.1 shows that the average IES score of child survivors of road accidents can be quite high, while scores of anxiety and depression seem to vary. It is probable that the severity of stress reactions is directly proportional to the severity of the accident.

While the prevalence of PTSD in child survivors of road accidents has

Table 5.1 Screen ratings of child survivors of trauma

	Cruise survivors (n=24) mean (SD)	Minibus accident (n=7) mean (SD)	RTAs (n=28) mean (SD)	Comparison Data (n=126) mean (SD)
Impact of events scale	35.33 (15.09)	31.11 (18.21)	19.93 (15.06)	*38.00 (md)**
Anxiety	16.04 (7.53)	13.57 (5.75)	10.86 (7.00)	12.40 (6.10)
Depression	14.80 (5.80)	15.14 (4.79)	9.96 (6.94)	9.30 (4.70)

Note: * Average IES scores of 20 RTA survivors 4–6 months post-accident (Heptinstall 1996); ** md = missing data.

yet to be clarified, it is already evident that some survivors go on to develop chronic and disabling reactions as is illustrated in two case studies from our files.

CASE VIGNETTE 1

Three years to the day after his father had been badly injured in a car crash, Mike was in the back of the family car with his brothers and cousins when they collided while overtaking another car. Mike was 8 years old.

The car turned over, Mike was thrown through the window and got out, although he cannot remember actually getting out of the car. He was aware that the others were still in the car. He remembers going in the ambulance. The next he knew he was in theatre where his clothing was cut off. He was given an injection in his arm that hurt him. The next thing he can remember he was in a wheelchair going up to the ward. He had a big bandage round his face and had a headache. He remained in hospital for nearly two weeks.

The first time he saw his scars, he was sitting in his bed playing a computer game when he saw his reflection in the screen. No one had told him his face was scarred and he tried at first to wipe the screen clean, then realised the scars really were there. The rest of his body was all right. He could not believe that no one had told him, and he sat on his bed and cried. When he returned to school, he was occasionally teased about the scars. He had plastic surgery over the following eight years. He had never really talked to his parents about the accident and its sequelae as he feared that his mother, especially, might be upset.

Mike was referred for assessment at age 15 and had not previously been assessed for his emotional reactions to the accident, nor for any help. At first he claimed to have few stress reactions, but was surprised at how upset he became when discussing the accident in detail. He was not keen on meeting new people and he feels embarrassed at having to tell people what happened to him when they comment on his scars. He remains wary of travelling in cars, especially when other cars overtake. He now always insists on wearing seat belts, but does not think he is unduly aware of dangers. For some time after the accident, he had bad dreams and intrusive thoughts, but these have greatly lessened over the years. However, he still actively avoids thinking of the accident and gets caught out occasionally if he is watching programmes on television.

On self-completed questionnaires, he scored as follows: Impact of Events (31); Birleson Depression (3); RCMAS-Anxiety (4). Thus his scores on anxiety and depression are within normal limits, but seven years after the accident his score on the Impact of Events Scale is higher than the average score (29) of teenage boys who survived the sinking of the cruise ship *Jupiter*, completing the form five months after the sinking.

Mike was developing normally prior to the car crash. Remembering that seven years had passed since the accident, he still reported high levels of both intrusive thoughts and avoidant behaviours and developed a positive psychiatric disorder, specifically PTSD (DSM-III-R) as a direct result of his experiences in the accident. He still has intrusive and upsetting thoughts about the accident, even though he usually manages to suppress them. He reports a lot of avoidant behaviour, and understates his symptoms. He still shows a few signs of increased physiological arousal. It appears that the disorder was of moderate severity earlier and it remained chronic and was of mild severity at the time of examination.

CASE VIGNETTE 2

Geoff was aged 7 when he was badly frightened in an unusual car accident. He was seated in the back of the car driven by his mother, waiting in a queue to enter a park when a car behind went out of control and hit their car, causing quite a bit of damage but no injury to the occupants. Three years later he was referred for treatment.

The car was hit on his side, and Geoff thought that he was going to be badly hurt, if not killed. Shortly afterwards, Geoff started to have nightmares and kept waking in the night. There were other times when he was too scared to sleep. He kept seeing pictures of the other car that hit him. He also developed a very strong fear of death.

When seen he still had worries about travelling by car. He still saw recurring pictures of what happened which were upsetting. His nightmares happened at least once a week. In the nightmare, the car turns over and goes into a ditch full of water. They fall down and with that he usually woke up shouting, with the bedcovers all over the place. He occasionally had flashbacks feeling as if it was all happening all over again. He felt shaky and scared. He did not like watching programmes on television that involved car crashes. He often had to sleep in his parents' bed. He felt that the accident had not really affected his future, although it may affect him when he starts to drive. Sleeping was a problem as he was waking up at least once a month. He denied being unduly irritable or having any concentration problems. He had become much more aware of dangers when he was in a car or walking on the pavement. He tries to stay in the middle of the seat when in the car. He said that he did not feel miserable or depressed, but was anxious. He worried about death. He got upset by sudden loud noises. There was no concern about his development before the accident, although this was followed immediately by the appearance of many symptoms of stress reactions and anxiety. As a direct consequence of the accident, Geoff developed a positive psychiatric disorder, namely, post-traumatic stress disorder of moderate severity, but which ran a chronic course still meeting criteria for the diagnosis three-and-a-half years later. On self-completed questionnaires at initial assessment in July, he scored as follows: Impact of Events (32); Birleson Depression (14); RCMAS-Anxiety (21).

Fortunately, following only two sessions of *Eye Movement Desensitisation and Reprocessing*, during which he recalled many details of the accident very vividly, there was a remarkable drop in the level of reported symptoms. On self-completed questionnaires, he scored at follow-up (September) as follows: Impact of Events (2); Birleson Depression (6); RCMAS-Anxiety (1). His mother confirmed that he was greatly improved and he no longer met criteria for a diagnosis of PTSD.

CONCLUSIONS AND DIRECTIONS FOR FUTURE RESEARCH

The research reported here indicate that some children suffer post-traumatic stress reactions following road accidents. However, at present there is a lack of systematic prospective research in this area. The growing number of studies within the adult literature support the view that road accidents carry a risk for psychological morbidity and also provide a model for future studies with children. In particular, the methodology described by Blanchard et al. (1995c), which provides categorical data on the proportion of adult road accident survivors meeting diagnostic criteria for PTSD as well as describing changes in symptoms over time, should be considered.

In addition, risk and protective factors which might influence post-traumatic responses in children involved in road accidents need to be examined. Studies of children exposed to other kinds of trauma have suggested that factors associated with the event, such as degree of exposure and perception of life threat, arc strongly related to subsequent adjustment. Factors associated with the child such as age, sex, academic ability and previous adjustment have received some attention in the literature but need further investigation.

At present it appears that psychological support is rarely offered to children involved in road accidents. The effects of the brief intervention described by Stallard and Law is encouraging but the efficacy of routine psychological debriefing has yet to be demonstrated (Raphael et al. 1995). Furthermore, Brom et al. (1993) found that a brief intervention with adult road accident survivors was no more effective than the passage of time. Systematic investigation of the prevalence, nature and duration of post-traumatic stress reactions in children involved in road accidents is essential in order to identify those children at particular risk and to target interventions appropriately. At the very least it is clear that professionals and parents need to be more aware of the emotional impact of road accidents on children, both to minimise subsequent distress and so that psychological difficulties can be identified early and appropriate help sought.

Chapter 6

Long-term outcome in whiplash injury

Bogdan P. Radanov, Matthias Sturzenegger and Giuseppe Di Stefano

When this study was designed in 1988 several reports existed regarding the consequences of whiplash injury (or soft-tissue injury of the cervical spine) (Balla 1982; Deans et al. 1987; Farbman 1973; Hodge 1971; Maimaris et al. 1988; Norris and Watt 1983). In our view, these had several serious limitations, among which were an unclear definition of the syndrome, use of a retrospective research design, selection bias (e.g. using records of insurance companies or patients involved in litigation procedure) and lack of comprehensiveness (i.e. studies have tended to isolate factors of interest to support the stated hypothesis but failed to investigate the relationship between different somatic or psychosocial factors in the longer term). In order to overcome these limitations we decided: to use a multi-disciplinary approach to investigate patients who had been injured in a motor vehicle accident and referred from primary care; to use a strict definiiton of the injury; to conduct the initial assessment as soon as possible after injury; and to follow-up these individuals for a period of two years.

SAMPLE AND METHODS

As reported in previous publications (Radanov et al. 1991, 1993a, 1993b, 1994a, 1994b, 1995; Sturzenegger et al. 1995), a non-selected sample was obtained by announcing the study in the *Swiss Medical Journal* and repeatedly distributing letters to primary care physicians in our catchment area. Physicians were asked to refer patients as soon as possible after whiplash injury. We used the strict definition proposed by Hirsch et al. (1988) that *common whiplash* is a trauma causing cervical musculo-ligamental sprain or strain due to hyperflexion / hyperextension. The term 'common whiplash' was chosen to indicate uncomplicated whiplash injury which, in contrast to those with associated fractures or dislocations of the cervical spine, is poorly understood as regards the development of long-lasting symptoms. Thus diagnoses excluded from our study were fractures or dislocations of the cervical spine, head injury or alteration of consciousness. In addition, in order to avoid cultural differences in illness behaviour we used only patients with German as their native language. Furthermore, patients with previous neurological deficits were excluded (because the neurological consequences of whiplash were of particular interest), as were injuries to other parts of the body, to avoid confounding of illness behaviour for reasons other than whiplash. Finally, patients over 55 years were also excluded because of the available norms on neuropsychological testing.

Over a period of two years, a series of 164 patients was referred, of which twenty-seven failed to meet the inclusion criteria and a further twenty dropped out during follow-up. The final sample consisted of 117 patients (mean age = 30.7 years (SD 9.6) years, range 19–51 years, 58 per cent women) all of whom had been injured in car accidents and were fully covered by accident insurance. Under the Swiss Accident Insurance System, if a person loses time from work because of injury, they receive a proportionate amount of lost wages, regardless of liability. Certification of disability is the task of the treating physician. The system does not provide compensation for non-financial loss such as pain or suffering. If permanent disability is expected (i.e. no therapeutic measure is likely to improve the patient's health status), a final disablity assessment is initiated. This usually happens several months after the accident.

Participants were assessed at referral (a mean of 7.2 days (SD 4.2) after the accident) and at three (T2), six (T3), twelve (T4) and twenty-four months (T5). During the follow-up period the patient's treatment was the responsibility of the referring physicians, who were sent detailed information on all aspects of baseline and follow-up investigations, although they were not given any treatment recommendations from our group (Radanov et al. 1995). Patients who had fully recovered at the six-month examination (i.e. they did not complain of any trauma-related symptoms) were released from the study, but were interviewed by phone two years later. However, these patients could be referred back to the study if any symptoms recurred.

ASSESSMENT

The assessment schedule is described in the authors' previous publications (Radanov et al. 1991, 1993a, 1993b, 1994a, 1994b, 1995; Sturzenegger et al. 1995) and readers are referred to these for further detail. Assessment included:

1 Semi-structured interviews which at referral assessed features of accident mechanisms, patients' assessment of accident, initial subjective complaints and the interval between injury and the onset of neck pain and headache as well as the latency to display initial symptoms (Radanov et al. 1994b, 1995). Attention was given to previous cervico-cephalic trauma as was any history of headache and its type (Radanov et al. 1993b, 1994b, 1995). In

addition, findings considered to be of prognostic relevance, such as shoulder and back pain, anterior neck pain and dysphagia were also assessed (Radanov et al. 1994b; Radanov et al. 1995; Sturzenegger et al. 1995). Injury mechanism was evaluated by recording the damage to the car, the patient's position in the car, the use of head rests and seat-belts, and the head position at the time of impact. Subjective appraisal of injury and judgement of outcome, including familiarity with symptoms of whiplash, current vocational disposition and job-satisfaction, were recorded at initial examination. A detailed analysis of symptoms and a symptom score was calculated for each patient at initial examination (using posterior neck pain, headache, shoulder pain, back pain, anterior neck pain, dysphagia, vertigo, unsteadiness, visual disturbance, tinnitus, symptoms of radicular irritation, and symptoms of myelopathy: each presented symptom was given a score of '1'). At follow-up, patients' subjective complaints were recorded according to an established structured interview.

2 A complete neurological and physical examination. In addition, the following grading system of severity of injury was applied (Radanov et al. 1995; Sturzenegger et al. 1995): Grade I: symptoms only; Grade II: symptoms and restricted neck movement; Grade III: symptoms, restricted neck movement and evidence of objective neurological loss. Complete neurological and physical examinations were also performed at T3, T4 and T5.

3 Cervical spine x-rays were performed at baseline and included antero-posterior, lateral, right and left oblique as well as lateral views inflexion and extension, the antero-posterior view in lateral inclination and the transoral view of the Dens.

4 Self-ratings of initial neck pain and headache intensity, using a scale from '0' representing 'no pain', to '10' representing 'maximum pain', were obtained at each investigation.

5 Patient's personal and family history, and current psychosocial disposition (Radanov et al. 1991, 1994a, 1994b, 1995).

6 A set of formal psychological (Radanov et al. 1991, 1993a, 1993b, 1994b, 1995) and cognitive tests (Radanov et al. 1993a, 1994a, 1994b, 1995) was used at each investigation including a measure of personality traits (the Freiburg Personality Inventory: Fahrenberg et al. 1984), in which the scales measuring nervousness, depression, openess, masculinity and neuroticism were considered important for reasons discussed in our previous publications; self-rated wellbeing (the Well-Being Scale (WBS): von Zerssen 1983) using parallel versions at follow-up; changes in trauma related cognitive ability (the Cognitive Failures Questionnaire (CFQ): Broadbent et al. 1982); a series of formal tests of attention (the Digit

Span: Wechsler 1945; Corsi Block-Tapping: Milner 1971; the Trail-Making Test Parts A and B, TMT-A and TMT-B: Reitan 1958; the Number Connection Test (NCT): Oswald and Roth 1987; the Paced Auditory Serial Addition Task (PASAT): Gronwall 1977).

At the two-year follow-up study, participants were divided into a symptomatic (persistence of any trauma-related symptoms) and an asymptomatic group (completely recovered). Using the X^2 test for dichotomous variables and Mann-Whitney U-test for interval-scaled variables to account for scores of different tests, the two groups were compared with the baseline examination. Changes in pain intensity and psychological measures between baseline and the two-year follow-up in the symptomatic patients was analysed, using the Wilcoxon matched-pair signed-ranks test; cognitive and psychological functioning was analysed during follow-up using scores of symptomatic and asymptomatic groups. Statistical analysis was performed using SPSS-X (SPSS Inc. 1988).

RESULTS

Persistent injury-related symptoms were found (symptomatic group) at three months in 44 per cent of the sample (n=51); at six months in 30 per cent of the sample (n=36); at one year in 24 per cent of the sample (n=28) and at two years in 18 per cent of the sample (n=21). Comparing the symptomatic patients after two years with those who had completely recovered, the following observations are noteworthy: symptomatic patients were significantly older (Table 6.1), reported significantly more rotated or inclined head position at the time of impact (Table 6.2), showed significantly more worry about the possibility of long-lasting symptoms or disability, and reported a greater range of subjective complaints at the initial examination (Table 6.3). Also, a significantly higher prevalence of pre-accident headache was documented, the onset of initial symptoms was quicker (not to statistical significance), initial pain ratings for headache and neck pain were significantly higher and on average remained high (Figure 6.1).

Additional findings included significantly more symptoms of radicular deficit, higher average scores on multiple symptom analysis and significantly more indications of osteoarthrosis on initial x-rays (Table 6.4). No differences were found between the groups on psychosocial variables assessed in interview (Table 6.5). Significant differences between the groups on psychological variables were found on tests requiring a more complex level of attentional processing, e.g. number connecting test, trail-making and auditory serial addition with the symptomatic group performing significantly more poorly, and on the Well-Being Scale (Table 6.6 and Table 6.7).

Table 6.1 Sociodemographic and work-related variables at initial examination

	Asymptomatic at two years (n=96)		Symptomatic at two years (n=21)		Difference	
					Coefficient	p
Female	n=55	(57%)	n=13	(62%)		
Male	n=41	(43%)	n=8	(38%)	0.15	n.s.
	mean (SD)		mean (SD)			
Age	29.7	(8.9)	35.4	(11.0)	709.5	<0.03
Educational attainment in years	12.9	(2.7)	12.1	(2.6)	761.5	n.s.
	n		n			
Type of work:						
Primarily intellectual	39	(41%)	7	(33%)		n.s.
Primarily physical	35	(36%)	9	(43%)	0.426	n.s.
Both	22	(23%)	5	(24%)		n.s.
Dissatisfaction with occupation[a]	14	(15%)	4	(19%)	0.263	n.s.

[a] Person has regrets about education and wishes they had some other occupation.

Table 6.2 Accident-related variables and injury mechanism

	Asymptomatic at two years (n=96)		Symptomatic at two years (n=21)		Difference	
					Coefficient	p
Accident-related variables						
Rear-end only	33	(34%)	11	(52%)	2.380	n.s.
Frontal only	27	(28%)	5	(24%)	0.161	n.s.
Rear-end followed by frontal	22	(23%)	4	(19%)	0.149	n.s.
Other	13	(13%)	2	(9%)	0.516	n.s.
Injury mechanism						
Patient driving at time of accident	74	(77%)	17	(81%)	0.149	n.s.
Seat belt not fastened	8	(8%)	3	(14%)	0.661	n.s.
No head restraints	8	(8%)	2	(9%)	0.031	n.s.
Seat upright broken	22	(23%)	5	(24%)	0.007	n.s.
Patient unprepared for collision at time of impact	70	(73%)	16	(76%)	0.094	n.s.
Head rotated or inclined	27	(28%)	12	(57%)	7.062	<0.008
Car stationery when hit	45	(47%)	14	(67%)	2.699	n.s.
Patient responsible for the accident	22	(23%)	4	(19%)	0.149	n.s.
Illness or disability worry, judges symptoms as serious	25	(26%)	11	(52%)	5.611	<0.017
Familiarity with symptoms of whiplash	47	(49%)	9	(43%)	0.257	n.s.

Table 6.3 Neurological history and initial subjective complaints (a combination of complaints should be considered)

	Asymptomatic at two years (n=96)		Symptomatic at two years (n=21)		Difference	
	n		n		Coefficient	p
History of blunt head injury	14	(15%)	6	(29%)	2.378	n.s.
History of whiplash	15	(16%)	2	(9%)	0.516	n.s.
History of significant debilitating headache	36	(37%)	18	(86%)	16.117	<0.0001
Initial subjective complaints						
Neck pain	88	(92%)	20	(96%)	0.309	n.s.
Headache	51	(53%)	16	(76%)	3.745	n.s.
Easily fatigued (no clear cut symptoms of chronic fatigue syndrome)	50	(52%)	16	(76%)	4.072	n.s.
Shoulder pain	44	(46%)	13	(62%)	1.781	n.s.
Anxiety[k]	38	(40%)	14	(67%)	5.118	<0.023
Sleep disturbances (due to pain)	30	(31%)	16	(76%)	14.585	<0.0001
Back pain	36	(37%)	9	(43%)	0.208	n.s.
Sensitivity to noise	26	(27%)	8	(38%)	1.013	n.s.
Impaired ability to concentrate	23	(24%)	8	(38%)	1.768	n.s.
Blurred vision	16	(17%)	9	(43%)	7.034	<0.008

Irritability	18	(19%)	7	(33%)	2.181	n.s.
Dizziness (mainly light-headed ness)	12	(12%)	6	(29%)	3.418	n.s.
Forgetfulness (couldn't follow information flow, although no real memory impairment)	10	(10%)	7	(33%)	7.286	<0.006
Difficulty in swallowing	8	(8%)	2	(9%)	0.031	n.s.
Jugular pain	8	(8%)	1	(5%)	0.309	n.s.
Time between impact and symptom onset (hours)	mean (SD)		mean (SD)			
Neck pain	11.5	(16.5)	8.1	(17.8)	636.5	n.s.
Headache	10.0	(14.2)	4.1	(8.3)	377.0	n.s.
Initial pain intensity (self-rating 0=no pain; 10=maximal pain)						
Neck pain	3.9	(1.9)	5.3	(2.2)	640.5	<0.008
Headache	2.6	(2.8)	4.8	(3.4)	622.0	<0.004

κ Phobic reaction as a consequence of being a driver (most subjects avoided driving after the accident) or when a passenger in congested traffic. PTSD could not be diagnosed because the accident did not fulfil the criterion of being outside usual human experience.

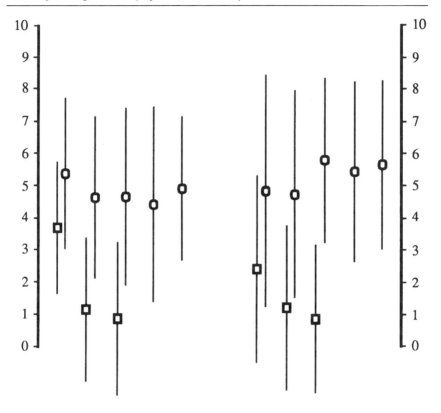

O   Patients who remained symtomatic
      at two years (T5)

□   Patients who recovered during follow-up
      being asymptomatic at two years (T5)

Figure 6.1 Course of neck pain and headache self-ratings during follow-up

Test scores on attentional functioning, self-rated cognitive ability (CFQ) and self-rated wellbeing (WBS) are shown in Figure 6.2. Although there is an apparent difference with regard to attentional functioning between symptomatic and asymptomatic groups at T1, T2 and T3 (Figure 6.2), group comparisons, using MANOVA with age and medication as covariates, showed no statistically significant differences.

Other important findings were apparent in the symptomatic group when comparing the initial (T1) with the final examination (T5):

1 Significant differences were found on the NCT, TMT-B and PASAT where, on average, an improvement was found ($z=-3.49$, p<.001, $z=-2.01$, p<.05, and $z=-3.13$, p<.002 respectively).

2 With regard to psychological variables (i.e. WBS, CFQ or scales from the Freiburg Personality Inventory), no significant differences between T1 and T5 were found on CFQ ($z=-1.66$, p=<.09), depression-scale ($z=-0.08$, p=<.93), openess-scale ($z=-0.69$, p=<.48), neuroticism-scale ($z=-1.03$, p=<.30) and nervousness-scale ($z=-1.90$, p=<.057). In contrast significant differences were found on the WBS ($z=-2.15$, p<.04) and masculinity-scale ($z=-2.51$, p<.02) which on average showed an improvement.

DISCUSSION

By evaluating cases directly from primary care we were able in the present study to assess an essentially non-selected sample of whiplash patients chosen according to clearly defined injury criteria. This design allows the unbiased evaluation of the significance of different aspects of the patient's history, various initial somatic and psychosocial factors, x-ray findings and features of injury mechanism as they may influence recovery from this type of injury. To our knowledge to date there is no comparably comprehensive assessement of the longer-term consequences of whiplash injury. As reported previously (Radanov et al. 1993b, 1994a, 1994b, 1995) the number of patients in our study was a reasonable representation of the total number of people with whiplash injuries in our catchment area. All patients were injured in automobile accidents, had similar socioeconomic backgrounds and educational attainment and were fully covered by accident insurance; this resulted in a highly homogeneous sample. Since the national insurance scheme provides only for financial loss, bias due to compensation-seeking behaviour in this sample is unlikely. We do, however, consider aspects of our country's insurance scheme of considerable importance when comparing our results with those of other researchers. The fact that we investigated an essentially unbiased sample according to a clear definition of whiplash injury revealed many differences when comparing the present results with those of previous studies (Deans et al. 1987; Maimaris et al. 1988; Norris and Watt 1983). We found a fairly high recovery rate after two years, with only 18 per cent of the sample still suffering from injury-related symptoms; we were unable to confirm the results of previous reports (Balla 1982) that gender or vocational activity may influence outcome.

One further important finding, not previously reported, is that there was no significant difference between groups with regard to initial subjective accident assessment. However, patients from the symptomatic group initially showed more illness or disability worry, likely reflecting a more severe

Table 6.4 Neurological and radiological findings

	Asymptomatic at two years (n=96) n		Symptomatic at two years (n=21) n		Difference Coefficient	p
Neck muscle tenderness	69	(72%)	18	(86%)	1.730	n.s.
Restricted neck movement	52	(54%)	14	(67%)	1.094	n.s.
Symptoms of radicular irritation[a]	12	(12%)	5	(24%)	0.625	n.s.
Symptoms of radicular deficit	11	(12%)	6	(29%)	4.063	<0.043
Symptoms of:						
Cranial nerve or brain stem disturbance	28	(29%)	13	(62%)	8.113	0.004
Diplopia	2	(2%)	2	(9%)	2.888	n.s.
Oscillopsia	2	(2%)	0		0.428	n.s.
Unsteadiness while walking or standing	12	(12%)	6	(29%)	3.418	n.s.
Vertigo	5	(5%)	1	(5%)	0.007	n.s.
Tinnitus	4	(4%)	1	(5%)	0.014	n.s.
Myelopathy[b]	3	(3%)	2	(9%)	1.724	n.s.
Signs of:						
Cranial nerve or brain stem dysfunction	7	(100%)	0		0.144	n.s.
Ocular motor dysfunction	7	(7%)	0		1.628	n.s.
Olfactory motor dysfunction	2	(2%)	0		0.445	n.s.
Trigemino-facial dysfunction[c]	3	(3%)	0		0.673	n.s.
Pupillomotor dysfunction	2	(2%)	0		0.445	n.s.
Radicular deficit	2	(2%)	1	(5%)	0.494	n.s.

Injury severity:						
Grade 1	15	(16%)	2	(9%)	1.813	n.s.
Grade 2	69	(72%)	18	(86%)		n.s.
Grade 3	12	(12%)	1	(5%)		n.s.
	mean (SD)		mean (SD)			
Multiple symptom score (calculated taking into account 12 symptoms as described in the method)	2.9	(1.4)	3.9	(1.9)	701.5	<0.026
	n		n			
Radiological findings						
Misalignment of cervical curvature	46	(48%)	12	(57%)	0.586	n.s.
Signs of degeneration (ostheoartrosis)	18	(19%)	9	(43%)	5.641	<0.017
Signs of restricted movement (lateral projection)	22	(23%)	7	(33%)	1.002	n.s.
Signs of restricted movement (frontal projection)	16	(17%)	3	(14%)	0.071	n.s.
Signs of restricted movement (both projections)	29	(30%)	8	(38%)	0.495	n.s.

[a] Dermatom-associated pain irradiation, paresthesia, numbness and radicularly distributed weakness. This was unilateral in 19 patients involving C8 dermatom in eight, and C7 dermatom in two, and biltaerla in four patients.
[b] Transitory tetra-parenthesis was suspected in three patients, transitory tetra-parenthesis in four, and transitory urinary voiding problems in three patients (combination should be considered).
[c] Sensory disturbance, asymmetry in corneal reflex, asymmetric facial innervation.

Table 6.5 Psychosocial stress assessed by interview, with examples of issues considered stressors (a combination of factors for each category is possible).

	Asymptomatic at two years (n=96)		Symptomatic at two years (n=21)		Difference	
	n		n		Coefficient	p
Neurotic symptoms in childhood: bedwetting, eating difficulties, passivity/absence of fantasy, negligible social skills, problems dealing with authority figures (e.g. teacher), socially withdrawn, anxiety, speech problems (e.g. stuttering), nailbiting	39	(41%)	7	(33%)	0.383	n.s.
Performance problems in school: difficulties presumably unrelated to intellectual ability (i.e. developmental arithmetic, expressive writing and reading disorders)	19	(20%)	4	(19%)	0.006	n.s.
Dysfunctional family: parental alcohol or drug abuse, physical or sexual abuse directed towards children, marital physical abuse, parental death	19	(20%)	5	(24%)	0.17	n.s.
Family history of somatic illness: illness of close family member interpreted as social modelling for illness behaviour of patients (e.g. neurological disorders, accident-related illness or impairment, headache, back pain)	37	(38%)	11	(52%)	1.364	n.s.
History of psychological or behavioural problems in adolescence and adulthood: problems during puberty (e.g. anorexia nervosa) and adolescence (e.g. drug abuse), and psychological problems such as depression, socalled nervous breakdown, suicidal ideation, previous psychiatric or psychotherapeutic treatment	24	(25%)	7	(33%)	0.614	n.s.
Current psychosocial stress: marital or relationship problems, family problems, difficulties at work, financial difficulties	29	(30%)	11	(52%)	3.764	n.s.

Table 6.6 Psychological measures (Freiburg Personality Inventory (FPI))

	Asymptomatic at two years (n=96) mean (SD)		Symptomatic at two years (n=21) mean (SD)		Difference Coefficient	p
Nervousness	4.6	(1.7)	5.4	(1.7)	771.5	n.s.
Depression	3.9	(2.0)	4.5	(1.7)	818.0	n.s.
Openess	5.6	(1.9)	6.4	(1.8)	760.5	n.s.
Neuroticism	3.9	(2.0)	4.1	(1.7)	919.5	n.s.
Masculinity	4.7	(1.7)	5.0	(1.6)	876.0	n.s.
Well-being scale	15.6	(12.0)	21.8	(12.3)	708.0	<0.033

Note: Scores on scales of the FPI between 4 to 6 are comparable with 54 per cent of a random sample. Scores over 6 on scales Nervousness, Depression and Neuroticism and scores below 4 on scales Openness and Masculinuty are considerd pathological.

Table 6.7 Cognitive measures

	Asymptomatic at two years (n=96) mean (SD)		Symptomatic at two years (n=21) mean (SD)		Difference	
					Coefficient	p
Score on self-rated cognitive ability (CFQ) (<30)	17.3	(14.4)	23.0	(20.3)	864.0	n.s.
Digit Span (total correct) (>10)	10.6	(1.8)	9.9	(2.1)	807.5	n.s.
Corsi Block-Tapping (total correct) (>10)	11.3	(1.4)	10.6	(2.0)	751.5	n.s.
Number Connection Test (seconds) (<85)	69.2	(14.6)	83.3	(14.8)	454.5	<0.0001
Trail-Making, Part A (seconds) (<27)	22.6	(7.6)	27.0	(9.6)	696.5	<0.026
Trail-Making, Part B (seconds) (<69)	66.1	(26.0)	76.4	(20.6)	655.5	<0.012
PASAT (average incorrect) (<15.4)	14.9	+7.9	20.6	+11.3	636.0	<0.023

Note: Normal ranges are given in parentheses.

injury in these patients. This explanation is supported by the evidence: patients in the symptomatic group had a greater number of complaints, higher prevalence of neck pain and headache, and higher scoring on pain ratings; their pain started sooner; they had a significantly higher score on multiple symptom analysis; and they reported significantly more rotated or inclined head position at the time of impact – making the cervical spine more susceptible to biomechanical damage (Severy et al. 1955; Tegenthoff Malin 1991; Wickström et al. 1967) pointing to more severe injury in this group.

The results of this study support the view that two pre-existing conditions are related to symptom persistence: cervical spine osteoarthrosis, which was significantly more frequent in the symptomatic group, and a higher prevalence of pretraumatic headache (Radanov et al. 1993b, 1994b, 1995). The latter is significant since the high percentage of patients suffering from pretraumatic headache in the study sample exceeds the prevalence of headache found in the general population (Linet et al. 1989). This may indicate that patients with a history of pretraumatic headache may be more susceptible to display symptoms following whiplash injury, headache being one of the prominent complaints because of headache-triggering based on a preformed pattern (Radanov et al. 1993b, 1995).

Consistent with previous results obtained with the same sample after a shorter follow-up period (Radanov et al. 1991, 1994a) psychosocial factors were not of prognostic relevance in the long term. Based on this, we believe that the significantly poorer scores with regard to wellbeing and cognitive functioning found in the symptomatic group at initial assessment, in reality indicate a reaction to a more severe injury. Similarly, in accordance with other results from the same sample (Radanov et al. 1993a) the data presented here do not indicate major impairment of attentional functioning in whiplash patients in the long term. Following an average improvement, regarding all aspects of attentional functioning in both groups during the first months, the subsequent performance of symptomatic patients was poorer on almost all tests of attention. This may be explained by the adverse effect of analgesics, used regularly by many of the symptomatic patients, or by their prolonged suffering from severe headaches, which, conceivably, could impair attentional functioning. As with average scores of headache rating, and scores on tests of attention, there was an increase in average scores of self-rated cognitive ability, providing further indication that these three aspects are closely correlated. It is thus conceivable that worsening of cognitive functioning, according to neuropsychological test scores, reflects that cognitive impairment may be due to psychological causes.

The present results suggest that a comprehensive multidisciplinary initial assessment of whiplash patients may help to identify patients at risk of poor

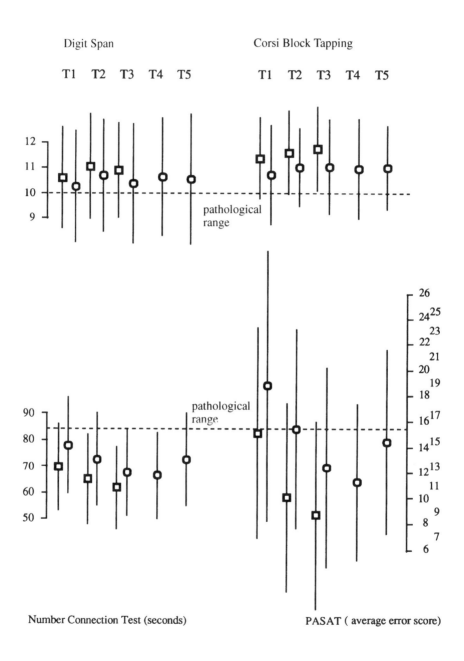

Digit Span   Corsi Block Tapping

Figure 6.2 Course of attention, wellbeing, and self-rated cognitive ability during follow-up

Figure 6.2 continued

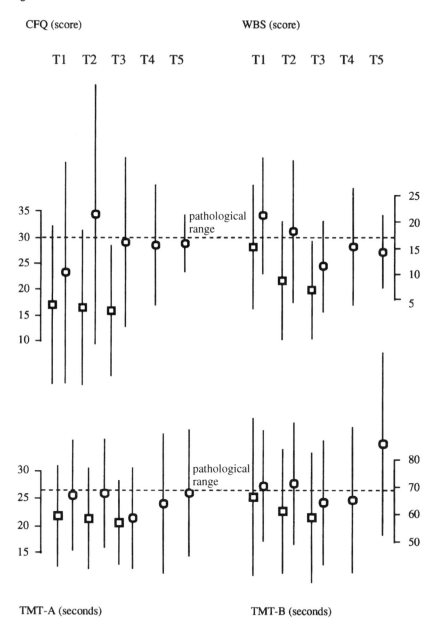

CFQ (score)

WBS (score)

TMT-A (seconds)

TMT-B (seconds)

O   Patients who remained symtomatic at two years (T5)

□   Patients who recovered during follow-up being asymtomatic at two years (T5)

prognosis, as well as to understand the course of psychological and cognitive factors in the long term.

Acknowledgements Some of the research reported in this chapter was presented at the symposium of the Physical Medicine Research Foundation in Banff, Canada (October 1995). Permission was also kindly granted by Williams and Wilkins for reproduction of some material.

Chapter 7

The psychological consequences of head injury in road accidents

Lindsay Wilson

Road accidents are the most common cause of head injury and account for approximately half of fatal head injuries (Frankowski 1986). In addition to those killed outright by head injury, many survive and are left with lasting brain damage and psychological impairment. Most of these head-injured survivors are young people with near normal life expectancy, yet many of them will never work again and some will remain permanently dependent on others for daily care. Some survivors are clearly disabled, but it is now well established that others can apparently make a good recovery from head injury, yet still have residual cognitive impairment and emotional disturbance (Stuss et al. 1985).

There are many good general reviews of the neuropsychology of head injury (e.g. Gronwall et al. 1992). It is not the purpose of this chapter to give an overview of head injury, but rather to focus on aspects of head injury which relate specifically to road traffic accidents. There are at least two reasons why the psychological consequences of head injury in road accidents may have a distinctive character. It is known that the pathology of head injury caused in motor vehicle accidents typically differs from that found after head injury arising from other causes, such as falls and assaults. Modern neuro-imaging techniques have allowed lesions to be identified, and have begun to lead to an appreciation of the neuropsychological significance of different patterns of focal and diffuse injury (Wilson et al. 1995). Another reason for distinguishing road accidents from other causes of injury rests, not on the type of brain injury involved, but on the circumstances of the injury. Among factors important for outcome are the emotional response of the individual to the accident and its aftermath. In this respect, the psychological effects of road accidents are likely to differ in important ways from other causes of injury.

Neuropsychological studies of head injury rarely distinguish patients on the basis of cause of injury, preferring distinctions based on severity of brain injury or underlying pathology. Although there may be good reasons for distinguishing head injury of different causes a limitation is that the relationship between aetiology and brain pathology is not simple and

Table 7.1 Causes of head injury in 103 patients admitted to an acute neuro-
surgical unit

Cause	Number of cases	
Motor vehicle occupant	13	
Pedestrian	9	
Motor cyclist	5	
Other road accidents	6	
Sub-total.		33
Assault	38	
Falls	11	
Accident at work	12	
Sports injury	5	
Other cause	4	
Sub-total		70
Total		103

direct. Road accidents are quite varied in nature (Table 7.1), and can lead to many different forms of brain damage. A reluctance to categorise patients on the basis of cause of injury, has led to there being little literature dealing specifically with brain damage caused by road accident. For the present purposes, in order to obtain information about the psychological effects of road accidents, data from a cohort of head-injured patients is analysed and the findings form the balance of this chapter.

PATHOLOGY AND ACUTE CONSEQUENCES OF BRAIN INJURY

The hallmark of brain injury in road accidents is immediate loss of consciousness at the time of the injury. The brain lesion particularly associated with road traffic accidents is diffuse axonal injury, that is, widespread damage to the white matter of the cerebral hemispheres due to sudden acceleration or deceleration of the head. Adams (1992) has identified other types of focal and diffuse brain injury such as contusion (bruising), haematoma (blood clot), and hypoxic-ischaemic damage (damage due to loss of oxygen and/or blood supply). The severity of diffuse damage of this sort (axonal injury) is indicated by the extent of loss of consciousness, and it is probable that any loss of consciousness, however brief, is indicative that some brain damage has occurred (Blumbergs et al. 1994). Head injury severity is usually classified clinically according to the depth of coma on admission to hospital: a Glasgow Coma Scale Score of 3 to 8 indicates a severe injury, 9 to 12 a moderate injury, and 13 to 15 a mild injury. This scale is applied appropriately to those injured in road accidents who sustain diffuse injury, but it does not indicate the extent of any focal injury such as contusions and haematoma.

Recovery of consciousness is followed by a period of post-traumatic amnesia (PTA), when the person is alert and may be able to converse normally but has lost continuous memory. The patient who has lost consciousness may remember the events leading up to the accident, but will never remember the accident itself or the events which occurred during the period of PTA. In the most severe injuries, PTA may last for several months, but patients usually emerge eventually from PTA. Duration of PTA is also used as a simple measure of injury severity in that it can be assessed simply by interviewing the person about the return of continuous memory. Anyone who reports loss of memory for more than 24 hours may be considered to have had a severe head injury and PTA of greater than seven days is considered a very severe injury (Russell and Smith 1961). Clearly, post-traumatic amnesia of two weeks or more is particularly likely to be associated with significant psychological problems, especially cognitive and emotional difficulties.

PSYCHOLOGICAL IMPAIRMENT AND RECOVERY OF FUNCTION

After recovery of normal day-to-day memory there is usually a gradual improvement in cognitive abilities, but some deficits can persist indefinitely. Psychological impairment after head injury is very variable, and individuals can demonstrate any of a wide range of neuropsychological deficits including problems of perception, movement, and communication. The areas in which cognitive problems are most commonly found are in memory and learning, in attention and information processing, and in executive and adaptive functioning. Tate and colleagues (1991) analysed the performance of one hundred people with head injuries and found that variability of type and combination of deficits was characteristic: one-third of patients had impairment in only one of the areas assessed. It is, therefore, unlikely that the pattern of cognitive impairment caused by road accidents is highly specific. Diffuse injury is particularly associated with mental slowing and attention deficits, and perhaps these may be evident even in relatively mild injuries. However, slowing can also result from focal injuries to the brain. Furthermore, patients with diffuse injury after road accidents will often show a number of other deficits including problems of memory and of executive function.

Head injury also often results in a variety of emotional problems and psychosocial difficulties. Stambrook and colleagues (1991) compared the effects of head injury and spinal injury, and found that severely head-injured patients reported more psychological distress and were rated by their spouses as more socially and psychologically disabled than wheelchair-dependent spinal injury patients. The psychological consequences of head injury also include the effects on the carers and relatives of the injured person (McKinlay et al. 1981).

It is generally agreed that most recovery of function occurs within the first year after injury. Change is possible beyond one year, but this may depend on adaptation or compensation rather than direct amelioration of the cognitive impairment. Just as there is variation in the deficits caused by injury, there is also variation in the rate and extent of recovery, which makes generalisation difficult. Broadly speaking, cognitive functions which are most impaired show improvement over longer time periods. So, for example, verbal abilities tend to recover relatively quickly, while memory and attention problems improve more slowly. However, prediction of rate and extent of recovery in individual cases remains uncertain.

Many studies have demonstrated broad relationships between the degree of cognitive impairment and the severity of initial injury, particularly the duration of post-traumatic amnesia. Emotional and psychosocial difficulties are also a feature late after injury, and may be quite enduring. Indeed, sometimes emotional problems may increase with time after injury (Fordyce et al. 1983), and sometimes they may be more apparent in patients with less severe injury (Novack et al. 1984).

MINOR HEAD INJURY AND THE POST-CONCUSSION SYNDROME

The majority of head injuries are minor, and may not involve hospital admission. There is acknowledgement that in some cases minor head injury can lead to significant psychological difficulties within the first few months of injury (Levin et al. 1987). However, there is controversy over whether there is a lasting post-concussion syndrome (PCS) (see Chapter 8). The features of post-concussion syndrome include irritability, depression, anxiety, memory and concentration difficulty, sensitivity to light and noise, headache, fatigue, and dizziness. Consideration of PCS often focuses on whether the symptoms reported are due to organic damage, and there is often a tacit assumption that if the symptoms are not organic then the patient is malingering. However, it is important to emphasize that psychological factors also play a role in the development of PCS (Lishman 1988): for example, affective disturbance can be caused by the circumstances of the accident and difficulties which arise as a result of the injury.

Some of the features of post-concussion syndrome overlap with post-traumatic stress disorder. Post-traumatic stress disorder (PTSD) appears to be relatively common after road accidents which do not involve brain injury: Green and colleagues (1993) recently found clinically significant PTSD in six out of twenty-four road accident survivors fourteen months post-injury. It is sometimes supposed that PTSD cannot occur without memory for the traumatic event. Bryant and Harvey (1995a) investigated acute stress responses in head-injured and non-head-injured road accident survivors. Amnesia about the traumatic event was associated with less acute post-traumatic stress, however, a proportion of head-injured patients reported intrusive and avoidance symptoms despite being unable to remember the accident itself. McMillan (1991) described the case of a young woman who was severely brain injured in a road accident, and who developed classic PTSD symptoms despite post-traumatic amnesia of six weeks. The woman's friend had died in the accident and she developed intrusive thoughts concerning her friend and the circumstances surrounding the accident. Although head-injured patients may not remember the accident, they will have memories of other aspects of the injury and surrounding circumstances, and may have information provided to them by others, which may be distressing.

ROAD ACCIDENTS VERSUS OTHER CAUSES OF HEAD INJURY

In order to address the specific effects of head injury in road accidents, data from 103 head-injured patients were analysed. These patients had originally been recruited for a study of recovery after injury conducted at the Institute of Neurological Sciences in Glasgow (further details are given in Wilson et al. 1996). Causes of injury are shown in Table 7.1. Patients were followed up at six months post-injury by interview and neuropsychological assessment. Twenty-nine of the thirty-three road accident survivors were assessed, two were lost to follow-up, and two were so severely disabled that they were not testable. Sixty-four patients with injuries from other causes were followed-up and were able to be tested. The mean age of the two groups was similar: 29 years for patients injured in road traffic accidents and 31 years for patients injured from other causes.

Severity of initial diffuse injury was assessed by the Glasgow Coma Scale (GCS) (Teasdale and Jennett 1974) on admission. Patients who had been involved in road accidents had lower GCS scores indicating a *deeper* coma on admission than patients injured from other causes (Mann-Whitney, $p < .05$). Nearly half (46 per cent) of patients injured in road accidents were in coma on admission, whereas only one-third (31 per cent) of patients injured from other causes were in coma. Only 27 per cent of the survivors of road accidents had mild injuries, but 56 per cent of injuries from other causes were mild according to coma scale criteria. The lower Glasgow Coma Scale score in the road accident group indicates greater diffuse injury in this group, and this is consistent with the evidence that road accidents are associated with diffuse axonal injury.

It should be emphasized, however, that the Glasgow Coma Scale does not reflect the extent of focal injury. The total mean volume of brain abnormality was 23 cc in the road accident group and 34 cc in the other group as measured from T_2 weighted magnetic resonance (MR) images obtained in the acute stage. This investigative method is designed to be sensitive to contusional lesions in head injury; so, if anything, the extent of focal injury was greater in the group injured from other causes. Further, the proportion of patients who had blood clot was very similar in both groups: 76 per cent of those injured in traffic accidents and 77 per cent of those injured by other means.

Despite the high proportion of severe initial injuries, the majority (69 per cent) of those injured in road accidents showed good recovery on the Glasgow Outcome Scale (Jennett and Bond 1975) at six months. The remaining road accident survivors who had neuropsychological assessment were in the upper band of moderate disability (this analysis excludes the two patients who were very severely disabled and could not be assessed). The proportion of patients head-injured from other causes who had good recovery was 64 per cent. Comparison of two groups on neuropsychological testing indicated they were matched on pre-accident IQ predicted by the National Adult Reading Test (NART), and performance was similar across a range of tests, including measures of learning and reaction time. In comparison to patients injured in RTAs, patients injured from other causes performed more poorly (p<.05 on t-testing) on four measures: Digit Span, Digit Symbol, Object Assembly, and Visual Pattern Span. Furthermore, patients injured from other causes reported significantly more malaise on the General Health Questionnaire (mean = 39.2 vs 31.1, p<.05).

As expected, the patients injured in road accident had more severe diffuse injury than those injured from other causes. However, severe diffuse injury does not lead to a particularly poor outcome in this group of patients. Overall outcome was similar in patients injured in road accidents, and the group injured from other causes performed less well on several neuropsychological measures. It is sometimes suggested that diffuse injury is the main determinant of disability in head injury (Adams et al. 1991), but these results suggest that focal injury also plays an important role. The current study indicates that the prognosis for patients severely injured in road accident is not particularly gloomy in comparison to other causes of injury. This is not to deny that there is considerable residual impairment in this group. Nor do the results imply that the prognosis for road accident survivors can always be optimistic, because two patients remained very severely disabled.

PSYCHOLOGICAL CHANGES DUE TO HEAD INJURY IN ROAD ACCIDENTS

In order to clarify the psychological changes in patients with head injury due to road accident, this group was compared with a group of twenty-six

Table 7.2 Comparison of patients head injured in road accidents and controls on neuropsychological testing.

	Head injured (n=29)		Controls (n=26)			
	Mean	SD	Mean	SD	t	p (2-tail)
Similarities	11.1	2.3	10.9	1.3	0.51	n.s.
Digit Span	11.6	3.3	11.5	2.8	0.11	n.s.
Vocabulary	10.4	2.8	11.0	2.3	−0.83	n.s.
Digit Symbol	10.1	2.8	11.2	3.2	−1.4	n.s.
Block Design	11.6	2.6	11.1	2.9	0.65	n.s.
Object Assembly	11.3	3.2	10.2	2.6	1.3	n.s.
Rey Figure Recall	23.4	6.9	22.1	5.1	0.78	n.s.
Logical Memory	13.6	3.8	13.1	2.7	0.60	n.s.
Paired Associate Learning	15.3	4.0	16.8	3.9	−1.4	n.s.
Visual Pattern Span	10.1	1.8	9.7	2.2	0.83	n.s.
PASAT	79.0	16.1	89.9	12.0	−2.8	0.01
Card Sort Categories	5.0	1.5	5.5	1.1	−1.5	n.s.
Word Fluency	40.9	10.9	49.1	10.1	−2.9	0.01
Simple RT:						
Decision	318	54	279	31	3.3	0.01
Movement	273	62	234	42	2.8	0.01
Choice RT:						
Decision	344	52	309	37	2.9	0.01
Movement	275	64	230	46	3.1	0.01

controls matched for age (head-injured mean = 28.9 years, control mean = 30.2 years) and IQ estimated by the reading test scores (head-injured mean = 107, control mean = 110). Controls were orthopaedic outpatients and volunteers from the general population. Head-injured patients performed as well as controls on a range of neuropsychological measures, but performed poorly on Paced Auditory Serial Addition Task (PASAT) (Gronwall 1977), Word Fluency, and all the Reaction Time Measures (Table 7.2).

Neuropsychological tests used

1 Wechsler Adult Intelligence Scale subtests (Similarities; Digit Span; Vocabulary; Digit Symbol; Block Design; Object Assembly).
2 Rey Figure Recall, Logical Memory and Paired Associate Learning are measures of the subject's ability to learn new visual and verbal material.
3 Visual Pattern Span is a measure of short-term visual memory.

4 The Paced Auditory Serial Addition Task (PASAT) is a demanding measure of attention and information processing.
5 The Wisconsin Card Sort and Word Fluency are sensitive to frontal lobe dysfunction.
6 Simple and Choice Reaction Time (RT) measures are divided into a movement time and a decision time (in milliseconds).

The results of neuropsychological testing show that the people brain injured in road accidents were not globally impaired. The simplest explanation of the particular pattern of deficits observed is that there is a slowing of mental processes and movement. Slow performance on the movement component of the reaction time tasks could be due to residual physical problems. However, the poor performance on PASAT and on Word Fluency indicates that mental slowing is a component of the disorder seen in these patients. In PASAT the subject is presented with a string of digits and must add each number in turn to the immediately preceding number; the task is relatively easy at slow presentation rates but is demanding when the rate is increased. Deficits on this task, reaction time, and many similar tasks appear to reflect basic slowing in mental processes after head injury. It is noteworthy that slowing in the road accident patients is relatively subtle and not evident on other timed measures such as Digit Symbol or Object Assembly. More demanding tasks such as PASAT or RT tasks are needed to demonstrate a deficit. Van Zomeren has argued that slowing results in reduced information processing and a deficit in divided attention (van Zomeren and Brouwer 1990). Reduced information processing capacity could account for a number of the complaints made by patients, including concentration and memory problems, and a tendency to become fatigued easily. Mental slowing also appears to be linked to diffuse axonal injury, and may be directly due to loss of information transfer capacity with axonal damage or may be a secondary effect of disconnection of brain regions. In keeping with the hypothesis of a link with diffuse damage, performance on PASAT was related to severity of injury. Mean number correct on PASAT was 70.1 in the severely injured patients (GCS <= 8) and 85.7 in the less severely injured (GCS 9–15), p<.05.

Common cognitive complaints reported by head-injured patients at six months concern difficulties with word finding, memory and concentration problems, and being fatigued easily (Table 7.3). The complaints are broadly in agreement with the results of neuropsychological testing. Although there was no objective evidence of primary learning deficit in this group, complaints of memory problems in everyday life may reflect attentional difficulties. Problems with an affective dimension are also very common: irritability, fatiguability, anxiety, being easily angered or depressed. It should be noted that some of these problems are also quite common in controls (Table 7.3). The head-injured patients reported significantly higher

Table 7.3 Percentages of patients head injured in road accidents and controls reporting problems. Probability levels are from Chi Square Test or Fisher's Exact Probability Test as appropriate.

	Head injured (%)	Controls (%)	p
Problem speaking or word finding	68	27	0.01
Irritability	68	35	0.05
Memory problems	68	23	0.01
Concentration problems	59	19	0.01
Tire easily	59	42	n.s.
Anxious	50	35	n.s.
Easily angered	50	12	0.01
Easily depressed	45	27	n.s.
Dizzy spells	41	15	0.05
Blank spells	40	8	0.01
Problem understanding	32	4	0.01
Hearing problems	23	4	n.s.
Vision problems	23	23	n.s.
Problem with sense of taste	19	4	n.s.
Problem with sense of smell	19	8	n.s.
Violent	18	0	0.05

levels of depression on the Beck Depression Inventory (BDI) than controls (head-injured mean = 10.5, control mean = 6.5, p<.05). Finally, level of depression was similar in the severely injured road accident patients (BDI=9.1) and less severely injured patients (BDI=11.9).

CHARACTERISTICS OF HEAD INJURY AFTER ROAD ACCIDENT

Any attempt to generalise concerning head injury must always be viewed with circumspection; the population is very heterogeneous and individual cases will always be found who form exceptions. Nonetheless, certain broad messages emerge about the effects of road accidents. Comparison of patients involved in road accidents with patients injured from other causes suggests grounds for both optimism and pessimism concerning the specific consequences of road accidents. Outcome after road accident is not necessarily as poor as the initial severity of injury would suggest. In this study, cognitive recovery was better than in patients injured from other causes, even though patients in road accidents were more severely injured initially. The core cognitive impairment in the patients injured in road accidents appears to be slowing of mental processes; such impairment is consistent with the concept that diffuse axonal injury is the dominant pathology.

Emotional problems include depression and a high proportion of subjective complaints. The study supports the idea that involvement in a road accident can produce long-lasting emotional disturbance. There was no evidence that emotional disturbance was directly due to brain damage; there was a trend for the less severely injured patients to be more depressed. An issue of obvious importance is the *cause* of emotional disturbance in these patients, and one can speculate that it arises primarily because of a reaction to the events surrounding the injury. There are a number of factors which may play a role here: distress at residual impairment, dwelling on symptoms, possible bereavement in the accident, concern at having caused injury or harm to others, returning to work too early and being unable to cope, conflict over compensation, and friction arising at home. The causes of emotional disturbance after head injury are undoubtedly complex and remain to be further investigated.

If emotional problems are not directly caused by brain damage, then they should be amenable to psychological treatment, but it is noteworthy that this form of help is not routinely offered to the survivors of head injury.

Acknowledgements   The author's work was supported by a project grant from the Wellcome Trust.

Chapter 8

Post-concussion syndrome after road and other accidents

Brain damage, somatoform disorder, or litigation induced?

James Youngjohn

Minor or mild head injury is a frequent consequence of motor vehicle accidents. These head injuries, many of which are seemingly trivial in nature, often result in a persisting constellation of subjective disabilities and complaints that have been termed the post-concussion syndrome (PCS). The most common complaints that are attributed to minor or mild head trauma include memory loss, headache, dizziness, concentration difficulty, blurred vision, photophobia, ringing of the ears, irritability, fatigue, anxiety, and depression (World Health Organization 1978). The consistency of the cluster of PCS symptoms has been held out as evidence for an organic aetiology (Alves et al. 1986; Binder 1986). Sweeney (1992) has extended this interpretation of the consistency of self-reported symptoms in PCS to argue that many personal injury litigants, who have never even hit their heads, suffer from brain damage.

However, PCS complaints are not specific for brain injury. Indeed, the base rates of PCS complaints from the normal, non-brain-damaged population is very high (Gouvier et al. 1988). Kellner and Sheffield (1973) found that approximately 90 per cent of healthy individuals reported experiencing various somatic symptoms during a one week period. The most commonly reported symptoms for these normal individuals were headaches (49 per cent), fatigue (47 per cent), somatic aches and pains (42 per cent), and irritability (34 per cent). Putnam and Millis (1994) reviewed the responses of the standardization sample of the Minnesota Multiphasic Personality Inventory-2 (MMPI-2) (Hathaway and McKinley 1989) to items associated with PCS complaints. Interestingly, 37 to 40 per cent of these normal individuals endorsed the item 'I forget where I leave things'; 65 to 67 per cent endorsed the item 'At periods my mind seems to work more slowly than usual'; and 30 to 36 per cent endorsed the item 'Often I can't understand why I have been so irritable and grouchy'. Remarkably, 96 to 98 per cent of the normal population endorsed the item 'I get angry sometimes'. Mittenberg and colleagues (1992) found that naive subjects with imaginary concussions endorsed a cluster of symptoms virtually identical to PCS and that actual patients consistently underestimated the premorbid prevalence of these symptoms compared to the base rates in the general population. They interpreted these findings as indicating that patient expectations may play a substantial role in the cause of PCS. They proposed a model in which the event of a mild or minor head injury resulted in a selective or searching attention to one's internal state, based on expectancy for symptoms. The consequent attentional bias and arousal would therefore augment symptom perception.

Putnam and Millis (1994) have proposed that persisting PCS after minor or mild head injury can best be conceptualized as a type of somatoform disorder. They note that many of these patients with persisting complaints have concomitant psychosocial factors, such as growing up in aversive school and/or family environments, which may lead to illness behaviour and susceptibility to secondary gain. They note that children learn at an early age that stomach aches are often the means of avoiding what they perceive as unpleasant experiences such as going to school or separation from parents.

Well-controlled prospective studies examining minor and mild head injury have consistently found the presence of fairly subtle and temporary cognitive deficits immediately following the trauma (Barth et al. 1989; Dikmen et al. 1995; Dikmen et al. 1986; Gronwall and Wrightson 1974; Hugenholtz et al. 1988; Levin et al. 1987). These studies have also shown that most patients make complete recoveries within several months of injury, with little or no persisting disability. Dikmen et al.'s (1995) recent neuropsychological outcome study demonstrated that mild head injury patients were indistinguishable from non-head injury trauma controls at one year post-injury. Alves et al. (1993) characterised the continuation of persistent, multiple symptom constellations such as PCS in their large sample as 'extremely rare'.

In spite of the extreme rarity of persisting PCS after minor or mild head injury demonstrated by the prospective outcome studies, these patients represent a frequent source of referrals to many neuropsychologists and other neurologic health care professionals. Consequently, persisting PCS has been the subject of a great deal of debate in the professional literature, between professional disciplines, among colleagues and in the courtroom (Romano 1992). Miller (1961, 1966; Miller and Cartlidge 1972) proposed that persisting complaints following minor head trauma were a function of unconscious or conscious exaggeration of symptoms, or 'compensation neurosis', rather than organic injury. Auerbach et al. (1967) surveyed neurosurgeons and found opinion to be evenly split on the question of the underlying mechanism of PCS: 56 per cent felt that it was chiefly organic, 39 per cent felt it was secondary to emotional factors, and 5 per cent indicated that it was probably compensation related.

Twenty-five years later, McMordie (1988) attempted a replication of the Auerbach et al. (1967) study and found some shifting of opinion. About the same proportion of neurosurgeons still felt that PCS was chiefly organic (55 per cent). However, compensation factors appeared to be playing an increasing role, at least in the minds of the neurosurgeons (emotional causes: 26 per cent; compensation factors: 19 per cent). McMordie (1988) surveyed a new profession that had not yet been recognized at the time of the Auerbach et al. (1967) survey, that is, neuropsychology. Neuropsychologists were much more likely to ascribe a chiefly organic cause to PCS (72 per cent) and much less likely to relate it to compensation factors (9 per cent).

Mild head trauma is rarely associated with abnormal computed tomography (CT) scans. Magnetic resonance imaging (MRI) appears to be more sensitive to abnormal results (Eisenberg and Levin 1989), but these lesions are frequently unrelated to the injury in question. For example, the base rates of high-intensity lesions of the white matter are quite common in the normal population. Animal model studies of mild-to-moderate head injury have elicited some relatively subtle microscopic morphological changes not observable on CT or MRI (e.g. Povlishock and Coburn 1989), but the clinical significance of these changes is uncertain.

Consequently, the most commonly cited evidence in favour of an organic cause to PCS is neuropsychological test results (Binder 1986; Kay 1992; Leininger and Kreutzer 1992). Unfortunately, neuropsychological test results may not be as objective as we might wish, because valid test results are dependent upon the best efforts for success on the part of the patient (Rogers et al. 1993). Patients involved in personal injury or disability claims have a very unfavourable motivational context for neuropsychological assessment, in that they are rewarded with financial compensation for poor performance. Indeed, it has been suggested that entirely different sets of norms be used when interpreting the test results of litigating patients, because of the high occurrence of poor motivation and symptom exaggeration in this population (Fox 1994).

Given the increased likelihood of inadequate motivation for valid test results when in a litigation context, it is necessary to assess for co-operation and motivation for success when the patient is being, or potentially could be, compensated for their injuries. Perhaps the best validated instrument of this genre is the Portland Digit Recognition Test (PDRT) (Binder 1990, 1992, 1993; Binder and Willis 1991). It is based on forced choice symptom validity methodology, whereby patients who choose significantly fewer correct answers than would be expected if they were responding randomly, are specifically demonstrated to be either consciously or unconsciously motivated to do poorly. It has the advantage of extensive validation data on groups of normals, patients with documented brain damage but no financial incentives for doing poorly, uncompensated patients with emotional disturbances, and simulated malingerers (Binder and Willis 1991; Binder 1993).

A number of other measures of motivation and co-operation during neuropsychological testing are available which do not rely on forced choice methodology (Lezak 1983). One of these measures is the Dot Counting Test, which is based on 'the performance curve' approach to identification of inadequate motivation (Rogers et al. 1993). On this instrument, patients are required to count groups of randomly and geometrically arranged dots as quickly as they can. Motivated patients should require more time to perform difficult tasks than to perform easier tasks. Specifically, patients should require increased time to count increased numbers of randomly spaced dots. Additionally, patients should require less time to count geometrically placed dots than to count the equivalent number of dots spaced randomly (Lezak 1983). When multiple deviations from the expected performance curve occur, the patient's motivation becomes suspect.

We recently reported a series of fifty-five consecutive patients presenting with persisting PCS (Youngjohn et al. 1995a). One-third of the sample suffered their injuries in car accidents, with falls causing the majority of the remaining injuries. All patients satisfied the selection criteria of suffering from minor or mild head injury, which was defined by no more than thirty minutes' loss of consciousness (LOC), less than 24 hours' post-traumatic amnesia (PTA) and no intracranial abnormalities on CT, which were available on about half the sample. Furthermore, only patients with PCS persisting for at least six months after the original injury were eligible for the study.

Remarkably, all fifty-five persisting PCS patients were involved in litigation or were pursuing or receiving Workers Compensation or other disability payments. No patients with PCS were referred over the two years that we collected data, who were not litigating or pursuing or receiving compensation. One patient denied the presence of litigation, but a request for records was received from her attorney within weeks of the evaluation. One patient was excluded from the study, because his attorney admitted to an administrative law judge that he had explicitly coached his client as to how he was to respond to the test items. This case has been reported elsewhere (Youngjohn 1995).

Table 8.1 presents the frequencies and percentages of patients reporting common PCS symptoms from this series. The most frequently reported symptom was poor memory, followed closely by headache. Depression and insomnia were both reported by more than half of the patients. Concentration difficulty, dizziness, irritability, and ringing in the ears were each reported by about a third of the patients. Blurred vision was common, but photophobia and diplopia were relatively rare.

A remarkably high portion of patients (sixteen patients or 30 per cent of the sample) reported unusual or anatomically improbable symptoms. For example, two patients reported suffering from monocular diplopia (double vision with one eye closed), which is exceedingly improbable from a

Table 8.1 Frequency of reported post-concussional symptoms

Symptom	Number of patients reporting	% of total
Headache	40	75
Dizziness	15	28
Blurred vision	10	19
Diplopia	6	11
Photophobia	5	9
Tinnitus	16	30
Memory problems	45	83
Concentration problems	19	35
Fatigue	7	13
Insomnia	30	57
Irritability	16	30
Anxiety	11	20
Depression	30	56
Other symptoms	50	93

neuroanatomic perspective. One patient reported experiencing double vision only when she was crossing through a doorway. One patient reported experiencing *triple* vision. Several patients claimed extended periods of autobiographical or retrograde amnesia for all events preceding their mild head injuries. Periods of extended, dense, autobiographical amnesia has been related in the literature to psychogenic amnesia (Binder 1994).

Also noteworthy were a number of unusual performances during sensory perceptual testing. One patient's response after the very first trial of double simultaneous stimulation was 'only the left' (he had not been previously informed that both sides would be stimulated at the same time). Several patients who claimed total anaesthesia of some portion of their body were subjected to forced choice symptom validity testing. They were required to choose between the number '3' or the number '8' that was traced on the affected area. Feedback was provided after each trial. Of the patients tested in this manner, a majority obtained significantly fewer items correct than would be expected had they been responding randomly. We also performed forced choice validity testing on the three patients who claimed total loss of smell by subjecting them to forced choice olfactory testing. One patient only obtained four trials correct out of eighteen total (p <.05), suggesting that his sense of smell is better than he wanted us to believe.

Table 8.2 presents the average performances of our series of PCS patients on the PDRT. No patients performed worse than chance (p <.1) on either the 5 second or the 15 second delay trials. Seven patients performed below chance on the 30 second delay trial, demonstrating it to be the most sensitive trial to poor motivation. When the different trials were combined, eight of the patients from our sample (15 per cent of them)

Table 8.2 Performance on the PDRT

	n	Mean % correct	SD
PDRT 5-s delay	54	79	22
PDRT 15-s delay	54	66	19
PDRT 30-s delay	54	62	21
PDRT total	54	67	18

performed below chance on either one of the PDRT trials, or the whole test, demonstrating that they were consciously or unconsciously motivated to do poorly on at least part of the examination. These rates of below chance responding on the PDRT are quite similar to those of compensated minor head trauma patients recently reported by Binder (1993).

It has been noted by a number of investigators that relying solely on below-chance responding on symptom validity testing to identify poor motivation, yields very high false negative classification rates (Guilmette et al. 1993; Rogers et al. 1993). Consequently, we determined the number of patients in our group who fell below the cutoff scores on the PDRT for poor motivation established by Binder (1993). Specifically, none of the 120 uncompensated patients with documented brain damage that he has examined has obtained fewer than 54 per cent of the items correct on the entire test or fewer than 50 per cent correct of the hard items with a 30-second delay. Sixteen of our patients (30 per cent) fell below the cutoff of 54 per cent of the items correct on the whole test, indicating the lack of co-operation. Eighteen of the patients (33 per cent) fell below the cutoff of 50 per cent correct on the hard items. These rates of poor motivation are again quite similar to those of the compensated minor head trauma patients reported by Binder (1993).

We also compared the PDRT performances of our patients to the average performances of uncompensated patients with documented brain damage, as reported by Binder and Willis (1991). Binder and Willis's group of brain damaged patients obtained a mean of 78 per cent of the total items correct and a mean of 75 per cent of the hard ones correct. Only fifteen of our patients (28 per cent) performed at or above these levels. This should be somewhat surprising, given the mild nature of trauma experienced by our PCS group and the relatively severe injuries experienced by Binder and Willis's (1991) documented brain damage or uncompensated group.

A subgroup (thirty-eight) of our patients were given another measure of co-operation, the Dot Counting Test (Lezak 1983). Table 8.3 presents a number of indices from this test, including frequencies of errors in counting both the grouped and ungrouped dots, frequencies of out-of-sequence response latencies for counting the ungrouped dots, and frequencies of equivalent or greater response latencies for counting grouped dot cards relative to the analogous ungrouped dot cards. Ten of the thirty-eight

Table 8.3 Dot Counting Test performance in 38 PCS patients

	Frequency of occurrence					
	0	1	2	3	4	5
Ungrouped dots errors	14	13	2	4	3	2
Ungrouped dot counting: times out of sequence	12	16	9	1	—	—
Grouped dots errors	32	4	1	1	—	—
Times grouped dot card equalled or exceeded ungrouped dot card	14	12	8	2	1	1

patients (26 per cent) had two or more out-of-sequence response latencies on the ungrouped dot cards and four patients required as much or more time to count grouped dots as analogous ungrouped dots on three or more occasions. While these performances do not demonstrate a volitional cause for poor performance, they do suggest variable attention, motivation, and/ or co-operation with the measure.

When the Dot Counting Test and the PDRT were considered together, twenty-six patients our of our entire sample (48 per cent) had poor performance on one or both measures of co-operation. These results indicate that motivational factors may have adversely affected neuropsychological test performance in almost half of our cases.

The relatively high number of patients in our sample in whom motivational factors may have adversely affected test performance is of particular interest. It is quite common to encounter statements in the literature indicating that the incidence of malingering on neuropsychological tests is quite low (e.g. Kay 1992), although these statements are rarely accompanied by empirical support. Snow (1992) estimated the incidence of malingering in neuropsychological settings to be between 5 per cent and 20 per cent. In contrast, he has indicated that the base rates for brain damage will likely be greater than 50 per cent. Given that psychologists are often unsuccessful at detecting persons feigning neuropsychological deficits (e.g. Faust et al. 1988a; Heaton et al. 1978), and that, when administered, current measures of co-operation on neuropsychological testing have relatively low sensitivity to malingered performance (Rogers et al. 1993) it is reasonable to suggest that the frequency of fabricated or exaggerated neuropsychological deficits may actually be higher than these estimates.

We also examined MMPI-2 (Hathaway and McKinley 1989) personality profiles in our series of persisting PCS patients. Figure 8.1 presents their mean basic-scale profiles. Also presented in Figure 8.1 are mean MMPI profiles from two independent series of patients with documented brain damage after moderate or severe closed head injury. These independent

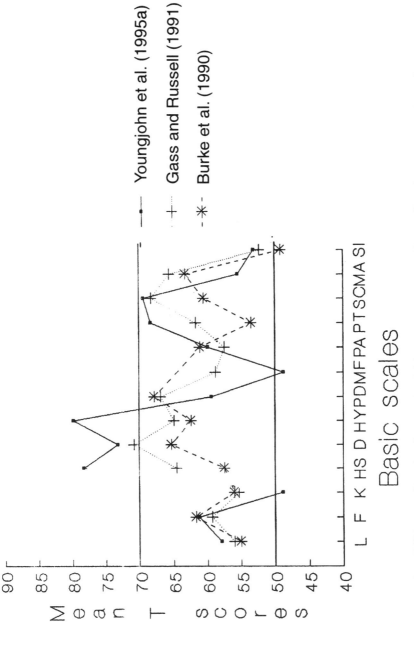

Figure 8.1 Basic scale MMPI-2 profiles for forty-eight PCS patients and MMPI profiles for two samples of patients with documented brain damage

Source: Reported by Youngjohn et al. (1995a); Burke et al. (1990); Gass and Russell (1991)

samples were composed of sixty-six patients (Burke et al. 1990) and fifty-eight patients (Gass and Russell 1991), respectively. The average PCS profile demonstrated clear elevations over those of brain injured patients on two scales in particular (Hs and Hy). These differences are especially notable in light of the normative differences between the MMPI and the MMPI-2 (Butcher et al. 1989). Specifically, equivalent responding to the test items on both tests would result in lower T score elevations on the MMPI-2 and higher elevations on the MMPI.

This finding of greater MMPI-2 elevations in persistent PCS patients, relative to actual brain injury patients, replicates the findings of previous investigators, who have discovered that more severely brain-injured patients paradoxically have lower MMPI elevations than patients complaining of PCS after minor head trauma, particularly on scales Hs and Hy (Leininger et al. 1991; Novack et al. 1984). It has been confirmed by a recent investigation comparing a series of thirty consecutive minor or mild head injury patients to thirty consecutive referrals of documented moderate or severe head injury (Youngjohn et al. 1995b). Our results suggest that PCS patients view themselves as having more physical symptoms and being more disabled by their symptoms than patients with documented brain damage. They also suggest the presence of significant elements of somatization and/or functional overlay to the patients' self-reports.

We would like to emphasise that there is nothing in our data which demonstrates conclusively that our PCS patients did not suffer some form of subtle brain injury. However, these results do suggest that the predominant causes of persisting complaints in our PCS patients were functional rather than organic. These conclusions are contrary to the opinions expressed by a large majority of neuropsychologists in a recent survey (McMordie 1988).

One criticism that might be argued regarding our investigation is that in order to better understand the influence of compensation and litigation factors on PCS, it would be necessary to include a control group of patients suffering from PCS who were not litigating or compensated. Unfortunately, no patients of this sort were referred during the two years that we were collecting data. In fact, our experiences in a variety of medical and rehabilitation settings suggest that patients with persisting PCS after minor or mild head injury who are not litigating or pursuing/receiving financial compensation for their symptoms are exceedingly rare. There have been a number of other recently published investigations of patients with persisting PCS. Remarkably, when the litigation issue was examined, these studies have revealed a virtual 100 per cent incidence of litigation and/or pursuit of financial compensation in patients with persisting PCS after minor or mild head injury (Binder 1993; Binder and Willis 1991; Cicerone and Kalmar 1995; Greiffenstein et al. 1994; Greiffenstein et al. 1995; Millis 1992; Youngjohn et al. 1995a, 1995b). The overwhelming prevalence of litigation in persisting PCS patients stands in stark contrast to the much lower prevalence of litigation in survivors of moderate and severe head injury (Youngjohn et al. 1995b). It is common to see moderate and severe head injury patients referred for neuropsychological evaluation or treatment, when no avenues for compensation exist or long after any litigation or compensation issues have been resolved.

In a recent MMPI-2 study investigating litigation in head injury, the authors found that paradoxically, head injury patients in litigation had *less* severe injuries overall than those who were not in litigation (Berry et al. 1995). Fee and Rutherford (1988) performed a prospective investigation examining outcome after minor and mild head injury. All patients were equated for severity of the initial injury. Remarkably, they found that on follow-up, those patients involved in litigation reported twice as many symptoms and complaints as those who did not enter litigation and/or declined to pursue financial compensation. They interpreted these results as suggesting that the decision to pursue financial compensation and/or the retention of an attorney in and of themselves delay recovery and increase symptom reporting.

The presence of litigation clearly plays a substantial, causative role by increasing the frequency and intensity of subjective complaints after personal injury. Lees-Haley and Brown (1993) looked at the base rates of symptom endorsement on a neuropsychological symptom checklist in personal injury litigants whose claims did not involve central nervous system (CNS) injury or illness. Indeed, patients were excluded from the study sample if they reported a history of head injury or other CNS conditions. Remarkably, they found that many symptoms often included as part of the PCS were reported by the non-head-injury litigants at a much higher rate than the control group. For example, 88 per cent of the litigants reported headaches, 78 per cent reported concentration problems, 77 per cent reported irritability, and 53 per cent reported memory problems. Consequently, PCS symptoms were felt to be more a function of litigation than brain injury. In a recent epidemiological investigation of PCS complaints, the authors found that being in litigation and/or psychiatric treatment were almost as powerful predictors of the presence of PCS complaints as having suffered a head injury (Fox et al. 1995).

Binder and Rohling (in press) have performed a comprehensive, meta-analytic investigation of the effects of litigation on neuropsychological complaints and test performance. Their results demonstrate consistent, significant effects leading to decreased neuropsychological test performance or increased symptom reporting, across virtually all studies that were examined.

One model that has been proposed to explain the increased intensity and frequency of complaints in litigating patients, as well as their extended periods for recovery, is that these individuals have financial incentives to remain in a sick role and report relatively more severe disabilities (Rogers et al. 1994). Alternatively, certain personality factors may predispose some individuals to be particularly susceptible to secondary gain and symptom exaggeration (Youngjohn et al. 1995b).

On the other hand, there is some evidence to suggest that retaining an attorney for litigation purposes may have a more direct effect on symptom reporting than the models described above. Specifically, it is common practice for some attorneys to show their clients lists of symptoms associated with various disorders, such as post-traumatic stress disorder and/or post-concussion syndrome, in order to enhance the likelihood of financial recovery (Lees-Haley 1992). Indeed, a 'how to' manual on preparing mild head-injury plaintiffs has been published in the legal literature (Taylor et al. 1992). Not surprisingly, it has been reported that attorneys have suggested overtly to their clients that they complain of symptoms consistent with post-traumatic stress disorder (Rosen 1995).

Wetter and Corrigan (1995) surveyed seventy practicing attorneys and discovered that four-fifths of them believe that they should educate their clients regarding psychological testing prior to forensic evaluations. One-half of the practicing attorneys in this survey felt that they should routinely provide specific information regarding symptom validity scales to their clients prior to psychological testing. Consequently, it should not be surprising that there is a confirmed case of attorney coaching on neuropsychological testing prior to evaluation, in which the attorney actually admitted to an administrative law judge that he had provided specific information regarding symptom validity tests (Youngjohn 1995).

Our results and those of previous investigators indicate that financial compensation can be a powerful disincentive for valid test performances and result in increased symptom reporting after minor or mild head injury. While controversy remains, there appears to be an emerging consensus in the literature that the predominant aetiologies of persisting PCS complaints after minor or mild head injury are related to litigation, hysteroid and other dysfunctional personality characteristics, the pursuit of financial disability compensation, and/or other functional (non-organic) factors. Our results also suggest that when financial compensation for brain damage is sought by litigants after minor or mild head traumas suffered in road accidents, physicians, neuropsychologists and attorneys should be particularly sceptical of their claims.

Part II

Legal consequences

Chapter 9

At the scene

Road accidents and the police

Angela Hetherington, Alan Munro and Margaret Mitchell

This chapter provides the first perspective on the legal context of death and injury on the road. The first part, by Angela Hetherington, is based on her research on the response of road traffic officers to trauma on the roads and is a bridge between our consideration of the psychological impact on survivors and our consideration of the impact on the emergency services – in this case, the police. The second part, by Alan Munro, an Inspector in Strathclyde Police, presents data from interviews with regular patrol officers which emphasises their often competing roles at the scene of a road accident. Together these contributions describe the impact on police officers of their work with road accidents, and with bereaved relatives and survivors.

THE RESPONSE OF ROAD TRAFFIC POLICE OFFICERS TO TRAUMA ON THE ROADS

Professionals who are involved in the emergency response to disaster can be more adversely affected (on some measures) by their experience than the victims of the event (Green et al.1985), and these effects are not necessarily limited to large-scale traumatic incidents. Recent studies indicate that over 85 per cent of emergency personnel involved in critical incidents have at some time in their career experienced traumatic stress reactions (Mitchell 1985; Mitchell and Bray 1990).

Research into the everyday trauma of police work is largely descriptive in nature and is documented as subjective reports (Kroes 1976; Newton 1989). Like much of the research into occupational trauma it lacks methodological rigour, partially due to the nature of the subject and the ethical difficulties involved in ascertaining the effects of trauma.

Individual perceptions of traumatic reactions are subject to distorted recollections and, as such, are limited in the degree to which they can be generalised. Such statements can, however, support and provide substance to empirical research by providing insight into the impact of traumatic experiences on police officers (Mitchell 1991b). Despite methodological difficulties it is recognised that post-traumatic stress reactions can result from prolonged exposure to smaller-scale traumatic incidents such as are commonplace in police work (Kroes 1976; Singleton 1978).

In the following example, Kroes (1976: 64) describes a severe reaction in a police officer after involvement in a road traffic accident:

> One patrolman saw a three year old child who had been catapulted through the windscreen of a car and decapitated. He went on a three-day drinking binge as a result of the experience, and when he returned he was disciplined. He would not explain why he had been absent for three days because it would have required acknowledging that he had been deeply moved by the experience.

Such accounts illustrate the nature of incidents with which officers have to contend. Although one traumatic incident may be sufficient to incur a distressing set of reactions in an officer (Dyregrov 1989; Mitchell 1991b), such reactions may also be the result of an accumulation of events, referred to as 'sequential traumatisation' (Gersons and Carlier 1990). The nature of police work and the repeated exposure to traumatic incidents renders officers particularly vulnerable. For the officer, this may increase the 'unexpectedness' of his or her reactions because of the experience of having previously coped well with more serious incidents.

Recent research into the impact of traumatic events on road traffic police patrol officers found that over 40 per cent of officers reported incidents which had disturbing effects on them, characteristic of post-traumatic stress disorder (Hetherington 1992). Using both quantitative and qualitative measures, a significant number of patrol officers report experiencing intrusive thoughts and dreams relating to particular accidents. They also report using avoidance in an attempt to dispel the disturbing experience from their memory (Hetherington 1993a;1993b). Descriptions by patrol officers of disturbing incidents (from Hetherington 1994) illustrate traumatic stress reactions experienced by officers, and the nature of the events which gave rise to these reactions. These accounts emphasise the nature and variety of the reactions to trauma on the roads which, if not responded to, can result in severe and long-term effects on the officer. Incidents which officers consider disturbing often involve children:

> I was at an accident where a family of four died in a resultant fire. We could do nothing until the Fire Brigade arrived. Two children in the rear may well have survived. They were still in their seat belts. The thing that upset me most was that the two children died as they did. I later went home and burst into tears talking to my wife about it.

A sense of helplessness can add to the impact of the event: situations in which officers are unable to take any action can reduce their sense of

control, and heighten the emotional impact of the incident they are forced
to witness. One officer describes such a scene:

> I arrived at the scene of an accident where a youth was trapped by one
> leg in the car. [The car was] already burning fiercely. I had to stand by
> and watch while he burned alive. There was nothing I could do. That
> was the worst thing.

Anger is a characteristic reaction to traumatic incidents, where individuals feel a sense of outrage at the needless loss of lives (Duckworth 1990).
A sense of helplessness coupled with feelings of anger can also be directed
at the legal system: officers can feel angry about a legal system which they
see as insufficient in dealing with those who have caused death or injury to
another person. This theme is reflected in the following:

> [Attended] a fatal RTA involving an eight year old girl and her mother.
> Both died in my arms, and the guilty party was not prosecuted because
> of a delay in serving the summons. A lot of work for nothing. [I felt I]
> couldn't do justice to the dependants.

Identification with the victim or family can also increase the officer's
vulnerability (Raphael 1986; Bartone et al. 1989; Hetherington 1993).
Possibly this may be due partly to the intense psychological distress evoked
by everyday objects that are associated with the traumatic incident. The
following description illustrates this point:

> [A child death] When I arrived on the scene the only things visible were
> the dead child's legs. The child was wearing a pair of training shoes.
> When I returned home after my tour of duty, my son was wearing the
> same training shoes and I had to throw them away immediately as the
> sight of them upset me so much.

A characteristic reaction to traumatic incidents is recurrent and intrusive
distressing recollections or distressing dreams about the event (Horowitz et
al. 1980). A person may attempt to avoid stimuli associated with the
distressing event by deliberate avoidance of thoughts or associated images
it evokes. The mutilation resulting from a road accident can add to its
emotional impact, as follows:

> Three years ago I went to an RTA where a man was trapped in a vehicle.
> [The] car caught fire and I couldn't get him out. Watched him burn.
> From that day I have been unable to eat red meat or anything resembling
> it. The smell of cooked meat and the sight of it makes me feel ill.

Having to deal with distressed relatives, and informing them of a death,
has been reported by officers to be stressful, a finding replicated in the
present study. In addition, dealing with bereaved relatives after an incident at which an officer has attended, can revive their initial reactions.

Re-experiencing the incident in this way can also serve to stimulate feelings which the officer was able to control when dealing with the incident, but may find overwhelming when having to interact afterwards with survivors, or the victim's family.

Regular exposure to death can reduce the feeling most people have of invulnerability and can generate fears of imminent death (Peterson et al. 1991). In police officers these fears appear to arise most often in relation to the officer's children whose personal safety they feel responsible for, yet also feel they are unable to guarantee:

> [I attended a] fatal RTA, six year old hit by passing car after running out from between parked cars. I remember well his head being placed over a drain so that the blood ran down the drain. It made me over-protective for my children.

Fears relating to the safety of family members can be sustained by intrusive thoughts and images in which the real victims are replaced by members of the officer's own family. This can make it difficult for officers to disclose their feelings to their family, although when they are able to express their feelings, considerable support can be derived:

> I later went home and burst into tears talking to my wife about it. My wife is the main release from stress in these situations. Once I have related the event to her, whatever it might be, I can then forget it.

Through experiencing traumatic incidents officers can develop well-practised coping strategies, sometimes based on cognitive reappraisal of the events. The following may represent one person's attempt to depersonalise the incident, thereby allowing a focus on other aspects of the job, in order to cope:

> In general it is the transition of an injured party to a deceased. The injuries are usually such that you know it is inevitable, and there is little that can be done to help. Dead bodies are not people any more, and the injured who survive are no problem because you can help them.

Threat to life has been found to result in severe reactions in police officers (Solomon 1990); some officers in the present study reported severe stress reaction after accidents on duty in which they are involved.

> I was on police motorcycle duty when I chased a stolen car. The car deliberately rammed me to escape . . . I was absent for 95 days. I had serious mental problems following the accident. I had recurring nightmares and no concentration. I had flashbacks when I rode a motorcycle. I had no help from the police at all. Overall I felt I could not deal with the stress at work.

Some officers refer to the support and understanding from their workmates following such disturbing incidents which, when it is not forthcoming within the organisation, can result in strong feelings of anger or disillusionment. Distress, and anger towards the organisation, can also be the result of the officer's needs for a sense of security, to be appreciated, and to be with people he or she can trust. Answering these needs is an important factor in recovery after a traumatic incident and can prevent feelings of resentment arising. Duckworth (1990: 53) writes:

> Perhaps the scene is set for trouble because when supervisors feel that the officers' expectations are unrealistic, unjustified or out of order, they can so easily make the mistake of dismissing them rather than managing them – seeing them as a deficiency in the officers rather than as a problem to be managed.

The variability of the impact of traumatic events on an individual is related to individual differences, and to the use of coping strategies (Demi and Miles 1983; Raphael 1986). Strategies used most frequently by police officers are humour, talking to workmates, talking to friends and family, devoting oneself to one's work, physical exercise, working things out alone, and talking to a police counsellor (Silva 1990; Hetherington 1994). Kobasa (1979) suggests that training based on past experience can help develop a sense of mastery, reduce the unknown elements of incidents and prepare them for a subsequent similar event. Paton (1989) found prior experience of a stressor to be effective. Ways of coping with traumatic incidents can vary in effectiveness, while inappropriate strategies can compound the stressful impact (Raphael et al. 1984). Many also require the wider context of support from colleagues and supervisors. Leiter (1991) concluded that effective coping presumed to some extent a favourable environment, including supportive supervisors and associated organisational resources.

Reese (1990) emphasises the need for the individual to recognise and make it known that they need help, and to know how to obtain it, although research suggests that people may not recognise a need for additional support after trauma (Dunning 1990; Reese 1990). Similarly, Creamer et al. (1989) suggest that individuals not only fail to understand their own reactions to trauma but also, in the absence of psychological intervention, may be unable to conceive of improvement in their wellbeing.

Ultimately, the provision of appropriate and experienced counselling services, and its acceptance by officers as a necessary tool to recovery, remains the responsibility of the organisation (Hetherington 1993a). Reese (1990) recommends that some form of routine intervention should be made available to police officers following a traumatic incident, thus avoiding the problem of anyone standing out as needing help and of any disinclination to seek help. Although this may be changing in the light of new knowledge and raised awareness about vulnerability, emergency service workers including police officers, may not seek professional support due to the image of themselves as helpers (Mitchell et al. 1991; Paton 1989).

DISSONANT POLICE ROLES AT THE SCENE OF A ROAD ACCIDENT: INFORMATION AND SUPPORT

Road accidents are one of the most common type of incident that the emergency services are sent to, and police officers working with the Traffic Department and regular patrol officers are often involved. Such incidents vary from minor 'bumps' with no injuries, to those where passengers or pedestrians are seriously injured or killed. As a task which could be performed a number of times during an officer's working week, dealing with road accidents involves a great deal of routine activity to complete the procedural tasks involved in collecting and collating the evidence.

An officer may come across road accidents in the course of their regular patrol, or they may be sent to them by Force Control. Frequently, they are the first of the emergency services at the scene and, until other services arrive, officers can be called upon to rescue survivors and give first aid to the injured. Their main function at the scene is the overall control of the incident with the immediate priority being the prevention of any further escalation of the incident (Scottish Police College Training Notes 1991). Other traffic, and witnesses, need to be controlled so that the ambulance service and the fire service can do what they have to do, unimpeded, to rescue survivors or remove the injured. In some instances, a scenes-of-crime officer from the police might be called to photograph the scene.

Once these practical aspects of the incident are under control, the officer can focus on the more traditional role of the police in dealing with legal and procedural aspects. As much information as possible needs to be collected – through their own observations and by speaking to survivors and witnesses – in order to prepare a report on the circumstances leading to the accident. This role of information gatherer, the sheer amount of information which officers must collect and the time taken to do so – particularly if a death has occurred – can give the impression to witnesses and to others involved that completing a report is the only interest the police officer has in the incident. At a time when witnesses and survivors are shocked and have an acute need for support and for information, it may appear that an officer is emphasising legal and procedural matters at the expense of social and emotional support.

In order to maintain control over a volatile situation, the police officers need to be aware of potential hostility from witnesses and survivors towards those whom they see as having caused the accident. Dual roles are required of the police officer in switching between two distinct approaches: one in which they are understanding and caring towards the survivors and witnesses, and the other in which they are trying to prevent verbal or physical attacks. As one officer observed:

> We were at a fatal accident where a pedestrian was knocked down when a crowd of onlookers started threatening the driver of the car. The whole thing was becoming hostile and out of control at a time when you are trying to deal solemnly with a death.

Officers can find themselves getting frustrated as the situation becomes gradually more difficult to control. Officers are very conscious of the high profile and public nature of road accidents which place them squarely in the public gaze and give the sense that everything that they do at the scene is the subject of scrutiny. This is also reflected in the survey conducted by the Victim Support Scheme (1994: 4). As one officer, who attended an accident in which a pedestrian was knocked down in a busy city centre street, observed:

> You're under the spotlight at a road traffic accident. You've got this sense of an audience watching everything you are doing, so you busy yourself by taking endless statements from witnesses about what took place and how the accident happened.

Research on how police probationers learn to deal with sudden death found that distancing and detachment from the situation is a strategy frequently used by officers to help them control their emotions (Mitchell et al. 1996a). Certain deaths are perceived as being 'worse' than others in terms of becoming emotionally involved: the death of a child, in particular, is found to be the most difficult with which to deal. An officer attending a road accident in which an 8-year-old boy had been killed used detachment when dealing with a particularly disturbing incident: 'The Inspector wanted someone to take statements from a number of witnesses and I volunteered. I just kept my head down and thought about the job I was doing. I got through it OK.' The use of detachment in order to get the job done is a well-established coping strategy for many officers, but it can be a source of frustration to others. One officer who was dealing with a number of road crash survivors described his awareness that the people needed his support and help:

> You get a lack of sensitivity from some senior officers which really annoys you. They come along after you've been there for a while and you're doing what you can for those involved, and then they start telling you to attend to other things at the scene. All that does is separate you from the survivors who need you.

Police officers can often be caught between their dissonant roles at crash scenes. There is a need and requirement to control people and other traffic at the scene and to collect information. At the same time, there is an expectation on the part of witnesses and survivors that the police, as the authority figures at the scene, will also provide structure, support and comfort. To some observers, a police officer getting the job done by using personal detachment from the emotional implications of the accident may look cold and officious. A theme of the present volume is the importance to survivors of the particular way in which an accident is rendered within its legal and procedural context. When people are in shock and are angry and upset, they may try to find someone to blame for the tragic incident, and their first impressions of what may well turn out to be a lengthy and unyielding legal process are of the greatest significance.

Police officers also use anticipatory preparation to deal with sudden death incidents: in this way, an officer going to an incident will conjure up images of what they expect the scene to be like, and what the body will look like in an effort to diminish its impact and hence prepare themselves (Mitchell et al. 1996a). Often, this is not possible when attending road accidents, a particular feature of which, as distinct from injuries or fatalities caused in other ways, is the seemingly infinite variety of mutilations and crash scenes that can result. This is reflected in an officer's description of going to a road accident call: 'Its the unpredictable nature of [road traffic accidents]. When someone is shot or stabbed you have an idea what to expect as you attend the call, but with road accidents you can't visualise the scene, you can't prepare for it.' A young officer attending a road accident fatality commented: 'No human body should be twisted like that.'

The survey conducted by the Victim Support Scheme (1994) found that immediately following a fatality the victim's family has an acute need for information, and a police officer, most often, has the job of telling someone that a relative has been killed. Examples were found of good practice in the delivery of such messages in a caring and empathetic manner. On occasion, however, when 'impersonal remarks' were made or inadequate or hedging information was given, this was found to increase the distress felt by families, and added to their grief. Officers themselves openly acknowledge the task of delivering 'death messages' as extremely stressful (Holmes 1993). It can be made more difficult if the officer has attended at the accident scene, as is reflected in the following description by an officer, speaking of his difficulty in knowing how to convey information in a way which he felt was authentic:

I was at an accident where a passenger was killed and the body was badly damaged. Later I am telling a relative of the deceased of the death, and she asks me if I have seen the body and is it OK. What do you say? Do I tell her that her nephew was decapitated? Do you lie? Its very hard to deal with. You feel you must be honest with the next of kin. How can you lie to a person at a time like that?

Usually, the officer will often have time to prepare for how they are going to deliver the information, but occasionally they are unprepared – especially if they need to notify people at the scene. This could arise if other members of the deceased's family were involved, and can also arise in the situation when a driver has killed another person, as the following aptly describes:

> I was at a fatal accident, an elderly male pedestrian was killed, although he was alive when I first arrived. He died before the ambulance could take him away. I then had to tell the driver that the person she had knocked down was dead. She took it really bad. I felt as if I was accusing her of murder.

Such accounts bring into sharp focus the experience of drivers who themselves kill or severely injure on the roads, and the competing perspectives of the legal system, and the emotional reactions of the bereaved relatives, or the accident survivors. Indeed, there are many relatives who believe that drivers who kill – especially if that person is driving without a license or is drunk – should be charged with murder (see Chapter 12). Research in this area is very limited, although the extreme guilt or lack of guilt experienced by drivers who kill, and the anger felt by relatives at the apparent diminishment of responsibility of drivers who kill would make a very fruitful area for study. Again, the social context within which road accidents are interpreted, appears to treat death caused by a road accident as a very different entity than death caused in other ways.

As a consequence of the procedural and legal responsibilities of the police, training in dealing with sudden deaths is generally delivered during the officer's basic training and focuses on the initial investigation and the completion of a report. In other words, it is a task-oriented approach. Individual differences between officers result in some of them dealing with such incidents in a sensitive, caring and empathetic way, while some do not. Officers often learn on the job from more senior colleagues in an informal way about how to deal with people involved in road accident trauma. Mitchell et al. (1996a) has found that this can account for much of the variation.

There is considerable evidence to suggest that training is necessary to better prepare officers in working with road crash survivors and victims' families, and in dealing with their own emotional reactions. Such initiatives are well advanced in some police services, and relatively lacking in others. Overall, however, training approaches are changing as the police service increasingly recognises its importance and potential value to those affected by road accidents. Initiatives addressing these aspects could be integrated with the critical incident debriefing programmes which have now been adopted by many police services throughout the UK.

As an example of the increasing awareness of the part the police can play in exacerbating or ameliorating the emotional impact of road accidents, Essex Police have adopted a *Service Delivery Standard* setting out guidelines for procedure following a road crash. Pivotal to this is a strategy which is used in managing other categories of sudden death incidents, for example a murder, or a major disaster: the appointment of a named liaison officer as a point of contact for bereaved families. This expands police involvement with the survivors of a road accident up to any inquest or prosecution.

In conclusion, there is a need to provide officers with the confidence to deal with grieving relatives, an aspect of police work which has been identified by them as one of the most problematic aspects of dealing with sudden death (Mitchell et al. 1996a), in addition to training officers to collect evidence and information in an efficient and straightforward way. All of this requires a greater understanding of the many people who are affected by a road accident, identified by Victim Support (1994) as: bereaved family and friends of the deceased; witnesses to the crash, other drivers and injured passengers; professional personnel dealing with the crash and its aftermath. The emotional impact of a tragedy such as a serious or fatal road accident is an experience and image which can stay with a person for the rest of their lives. It is important that the memory of what took place is not made worse by any possibility that the police, as they carry out their work, are seen as uncaring.

Chapter 10

Claiming damages for psychiatric injury following a road accident

Kay Wheat and Michael Napier

Road accidents and their consequences raise issues in a number of areas of the law. These include criminal law, ranging from fairly minor infringements to death by reckless driving and manslaughter. European law is also relevant, particularly in relation to safety and the regulation of heavy goods vehicles, and a number of aspects of civil law such as insurance law, and of course, tortious liability. Given the theme of the present collection, we will concentrate on tortious liability and, in particular, certain medico-legal aspects of personal injury claims.

Even a minor road accident can be an alarming or traumatic event and can result in physical and/or psychiatric injury. Although there is often dispute about the liability of the road user who is alleged to have been negligent, liability is much easier to establish in road accident cases than in many other types of personal injury cases. The problems tend to arise with regard to the type(s) of injury sustained, and the losses for which compensation is recoverable by injured parties, as well as some aspects of the litigation process involved in recovery of compensation. This chapter will examine these issues, but first, it is necessary to outline the legal framework.

NEGLIGENCE

Most road accidents are caused by negligence, and for the purposes of the civil law of tort (which, roughly speaking, is non-contractual civil liability), this includes more serious acts which may be regarded as reckless. Negligence has a special definition in civil law. In order for a person to be held to be negligent, that person (the defendant) must owe a duty of care to the injured party (the plaintiff or victim). Here we mean 'injured party' in the wider sense, that is, someone who has suffered loss. The defendant must be shown to be in breach of that duty of care, and the breach must, in turn, have caused the loss suffered by the plaintiff.

Although the concept of a duty of care has long preoccupied tort lawyers, in the case of road traffic accidents, as far as physical damage is concerned, that there is a duty of care owed to other road users (whether drivers or pedestrians) is uncontroversial. Similarly, there is a clear duty of care owed to those whose property abuts the highway so as to be in the ambit of physical damage. However, special conditions are imposed by the law when there is no physical damage caused to persons or property, that is when the damage is purely financial, or where there is personal injury but of a psychiatric nature only.

Further, in order to establish breach of the duty of care it is necessary to apply a certain standard of care to the negligent road user – the central principle being that the standard is objective. It does not take into account the lack of experience of a driver, but imposes the standard of the reasonably competent driver upon everyone. Clearly, there are good pragmatic reasons for this; it would be unsatisfactory to apply different standards of care depending upon the experience of the road user, entailing the evidential problems that this would create.

The final component of the tort of negligence is that the breach must have caused the damage complained of. At first sight this seems obvious, but it is important to remember that there are two aspects to causation in this area. First, *factual* causation must be proved so that, for example, any illness, disability, or other loss suffered by the plaintiff must be causally linked to the particular impact of the accident in the physical sense, that is, the everyday meaning of causation. Second, however, there must be *legal* causation, which is usually described by saying that the damage must not be too remote. This means that although there is a factual causal link between the initial event and the resulting loss, it has been decided by the courts that it is not appropriate to hold the defendant responsible for every consequence of a negligent act. Analogously, only a limited number of the ripples in the pool will be deemed to be 'caused' by the pebble dropped into it. So, for example, the person who fails to post his winning football coupon because he has been the victim of another's careless driving, will not recover the lost £500,000 from the other party. For a real example of remoteness of damage, see the case of *Meah* v *McCreamer* [1985] 1 All ER 367 (below).

It is often said that for damage not to be too remote, it must be foreseeable. For the purposes of describing the basic concepts of negligence law, we have used the terminology of 'duty of care', 'remoteness of damage' and 'foreseeability'. It is important to know, however, that lawyers often use these concepts interchangeably, frequently with a confusing lack of clarity. The reason for this overlap is that the concepts have been created by judges to restrict the type and number of claims that can arise out of an act of negligence. This was summed up by the American judge, Cardozo CJ in *Ultramares Corporation* v *Touche* (1931) 255 NY 170, 179, as the law seeking to avoid 'liability in an indeterminate amount for an indeterminate time to an indeterminate class'. This is a public policy issue, and the concerns are twofold: the cost and availability of insurance, and the effect on the ability of a civil justice system to process large amounts of litigation. These concepts are reflected in expressions of fear about the 'floodgates' of litigation being opened. The floodgates argument has played a prominent part in the restricted and unsatisfactory development of recovery of damages for negligently inflicted psychiatric injury. It is our view that the argument has been much exaggerated and, when it results in legal formulations which deny justice, cannot and should not be sustained. In the context of road accidents, while *physical* injury is usually foreseeable, many of the difficult issues in personal injury litigation surround the question as to whether *psychiatric* injury is foreseeable. For further discussion of these and other issues related to recovering damages for psychiatric injury, see Napier and Wheat (1995).

INJURIES

Physical injury

If it is clear that the other road user has failed to meet the required standard of care and hence liability is not in issue, it may be thought that the resolution of the claim will not be difficult. However, commonplace as they are, road accidents can result in a variety of complex physical injuries, such as brain injury and catastrophic spinal damage. The social and economic consequences can be huge, requiring much expert help from carers and personal injury lawyers. Such injuries give rise to a range of interesting questions: for example, deciding on the most appropriate time following the accident (i.e. when the best prognosis can be given) to seek settlement of the claim, either by agreement or through the court process; deciding the settlement which is best for the injured party, whether 'structured settlements', where effectively the injured party receives guaranteed income, rather than a lump sum; deciding future loss in terms of the need for care, loss of earnings, and so forth, and obtaining actuarial evidence to support the claim; and whether it is necessary to apply for an interim payment if settlement will take some time to reach. These questions arise in cases of psychiatric injury, but are more common when there is severe and irreversible physical disablement.

Psychiatric injury

There have been major developments over the past ten years in recovering damages for psychiatric injury. The disturbing catalogue of disasters in the 1980s (e.g. Hillsborough, the King's Cross fire, the capsize of the *Herald of Free Enterprise* at Zeebrugge, the *Piper Alpha* fire, the Lockerbie bombing) meant that doctors and lawyers were confronted with survivors of those disasters who had been psychologically traumatised by their experiences. Sometimes psychological trauma accompanied physical injury, and sometimes it stood alone. Much was learned about recognising the psychiatric injury suffered, its disabling effect, and ways in which it could be treated. A number of key cases came before the courts, such as *Alcock* v *Chief Constable of South Yorkshire Police* [1992] 1 AC 310, and the *Herald of Free Enterprise* Arbitrations (Personal and Medical Injuries Law Letter, June 1989), which examined the legal and the medical issues involved.

Despite the increasing awareness of the extent of psychiatric injury (particularly post-traumatic stress disorder, PTSD), the law still restricts the circumstances in which damages can be recovered. These will now be examined.

Psychiatric injury with physical injury

If psychiatric injury accompanies physical injury, generally the law will allow damages to be recovered for the psychiatric injury. It is important to remember, however, that certain physical injuries make psychiatric injury more likely, for example head injury. In the case of *Meah* v *McCreamer* [1985] 1 All ER 367, in a road traffic accident Mr Meah suffered head injury resulting in significant personality change. As a result he committed acts of sexual violence, culminating in a long prison sentence. The case is a good illustration of the remoteness of damage issue. Mr Meah recovered damages to compensate him for the loss of his liberty, but he could not recover damages in respect of the compensation he had been ordered to pay to his victims. Apart from the remoteness point, it was also held that it would also be contrary to public policy for him to be indemnified in this way.

Obviously someone who has been involved in a disastrous road accident involving many vehicles, some in flames and so on, will be more likely to suffer a psychiatric injury as well as a physical injury, but it is important not to underestimate the effect of a relatively minor road accident (see below, the cases of *Brice* v *Brown* [1984] 1 All ER 997 and *Page* v *Smith* [1995] 2 WLR 664).

Psychiatric injury without physical injury

When there is no physical injury the law seeks to restrict claims by setting the following conditions. First, the person must have suffered the psychiatric injury as a primary victim, that is, they experienced reasonable fear of being injured themselves; or as secondary victim, that is, they experienced reasonable fear of, or actual injury, to another person. For this latter circumstance to be allowed, the secondary victim must stand in some special relationship to the person injured or imperilled, and must be present (in this case) at the road accident, or at its immediate aftermath. Second, the accident must also be 'shocking' to a person of, what is quaintly described in the cases as, 'customary phlegm' or 'normal fortitude'. And finally, any psychiatric illness must be one which is 'recognised' diagnostically.

THE 'PRIMARY' AND 'SECONDARY' VICTIM

The expression, 'primary victim', is used to describe the person who suffers psychiatric injury through fear for their own safety, and, generally speaking, contentious issues arise only when there is no physical injury. The right of such a survivor to recover damages was established in the case of *Dulieu* v *White & Sons* [1901] 2 KB 669, when a woman recovered damages following an incident in which a horse van came through the window of the public house where she was working. Although not really tested in English law, there seems to be no reason why damages cannot be recovered for the 'near miss', that is, the accident that never occurred. So, for example, imagine a car driver sees a large truck overtaking and coming towards him on his side of the road, although it manages to get back to the correct side of the road at the last minute. If the shock causes the car driver to suffer a psychiatric injury, then damages should be recoverable because physical injury is foreseeable by the driver and therefore psychiatric injury will also be foreseeable. This principle may sound fairly obvious, but has only just been established beyond doubt by the House of Lords decision in the case of *Page* v *Smith*, which we discuss in more detail below. In this case there was physical damage to the car, and as indicated, liability in a 'near miss' scenario has yet to be established in the English courts.

In all cases, however, what may be open to dispute is the question whether the survivor could reasonably have feared for his own safety. It could be argued that because of the security of the plaintiff's physical location in relation to the accident he could not have reasonably feared for his own safety. This would be a question of evidence in each case. From the legal practitioner's perspective, the importance of taking a full and accurate proof of evidence as to what was observed by the survivor, and the full details of spatial proximity, cannot be overestimated.

Real problems emerge when the survivor's psychiatric injury arises through fear for another, that is, when they are considered a 'secondary victim'. Again, the fear of injury must be reasonable: for example, a woman who sees a truck heading towards the car her husband is driving should recover damages if there is a near miss. The spectre of opening the floodgates alluded to above, however, has resulted in the imposition of two major restrictions on the right of a secondary victim to recover damages: first, the survivor must be in a special class of persons in relationship to the imperilled person; and second, the person must be imperilled by a shocking event, and the survivor must witness that event, or its immediate aftermath, with unaided senses.

It is evident why the courts wish to prevent the opening of floodgates – although we would strongly argue that the floodgates threat has never been proven and so any resulting injustice cannot be supported – but it may be less easy to understand why these two particular conditions should be imposed. It has to do with the legal concept of proximity, which in turn relates to foreseeability of damage. The law says that in order for a person to be liable for damage they must be able to foresee it occurring as a result of their own negligence. In consequence, the law has said that unless someone is 'close' in some way to the person injured, then it is not foreseeable that they will suffer psychiatric injury, nor is it foreseeable that they will suffer injury if they do not see the trauma, but are, for example, merely told of the death, some time later. What should never be lost sight of, however, is that these restrictions are conceptual developments to restrict the number of claims, and are nothing to do with the reality of psychiatric injury and its many and varied causes.

'SPECIAL RELATIONSHIP'

What kind of personal and social relationships are considered? The most obvious is a relationship of close love and affection. There are no English cases which involve relationships more remote than either spouse/spouse or parent/child, but the House of Lords in *Alcock* v *Chief Constable of South Yorkshire Police* [1992] 1 AC 310, confirmed that other close relationships may suffice if the evidence justifies this. The importance of the cogency of the evidence to show the closeness of the relationship cannot be over-estimated.

The relationship of rescuer and primary victim is also one of sufficient proximity, so that professional rescuers can recover damages for physical and psychiatric injury incurred in the course of a rescue. Problems can arise, however, as to precisely what must be done in order for the injured party to be accepted as a rescuer. In *McFarlane* v *E E Caledonia Ltd* [1994] 2 All ER 1, when the survivor was on a support vessel some 500 yards or so from the *Piper Alpha* oil rig when it exploded, and who helped assist the walking wounded was deemed not to be a rescuer. Clearly, the acceptance by the courts of the eligibility of rescuers to claim damages is based upon public policy reasoning, altruism being something to be encouraged. However, although on the basis of foreseeability any rescuer should recover compensation, the position of the professional rescuer is slightly different from a policy point of view, as the professional is paid to do the job, and presumably freely chose to undertake it. On the basis that 'if you can't stand the heat, get out of the kitchen', some would say that the professional should not recover because of the stress of the job (see the editorial 'Stress on the beat', *The Times*, 4 February 1995), following the settlement of damages to some of the psychiatrically injured police officers involved in the Hillsborough rescue). We would argue that this reflects a deplorable misunderstanding of the debilitating effects of psychiatric injury.

Other plaintiffs have recovered damages for psychiatric injury in a number of traumatic incidents when, for example, they believed themselves to be the cause of a fellow-employee's injury. In *Dooley* v *Cammell Laird Co Ltd* [1951] 1 Lloyd's Rep 271, a crane driver dropped a load into the hold of a ship, after the crane mechanism failed, causing him to believe he had injured his fellow-workers in the hold. Fortunately, they escaped injury, but the driver recovered damages for the psychiatric illness he subsequently developed. It has been suggested in both the *Alcock* case and by the Law Commission in their recent Consultation Paper on Liability for Psychiatric Illness (No 137, March 1995), that such an 'involuntary participant' should recover damages without the requirement of having to witness the accident with unaided senses (see below). The example given by the Law Commission is of a signalman who suffers a shock-induced injury when, due to the faulty signalling equipment he is operating, he believes he has caused a train crash. This would be pertinent to road accidents in the context of level-crossing collisions.

What of the person who witnesses a road accident, but has no special relationship with the primary victim(s)? Such a person is referred to in law as a 'mere bystander' (see Chapter 17), and the general principle is that such a person will not recover damages for psychiatric injury unless the accident is exceptionally horrific. In *Alcock*, an example is given of a petrol tanker running into a school playground and bursting into flames. In practice, however, the courts are reluctant to allow claims to bystanders under these circumstances (see *McFarlane* v *E E Caledonia* [1994] 2 All ER 1).

BEING PRESENT AT THE ROAD ACCIDENT OR ITS IMMEDIATE AFTERMATH

The development of the 'immediate aftermath' doctrine is an example of what is called the 'incremental development' of the law. Until the House of Lords considered the case of *McLoughlin* v *O'Brian* [1983] AC 410, there was doubt whether someone who did not experience the road accident itself, would be able to recover for resulting psychiatric injury. The point is illustrated by the facts of the case. Mrs McLoughlin received news that her husband and children had been involved in a road accident and had been taken to hospital. She arrived at the hospital several hours after the accident to find her family in an extremely distressed state, covered in dirt and blood. She was also told at the hospital that one of her children was dead. The court held that this scene of dishevelment formed part of the immediate aftermath of the road accident itself and therefore Mrs McLoughlin could recover damages for the psychiatric illness she had suffered. It is important to remember that the shock of this news, in itself, is not enough to enable a person in her position to be compensated: there has to be some sudden impact on the senses. This explains why it was said in *Alcock* that witnessing the Hillsborough tragedy through television broadcasts did not satisfy the 'event proximity' test.

IS A ROAD ACCIDENT ALWAYS 'SHOCKING', AND WHAT IS 'NORMAL FORTITUDE'?

The 'sudden impact' requirement can present difficulties in other areas of psychiatric injury, although there should be no difficulty in showing that a road accident will satisfy the requirement of being 'shocking' to both primary and secondary victims. But are all road accidents sufficiently shocking so that psychiatric injury is foreseeable? An answer recently has been provided by the House of Lords in *Page* v *Smith* [1995] 2 WLR 644. The accident was a relatively minor collision between two cars in which no one suffered physical injury. However, the driver, Mr Page suffered a recurrence of myalgic encephalomyelitis ('ME', also known as 'chronic fatigue syndrome'), which, it was claimed, was a direct result of the accident. The case was concerned with the 'normal fortitude' rule peculiar to psychiatric injury claims arising out of negligence. The rule says that in order for psychiatric injury to be foreseeable, the cause (i.e. the road accident), must be shocking to the psychologically 'normal' person. However, if the survivor is of a vulnerable disposition and suffers a psychiatric illness of great severity, then they will be compensated for this, that is, the negligent road user has to take their victim as they find them (sometimes referred to as the 'egg shell skull' rule). The question for the court to answer was whether someone of normal fortitude would have suffered such injury? The court provided a welcome clarification of the law: as Mr Page was a *primary* victim then the 'normal fortitude' rule did not have to be satisfied.

RECOGNISED PSYCHIATRIC ILLNESS

The survivor of a road accident, whether a primary or secondary victim, will not recover any compensation for 'ordinary' shock, that is, shock which does not result in a recognised psychiatric illness. Similarly, 'ordinary' grief is not compensatable. There have been cases (see *Hinz* v *Berry* [1970] 2 QB 40) where the courts have considered the difference between the natural grief which any bereavement can cause and what is described as 'pathological' grief which will attract compensation in the appropriate circumstances. However, it should be noted that illness need not be of any particular duration, so that what is classified as 'acute stress reaction' in both DSM-IV and ICD-10 may be compensatable. This is a condition, lasting between two days and four weeks, associated with symptoms such as sweating, palpitations and daze. This is a very important point. In the case of *Nicholls* v *Rushton* (1992) (*The Times*, 19 June 1992), it was held by the Court of Appeal that there could be no recovery of damages for 'ordinary shock'. However, if one considers the symptoms of acute stress reaction it is obvious that these are what the layman would describe as 'shock'. Damages can, therefore, be recovered as long as the symptoms described in the diagnostic manuals are present for at least two days, thus rendering it a recognised psychiatric illness.

The *Page* case, discussed above, did not of course concern a psychiatric illness as such, although it may well be that ME may have some non-organic component. What was interesting in this case is the judge's statement that there was no difference between physical and psychiatric injury, and that the general foreseeability requirements and so forth had to be applied in the same way. It remains to be seen how this will help the victims of psychiatric injury, because it will still be open to the courts to decide that the psychiatric injury was not foreseeable.

CAUSATION IN PSYCHIATRIC INJURY

As in all personal injury cases, the person must show that the injury complained of was caused by the tortious act. This may be difficult in cases of psychiatric injury, or certain unusual physical injury cases if the incident was of a relativel y minor nature. The case of *Page* v *Smith* has been decided by the House of Lords in relation to the normal fortitude rule but was referred back to the Court of Appeal on the issue of causation. Although ME, the subject of this case, is exemplified by physical symptoms, its pathology and aetiology are not well understood, and so the link with the road accident is difficult to establish. It is pleasing to note that the court has declined to interfere with the trial judge's finding of fact that the accident materially contributed to the recurrence of the ME and reinstated the award of damages (*Page* v *Smith* (No 2) [1996] 1 WLR 855).

PRE-EXISTING VULNERABILITY TO INJURY

Mention has already been made of the fact that, generally, one must take the survivor as one finds him. If a person has a pre-existing vulnerability, and suffers catastrophic head injury following a very minor road accident, as long as *some* physical injury was foreseeable, it does not matter that the *extent* of it was not foreseeable. In this case the survivor will recover full damages. Similarly, someone who is psychologically vulnerable will succeed as long as some psychiatric injury was foreseeable. An illustration of this point is provided by *Brice* v *Brown* [1984] 1 All ER 997. In a minor road accident, the plaintiff was not physically injured, although her daughter sustained an alarming-looking, but not serious, laceration. She was able to recover damages on the basis that the incident aggravated, and brought to the fore, an underlying personality disorder. Mrs Brice had suffered previous bouts of psychiatric illness, although none had been serious. Following the accident, however, she displayed startling and frightening behaviour, alternating between refusing to leave her room and wandering the streets, often scantily dressed; refusing to use the toilet; living mainly on biscuits; and going through episodes of severe hysteria and screaming. The judge accepted that this condition which, at the time of the trial had been going on for four years and had only improved marginally, was caused entirely by the accident, notwithstanding her pre-existing vulnerability.

COMPENSATION

Compensation is awarded in the form of general damages, special damages and (very occasionally) exemplary damages or punitive damages. As far as the latter are concerned, they are usually awarded against government bodies, for instance, as punishment for an abuse of power, and will not usually arise in road accident litigation.

General damages

General damages are to compensate the survivor of a road accident for pain and suffering and loss of amenity. Contrary to much popular opinion, the level of damages in the UK is modest, and reports in the media of seven figure 'settlements' are often largely made up of special damages, that is, quantifiable pecuniary loss (see below). General damages for the loss of an eye will be in the region of £25,000; general damages for injuries of the utmost severity, for example paraplegia, may be less than £100,000 (see the Judicial Studies Board, *Guidelines for Assessment of General Damages in Personal Injury Cases*, Blackstone Press, 1994). For psychiatric injury, the guidelines range between £1,500 and £45,000, depending upon the severity of the injury. The *Herald of Free Enterprise* Arbitrations (Personal and Medical Injuries Law Letter, June 1989) are a good guide to the level of damages for PTSD: damages ranged between £2,275 and £39,000 (1994 figures).

Special damages

Special damages compensate for actual financial loss: for example, damage to a vehicle or the need to hire a car for transportation. In the case of personal injury, past and future loss of earnings can be calculated. Where there is no provable future loss of earnings, potential loss due to the injury associated with the disadvantage of having to compete for other work in the event of job loss, due to the injury can also be calculated. Other special damages include the cost of future care, special housing and physical aids, which can be substantial in cases of severe injury. Since the accident survivor is not expected to rely on health care provided by the National Health Service, the cost of past and future medical care is also allowed.

MITIGATION OF LOSS

All survivors of road accidents must take steps to mitigate their loss. So, for example, those who have suffered personal injury should consider carefully the advice of their doctors, should return to work as soon as they are able to do so, and so on. However, it is important to personal injury lawyers to be aware that there are circumstances in which insurers and their legal advisers will allege failure to mitigate loss even when the survivor's behaviour has been reasonable. For example, in some circumstances it may be reasonable for the survivor to refuse a course of medical treatment because of the risks involved. In the context of psychiatric injury, this was recognised by the *Herald of Free Enterprise* arbitrators when they found that it may be reasonable for people suffering post-traumatic stress disorder to refuse psychiatric treatment for their condition if they could not face reliving their traumatic experiences. It is also important to remember that physical injuries can be exacerbated by psychiatric injury, the stress of the litigation process, and financial hardship brought about by loss of earnings. These factors should be taken into account when the plaintiff is accused of making an inappropriately slow recovery.

THE LEGAL PROCESS AND ITS SOCIAL AND PSYCHOLOGICAL CONSEQUENCES

Most accidents involve more than one party, although occasionally a vehicle may crash with no other party being involved. On such occasions litigation may ensue against the manufacturer of the motor vehicle which has the potential of leading to improved vehicle safety (USA litigation led to the introduction of driver air bags), with beneficial social consequences. Personal injury litigation, however, is by far the most common aspect of the civil law to result from road accidents, and the Law Commission Report No. 225, 'Personal injury compensation: how much is enough?' (Genn 1994: 204–214) emphasises that even injuries classified as 'minor' can have profound effects on the lives of survivors and their families, and that survivors felt that health and normal life were far more important than financial compensation. Although the potentially deleterious effects of the litigation process upon the accident survivor is dealt with elsewhere (see Chapter 11), it is worth looking briefly at some aspects of the process in the context of civil law. Perhaps a brief mention should be made here about the role of the coroner's inquest. This is a civil process whereby the way in which the deceased met his or her death is classified (e.g. accidental death), and it is not *determinate* of liability of any party (see Chapter 12).

It is important to note the advantages of the recent developments in motor insurance, where many drivers, as part of their motor insurance policy can obtain access to free legal advice. Although a lot of motor claims are relatively small (e.g. claims for damage to a vehicle only), there can still be a need for legal advice in respect of aspects of a claim which are not covered by the driver's own insurance policy. Another fortunate aspect of civil litigation resulting from a road traffic accident is that insurance will be available to compensate the victim of negligence, even if the driver at fault is not insured or cannot be traced. In such a case, the Motor Insurers Bureau scheme ensures that all survivors of road accidents are compensated for personal injuries and all but the most minor property damage. This situation, coupled with the fact that most claims settle out of court, may make the litigation process appear less stressful than in other circumstances. However, against this, it has to be remembered that the survivor of a road accident will always have a large and powerful organisation – that is, an insurance company – as the opponent. It is interesting that the person who caused the accident often drops out of the picture altogether: for example, if liability in the sense of carelessness is accepted and the dispute is about causation or quantum of damages.

Another interesting development is the introduction of conditional fees for personal injury claims as from July 1995. This means that solicitors may now enter into an agreement with the client that if the client loses the case he or she pays no fee to the solicitor, but pays an agreed percentage of the damages awarded if he or she wins. This will make litigation possible in cases where the client has modest means but is still ineligible for legal aid. It remains to be seen what effect this will have.

It should be remembered that the survivor of an accident will often have suffered serious and painful injuries, the effects of which remain for the rest of that person's life. The legal process is an added burden, and a constant reminder of the accident itself.

Chapter 11

The natural history of claims for compensation after an accident

Sally Lloyd-Bostock

Victims negligently injured in an accident can, in principle, claim compensation from the person at fault, under the tort system of compensation (see Chapter 10). For many types of accident the system is of little practical significance. Survivors of domestic, leisure and sporting accidents rarely seek tort damages, whether or not someone else was at fault (Harris et al. 1984). However, in road and work accidents tort claims are a significant source of compensation and support. Approximately a third of all people seriously injured in road accidents embark on a compensation claim, and road accidents account for about half of all claims for compensation under this system in the UK (see Harris et al. 1984; Law Commission 1994). For many people injured in road accidents and their families, therefore, the accident leads to involvement with solicitors, insurance companies and others as they attempt to make a claim under the tort system. That process is the subject of this chapter which draws on a large-scale survey of accident survivors carried out by the Centre for Socio-Legal Studies in the 1970s (Harris et al. 1984), and a more recent prospective study of road accident survivors carried out in the 1990s (Bryant et al. in press). Other important studies providing empirical data about the workings of the system in the UK include those by the Law Commission (1994) and Genn (1987).

It may seem only fair that someone who negligently causes injury should compensate the injured person. Unfortunately, there is a large gap between the *principles* underlying the tort system and the way it actually works in practice. Accident victims who embark on making a claim for compensation grow frustrated and disillusioned as they discover that the path to tort damages is littered with obstacles, and that justice is somewhat elusive. The difficulties, uncertainties, delays and hazards of pursuing a compensation claim often come as something of a shock to injured survivors and their families.

The shortcomings of the fault-based system of compensation are well documented (Cane 1987). The system is widely acknowledged to be inefficient, costly and something of a lottery. It has been estimated that as much money is spent on legal expenses as is paid out to victims. In many other countries (notably many States of the US and Canada), such systems have been replaced with no-fault compensation schemes for road accidents. In New Zealand the tort claim was abolished for all categories of accident in 1974 and replaced with a comprehensive state scheme to compensate *all* those injured in accidents irrespective of the place or cause of the accident. In Britain the Royal Commission on Civil Liability and Compensation for Personal Injury (Pearson 1978) proposed the partial abolition of the tort system in this country, but the recommendation has not been acted on.

EMBARKING ON A CLAIM

Most people injured in accidents do not even consider making a damages claim, although those injured in road accidents, as we have seen, are much more likely to claim than those who have been involved in other types of accidents. But even among road accident victims, many who might claim do not. What, then, leads an accident victim to embark on a claim in the first place?

The study by Harris et al. (1984) provided information about the demographic and other characteristics of those who bring claims, based on interviews with a nationally representative sample of 1,014 people injured in road accidents who had suffered at least three weeks' interruption with normal living. As already indicated, the most important factor predicting who will make a damages claim was the type of accident. Road or work accidents accounted for nearly 90 per cent of all claims; 33 per cent of road accident victims and 25 per cent of people injured in work accidents took steps towards a claim, compared with only 3 per cent of all other accident types. No claims were made at all for domestic accidents, one of the largest categories of accident. Data from the Harris et al. (1984) survey also provide much more detailed information about victims' beliefs about whose fault the accident was; who if anyone they thought should compensate them; and how the belief that they *should* be compensated related to their decision to embark on a legal claim (Lloyd-Bostock 1979a; Harris et al. 1984).

The findings, summarised below, cast an unexpected light on how people come to view compensation as an appropriate and possible consequence of their accident, and what factors influence them to pursue a claim or reject this option. The link between thinking the accident was someone else's fault and making a claim for compensation is far from straightforward. Such factors as whom people contact after the accident; their pre-existing relationship with the person who might be sued; and the chance that that person will be insured, appeared to have a far stronger and more direct effect on the decision to claim. Since the whole system is based on the principle that the person at fault *should* compensate, we examine first how far attributions of fault lead to claims.

BELIEFS ABOUT FAULT AND WHO SHOULD COMPENSATE

Legal discussion generally assumes that ordinary people, as well as the law, view fault as a fair basis for liability to compensate; and that this belief in turn leads them to initiate a claim (Lloyd-Bostock 1979a, 1979b, 1991; Harris et al. 1984). Accident victims in the Harris et al. (1984) survey were asked a series of questions to test how far they did in practice follow the sequence of reasoning and action which this idea implies. The questions were divided between two different sections of the questionnaire to avoid suggesting a connection between fault and liability to compensate. The interview began with questions about how and where the accident happened, whether it was anyone's fault, and if so in what way. A section of the questionnaire administered perhaps half an hour later was concerned with who the survivor thought should compensate him or her and why, and with any damages claim that had been made. The sample was 1,014 accident victims who had suffered at least three weeks' interruption with normal life.

The results showed that their attributions of fault did not go far towards accounting for whether or not a legal claim was initiated. First, blaming someone and embarking on a compensation claim against them did not necessarily go to together. Only half (52 per cent) of those who took steps towards a legal claim said they thought the accident was someone else's fault and that that person should compensate them. A further 27 per cent of those beginning a claim had blamed someone else for the accident – but a different person or organisation from the one they were claiming against – while 21 per cent of those beginning a claim had said their accident was no one else's fault.

Those who thought someone else was at fault, but not that the person should compensate them, were asked if they could say why not. Sometimes payment of money was seen as inappropriate because there was no financial loss. Or the other person may have already 'paid' in some other way: for example, he or she may have been very upset, prosecuted, or trying to help. Making sure it does not happen again was sometimes seen as more appropriate than compensation. Sometimes the type of fault was not seen as being of the appropriate kind, which was reflected in such statements as, 'He couldn't really help it', 'You couldn't blame him', 'He didn't mean to do it', or even 'It was just an accident'. Their apparent ambivalence over fault and blame need not mean that the respondents were confused, but rather that the principles involved are complex and flexible, depending on the context and consequences. Fault might or might not imply liability, and in their particular case, it did not.

Furthermore, even where blaming and claiming did go together, the patterns of responses from accident victims suggested that the existence of the tort system itself gives rise to attributions of fault that provide the basis of a viable compensation claim. Fault was attributed overwhelmingly most often in those accidents where a compensation claim is most likely to occur to the victim, and was attributed to the person or organisation most likely to be able to pay: that is, to the employer in work accidents and to the other driver in road accidents. Those injured in road accidents are very likely to have contact with the police and insurance companies, and to regard claiming compensation as normal following road accidents. In addition, both drivers and employers are covered by compulsory liability insurance. Tables 11.1 and 11.2 show these marked patterns.

It seems, then, that rather than attributions of fault leading to use of the legal system, we are seeing the legal system producing attributions of fault. The effect is indirect as well as direct. The prospect of a damages claim, and the process of pursuing it, may directly affect the victim's perception

Table 11.1 Type of accident by whether anyone else at fault, and whether anyone should pay compensation

Type of accident	Someone at fault		Someone should pay		Total accidents
	n	%	n	%	n
Road	165	67	132	54	246
Work	155	38	217	53	409
Other (leisure/sport)	44	21	35	19	184
Domestic	7	4	0	0	142
Assault	19	90	13	62	21
Industrial illness	3	25	5	42	12
Totals	393	39	402	40	1014

Note: The figures in this table are unweighted and exclude survivors who could not be interviewed in person (thus excluding children). The table should not be taken as showing the relative frequency of different types of accident. Accidents other than road or work were sub-sampled at approximately one in two.

Table 11.2 Breakdown of who was said to be at fault

	n
Other driver	145
Other road user	3
Employer	85
Workmate/colleague/immediate superior at work	40
Child	2
Other individual or group of individuals	74
Organisation/system/corporate body	34
Don't know, not stated	10
Total where someone at fault	393

of the accident. In a more general, background sense, social norms and rules provide a framework for deciding both whose, if anyone's, fault an accident was, and the injured person's entitlement to compensation. Especially in the case of road or work accidents or assaults, those rules and norms are very likely to be, or derive from, legal norms of some kind.

Thus driving is governed by all kinds of legal rules about speed, right of way, and so on, which provide guidelines for establishing who was in the wrong. The police are likely to be called where injury is suffered in a road accident and the account they are looking for will be in terms of who, if anyone, has broken the criminal law, which is likely to be determined by the person's actions at the time of the accident. In most road accidents where someone else was said to be at fault (90 per cent), it was because of their actions at the time. More background factors such as road maintenance, road design, or car design, did not feature, even though road research shows these are frequent contributory causes of accidents.

At work, on the other hand, there is a variety of rule systems with a long historical tradition putting responsibility on the employer for ensuring safety and compensating the injured, moving the emphasis away from 'fault' in the more immediate sense. There are statutory duties, strict and vicarious liability, and other compensations systems, such as industrial injuries compensation, where fault is irrelevant anyway. In 80 per cent of work accidents where someone was said to be at fault, it was in terms of responsibility for safety, good management, and other remote causes and conditions. Moreover, in 22 per cent of the work accidents where the victim said someone should compensate, it was said that the employer should pay simply because the accident happened on his premises or in the course of employment.

As well as the influence of legal rules on when and how fault is attributed, the Harris et al. (1984) study found some general mixing and confusion of rule systems. Losses arising from accidents may be covered by a variety of systems, such as social security benefits, sick pay schemes, and industrial injuries benefits, besides any tort claim. The criteria for eligibility under these systems were often mixed. Thus one person who had been involved in a work accident thought he should get compensation because he had paid his stamp; another because he had been off work six months and therefore qualified (he was, in fact, claiming under tort). Respondents talked about what they felt should happen very much in terms of existing systems, whether or not these were fault based.

The picture which emerges is not so much one of the tort system providing a means for those who feel someone else was at fault to pursue a compensation claim, but rather one of the tort system obliging people to blame others for their accident if they are to obtain compensation. Accident victims are drawn into a process that obliges them to lay the burden of their losses at the door of someone who perhaps contributed one of the many causal factors to the accident, perhaps in a momentary lapse of concentration. As a claim progresses, plaintiffs are indeed likely to come to see that person as responsible for their suffering. The fact that obtaining damages involves blaming someone else has a very significant effect on people's willingness to embark on a claim, as well as on relationships between the people involved in claims that are brought. The detrimental effects on existing relationships and other anticipated social or material costs of blaming and claiming was evident throughout the accident victims' replies.

THE COSTS OF BLAMING AND CLAIMING

Even where a case is very likely to succeed if it is brought, the injured person may be unable to afford the costs of claiming and be ineligible for legal aid. However, the financial costs are by no means the only costs of legal action. Attributing fault brings with it potential conflict which people may prefer to avoid altogether. Blaming, holding people liable, and pursuing a legal claim will obviously have different sorts of impact on relationships between friends, family members, employer and employee, fellow-employees, and those who were strangers until the accident. Where the social and psychological costs of blaming are high and the prospects of benefit in the form of compensation remote, accidents are more likely to be seen as 'just accidents'. Burman et al. (1977) found that people who have been injured in domestic accidents very rarely sue the person they blame. The data from Harris et al. (1984) suggest that most potential legal cases arising from such accidents are filtered out at an earlier stage, since the injured person does not even attribute fault in the first place. Even accidents at work arc seen far more often as the fault of the employer than of a fellow-employee, although either could provide grounds for a claim against the insured employer.

Accident victims themselves mention these kinds of considerations when they give reasons for saying that someone at fault should not pay them compensation, and when they give reasons for not pursuing what they thought might be a legal claim. The injured person may appreciate that the person at fault *could* be thought liable, but prefers not to take this view because he or she is a friend, neighbour, or family member. Taking legal action is seen as a rather nasty, vindictive thing to do. As one respondent put it, 'I didn't want blood money'. Another said she would not 'do something like that – though an American probably would'. A number were worried about causing trouble with their employers. In fact, there were cases where employers were obstructive and even threatened to sack or blacklist employees who claimed, or gave evidence against them. People often choose not to pursue a claim following road accidents in which their spouse was driving, and hence the person claimed against. In most road accidents the person most likely to claimed against will be a stranger, but even so the injured person may feel sympathy for them, especially if they have also been injured, and may not want to claim against them. It has been suggested (Ehrenzweig 1953; Linden 1977) that vindicating an angry accident victim can be one function of the tort system. It would seem that taking legal action can indeed be a way of getting back at the person at fault, but that this prevents the system from working by inhibiting claims.

Although in formal terms a legal claim usually must come from the accident victim, those who did pursue a legal claim almost always said that the idea of claiming came from someone else, and that the amount of damages they hoped to receive was based on others' suggestions. What the victim felt about compensation by the time of the interview was, therefore, largely the result of what a lawyer, trade union official, the police, friends, and others suggested to him or her after the accident. People injured in accidents rely on experts to interpret and define what has happened to them and what they are entitled to receive. Their decision whether to pursue a legal case seems to be based not so much on what they see as the justice of the situation, as on the balance between the anticipated expense, trouble, upset and uncertainties of claiming on the one hand, and the prospect of compensation on the other. Some of the costs of claiming are, as already mentioned, its damaging effects on the person's relationships with the other party, but most costs (financial and otherwise) mentioned by those who got as far as considering a claim, arise out of the claiming process itself.

THE CLAIMING PROCESS: WHY ALL THE UNCERTAINTIES AND DELAYS?

Sources of delay and uncertainty lie in the nature of the tort system itself, as well as in the way it is operated by representatives or advisers of the parties, such as their lawyers or insurance companies. The scheme provides (with few exceptions) for a once-and-for-all lump sum payment, making it crucial to assess the extent of disability and consequent losses, not only up to the present, but for the rest of the plaintiff's life. This naturally leads to delay in cases where the prognosis is uncertain. To win a case in court the plaintiff must not only prove that he or she has suffered injury leading to various specified losses, but must also prove that the injuries were caused by the fault of the defendant. The basis of the case is the information available to each side, and the facts they can call on. If information is not available, then the facts might as well not exist. Even where an accident was someone else's fault, there may be no witnesses available, making proof impossible. This is a very common difficulty in road accidents.

It can be very difficult to predict what the outcome would be if a case went to court. It is uncertain whether damages would be awarded at all, and it is uncertain what amount of damages could be expected. The law itself can be uncertain (see Chapter 10) and much can depend on the individual judge. Genn (1987: 97), for example, quotes one solicitor: 'you never can tell. I mean, what's a case worth? It's as long as a piece of string.' It is not surprising that accident victims are dismayed by the inability of solicitors to be more accurate and definite in their predictions.

People who have no previous experience of making a compensation claim are often astonished to discover that the vast majority of claims do not go to court, but are settled out of court. The process inevitably gives rise to uncertainty, delay, and a sense of being 'messed about' by insurance companies and lawyers. Settlement is reached through a potentially very lengthy and unpredictable process of negotiation between their own solicitor (or other adviser such as a trade union official) and representatives of the other side (usually the defendant's insurance company or solicitors acting for the insurance company). The negotiations are thus conducted, not by the plaintiff and the person he or she is claiming against, but by proxy through professionals. This in itself can lead to frustration for the plaintiff, and a feeling of not being kept informed.

There is a common pattern to personal injury negotiations, which will usually involve a series of offers. If the insurance company (or its solicitor) thinks that the claimant has a reasonable chance of proving some fault on the part of the defendant, it will make an offer to pay a definite sum of money in full and final settlement of all claims the defendant might have arising out of the accident. If the offer is accepted by the claimant, a binding legal agreement is created. The defendant is bound to pay the agreed sum, and the claimant is precluded from pursuing the claim to a court hearing. If it is rejected, it lapses altogether and the claimant cannot later change his or her mind and accept it. Offers to settle a claim are understood in law to be 'without prejudice' to any litigation which may follow if there is no agreement on an out-of-court settlement. What this means is that the willingness of the defendant to pay something to settle the claim cannot be given in evidence to the court. A claimant who rejects an offer, therefore, not only faces the risk of further delay, but also the risk that he or she may fail to prove his or her case in court and so recover no damages at all.

It is easy to see that there is considerable temptation to accept an early offer, but if it is rejected, higher offers may well be made. In the survey by Harris et al. (1984), for example, almost a third (62 per cent) of those obtaining damages accepted the first offer; but 38 per cent rejected the first offer and ended up with more. In some cases as many as five offers were made before the claim was settled.

It cannot, of course, be concluded that in cases where an offer was accepted, a higher offer would have been made; the decision to accept may have been based on an accurate assessment of how high the defendant will go. But the outcome of the negotiations depends not only on the strength of the claimant's case, but also on the relative bargaining strengths and experience of the two sides. This systematically tends to disadvantage the plaintiff. A study of negotiation and settlement in personal injury cases by Genn (1987), aptly entitled 'Hard Bargaining', showed clearly how important it is for the plaintiff to have a solicitor who specialises in personal injury, and possibly in a particular branch of personal injury. Studies have also indicated that an insurance company, which is the most frequent defendant in road accidents, is a 'repeat player' and can afford to 'win some and lose some'; whereas the plaintiff is a 'one-shotter' and the case at hand is all-important. As a result, the insurance company is relatively indifferent to the uncertainties of litigation, and can afford to take more risks in the negotiating process (Galanter 1974; Ross 1980).

The settlement process almost inevitably means that the figure the plaintiff's solicitor originally asked for is more than the plaintiff eventually receives. Again, there is a built in probability of dissatisfaction for the plaintiff, who will often feel that the solicitor has failed to obtain the full amount, and advised him or her to settle 'too low' (Harris et al. 1984; Bryant et al. in press). This is ironic in that the plaintiff's idea of what the claim is worth almost always comes from the solicitor in the first place.

THE ROLE OF COMPENSATION IN MEETING THE NEEDS OF THOSE INJURED IN ACCIDENTS

When a plaintiff does obtain damages, even through a court, it is not at all clear that the system fulfils its goal of 'full compensation'. Although it is the large 'jackpot' awards that tend to be reported in the media, most damages awards are comparatively small. Harris et al. (1984) found that the average was around £2,000 in their sample of serious accidents which had taken place in the 1970s. Even large awards, however, are not simply a windfall but are based on an assessment of losses, and the recent survey by the Law Commission (1994) shows they may turn out to be inadequate. Nearly 40 per cent of their sample of people who had received damages thought that the amount had not been sufficient to cover their losses. The most frequent loss they felt was undercompensated was loss of earnings. The Law Commission study also clearly emphasises that money, however much of it, is inadequate to compensate people injured in accidents for what they have lost.

A further problem, particularly with large awards, was that few plaintiffs are experienced at handling large sums of money, and may make decisions about the use of the lump sum that they later come to regret. The growing trend towards structured settlements is a welcome development in this as well as other respects (Lewis 1993). Such settlements, which must be approved by the court, apply the award to purchase an annuity on the plaintiff's behalf, on tax-advantageous terms.

In the study by Bryant et al. (in press) a sample of accident survivors were interviewed at intervals from their arrival at hospital, and for the following five years. This made it possible to assess the person's financial needs at different times, and to see how compensation awards featured in meeting those needs. The results demonstrated what had been suspected, that accident victims' financial and other difficulties were at a peak in the year following the accident, but compensation payments usually came too late to prevent serious financial problems. Personal injury claims frequently take years, for the reasons outlined above. New provisions for interim payments and provisional damages are intended to address some of the problems of delay, but only apply in certain circumstances. Bryant and colleagues found that even where interim payments had been agreed, there were long delays in the payment actually being made.

These researchers also found that disillusioned road accident victims pursuing claims became resigned to settlements that would never recompense them for what they had lost or suffered. Their primary concern often became not how much compensation they would get, but rather when they would get it. Some felt that continuation of the legal process prevented them from putting the accident behind them.

CONCLUSION

It has been possible only to sketch the main features of the process of embarking on and pursuing a personal injury claim. Although the tort compensation system presumably is intended to benefit people injured in accidents by the negligence of someone else, it is clear that the process in practice causes those injured in accidents and their families a great deal of stress, often drawn out over many years and that the eventual compensation largely fails to meet their needs. Not surprisingly, accident victims express bitter criticism of the law and lawyers. Some problems could be alleviated by better care and sensitivity on the part of the solicitors handling claims, although the very nature of the system gives rise to delays, frustration and disappointment.

There is a pervasive misconception that people who have been injured initiate claims because they are litigious. Rather, what the research shows is a reluctance to use a system which obliges the plaintiff to blame the defendant and to take what is seen as a vindictive action. People injured in a road accident are among those most likely to embark on a claim, but not because they are litigious. They are drawn into doing so by the circumstances of their accidents, by what is 'normal' and expected after a road accident, and by the advice given to them by insurance companies, lawyers, and others. Most who embark on a claim will eventually obtain some compensation, and of course that will be welcome; but many social, psychological and financial costs inevitably are likely to have been involved in pursuing the claim.

Chapter 12

Death on the road
The role of the English coroner's court in the social construction of an accident

Glennys Howarth

In October 1995 Radio Southern Counties announced that, since records began, 500,000 people had been killed on the roads of England and Wales. Each road death is dealt with by the coroner system; the public office with responsibility for investigating, defining and processing every sudden death. This chapter considers procedures for managing road fatalities and argues that use of the term 'accident' in relation to road death may be inappropriate. This discussion is based on a study begun in 1993 of the coroner system in three distinct geographical regions of England. Data were collected through in-depth interviews with coroners, their officers, police officers, bereaved families, and other expert and lay witnesses. Lengthy courtroom observations were also undertaken.

THE CORONER SYSTEM IN ENGLAND

The coroner system exists to investigate sudden death: road, rail, sea and air fatalities; suicide; death at work; from industrial disease; death in custody; in disasters; from homicide; manslaughter; and all other unexpected death when the deceased had not seen a doctor for more than fourteen days. In all these cases the coroner must distinguish between non-natural death and death which occurred 'naturally' (see Prior 1985, for a discussion of the concept of 'natural' death). In England and Wales it is usual for the coroner to have medical and/or legal expertise since the primary responsibility of the post is to investigate the medical cause of death and to pass a verdict which will be influenced by and will subsequently determine the legal response.

The office of coroner is an ancient one dating back to the Articles of Eyre in 1194 (See Matthews and Foreman (1993), *Jervis on the Office and Duties of Coroners*). The incumbent at that time was 'keeper of the pleas of the Crown' and, being tasked with protecting the interests of the Crown, was responsible for the administration of criminal justice and for the

Crown revenue associated with it. It was also his duty to hold inquests into cases of sudden death. From around the sixteenth century, however, as the criminal justice system developed and centralised, the coroner lost many responsibilities, and criminal work other than that associated with death, was transferred to the justices of the peace. 'The only important duty that coroners retained was that of holding inquests into cases of violent or unnatural death' (Matthews and Foreman 1993: 5). A principle element of this work was the indictment of people to stand trial when death was found to be caused by homicide, manslaughter or infanticide. By 1977 the coroner's power to indict for homicide was perceived within the criminal justice system as irregular, and it was revoked. Although they may work together in cases where death occurs under suspicious circumstances, 'effectively, the coroner's role in the criminal justice system has now gone' (ibid. 8) and to all intents and purposes they are distinct offices. *It is not now the purpose of the coroner system to apportion blame for a death.* This prerogative lies with the criminal justice system, with the consequence that the coroner is associated with the death certification process, and accordingly has a *fact finding*, rather than a *blame apportioning* role in any investigation of death.

The limit of the modern inquiry or inquest is laid down in statute and is to determine *who* the deceased was, *how*, *when* and *where* he or she came by his or her death (Coroners Act 1988). *How* individuals meet their death is to be ascertained in relation to medical categories and legal verdicts, consequently the investigation and inquest are *inquisitorial* rather than *adversarial* processes. According to *Jervis*, the coroner's manual of law and practice:

A coroner's inquest is a rare . . . example of inquisitorial proceedings . . . The important distinction between an accusatorial process such as a criminal trial, and an inquisitorial process, such as a coroner's inquest, was stated by Lord Lane . . . in the following words: It should not be forgotten that an inquest is a fact finding exercise and not a method of apportioning guilt. The procedure and rules of evidence which are suitable for one are unsuitable for the other. In an inquest it should never be forgotten that there are no parties, there is no indictment, there is no prosecution, there is no defence, there is no trial, simply an attempt to establish facts. (Matthews and Foreman 1993: 6)

In undertaking an enquiry the coroner sets out to discover and record as many of the 'facts' surrounding the death as are deemed to be in the interests of the public; which is defined according to five criteria delineated by the Brodrick Committee. The enquiry should serve:

to determine the medical cause of death; to allay rumours or suspicion; to draw attention to the existence of circumstances which, if unremedied, might lead to further deaths; to advance medical knowledge; and to preserve the legal interests of the deceased person's family, heirs or other interested parties. (Brodrick Committee Report 1971)

In cases where there might appear to be the need to pursue criminal prosecution (an adversarial process) the coroner will pass the case over to the Crown Prosecution Service to determine the appropriate course of action. In the meantime, the inquest will be opened and adjourned. If criminal prosecution takes place the inquest may not be resumed or may resume only briefly to record a verdict, such as, for example, that of unlawful killing. These are some of the salient functions of the coroner's role in sudden death, so now let us turn to the process by which road fatalities come to be dealt with by these officials, beginning with a description of the *scene of death*.

THE SCENE OF DEATH

First at the scene are emergency service workers such as the police, ambulance personnel and firefighters. If there has clearly been a fatality the police will contact the coroner's office and one of his officers will usually be dispatched to the scene (in some districts all police officers are deemed to be coroner's officers and so would act on the coroner's behalf). An undertaker will also be called to remove the body to the public mortuary. Relatives will be traced and the next of kin informed of the death. Once informed, it is customary for them to be escorted to the public mortuary to identify the body of the deceased. Depending upon the coroner's district, relatives are sometimes taken into the viewing room by police, more often by mortuary technicians. As in other occupations, some public officials are more sympathetic and supportive than others. Dealing with sudden death on an everyday basis can mean that what constitutes one person's traumatic crisis is a routine and platitudinal activity for another (Howarth 1996).

Once the body has been identified, thus fulfilling the first imperative of the coroner's enquiry, the next step is to begin to *reconstruct* the incident. *When* and *where* the fatality took place are normally not in question, but it is for the coroner and his or her officers, with the help of the police, to determine *how* the death occurred. And so the piecing together of events to reconstruct the road death begins. Experts at the scene, typically the police, measure distances and skid marks, collect forensic evidence, draw diagrams, and attempt to gauge the absolute speed of the vehicles involved, and their speed in relation to other vehicles or bodies with whom they may have collided. Later, specialists examine the crash vehicle(s), taking them apart to check brakes, tyres, functioning, mechanical malfunction and bodywork corrosion, to discover any vehicle pathology. At the same time the pathologists at the mortuary examine the injuries to the body of the deceased, looking for signs of physical malfunction within it. For example, did the deceased suffer a heart attack or a stroke? From blood samples the experts will measure the levels of alcohol, drugs, or other stimulants or depressants present in the body. The body's organs will be removed, weighed and examined for every possible sign of damage. The injuries may also be photographed paying particular attention to the impact of the crash. From such signs the pathologist is able to estimate the position of the victim during the collision and the manner in which those injuries were sustained.

Meanwhile, as the experts probe the objects of their inquiry, lay witnesses to the incident are questioned closely in an attempt to reconstruct the event and the surrounding circumstances: Where were you in relation to the 'accident'? What did you see? How close were you to the incident? Where were you in relation to other cars? What distance? What speed? The street lighting? The weather conditions? What road signs? What road markings? Who else? . . . and so on. At the coroner's office, transcripts of the witness statements together with the professionals' reports (i.e. the evidence in the case) are collated, read, studied and discussed. The question asked by the coroners and their officers is: How did the *accident* occur?

The collection of evidence, however, is only one step on the way, for next there has to be a public inquest during which the evidence is delivered by witnesses. It is the coroner who decides which witnesses should appear before the court, chosen according to which testimonies will shed most light on the event. In the courtroom the coroner will publicly ask and attempt to answer the four questions: Who, when, where, and how, did the deceased meet with death?

DEFINING 'ACCIDENTAL' DEATH

Let us now focus on the manner in which a death on the road – commonly referred to as a 'road accident' – is processed through these structures in such a way as to reconstruct the incident, and so legally identify it as an 'accident'. We begin by comparing common-sense and legal definitions of 'accident'. An accident is defined in the Oxford English Dictionary as an 'event that is without apparent cause or unexpected' and notes further senses in which we understand an accident as an 'unlucky event', 'chance', 'misfortune' or an 'unintended act'. What these definitions all have in common is their *chance nature* and *blamelessness*. The definition of an accident in terms of coroners' verdicts also carries this same notion of blamelessness. According to *Jervis* (Matthews and Foreman 1993: 250), 'accident' connotes something over which there is 'no human control, or an unintended act'.

A further verdict which is becoming increasingly significant is that of 'misadventure'. This 'indicates some deliberate (but lawful) human act which has unexpectedly taken a turn that leads to death' (ibid. 250). Although the two – 'accident' and 'misadventure' – were once entirely separate categories, there is now a tendency for them to be linked and used interchangeably. As the coroner's manual points out, the two may be logically distinct but, in practice, coroners have chosen not to distinguish. One effect of this practice is that it enables the coroner, in cases of road death, to bring a verdict of accident even where the death was the 'unexpected result of a deliberate act' (ibid. 250). The decision as to whether a road death will be defined as 'unlawful killing' or as an accidental death turns on the distinction between 'objectively dangerous acts causing death', for example dangerous driving, and 'all other acts causing deaths', for example careless driving (ibid. 252), the latter carrying a maximum penalty of ten years' imprisonment. For the purpose of the inquest, however, coroners are advised, 'the proper conclusion for the inquisition in a case of this kind is "accident/misadventure" rather than "unlawful killing".' (ibid. 273)

The manner in which death on the road is generally defined and discussed has obvious repercussions for the social and legal status of this category of violent death. Quite apart from the inquisition and the verdict, the practice of automatically referring to death on the road as an 'accident' is prejudicial and the question of whether it was an 'accident' surely must be determined by the coroner after proper investigation and inquest. To refer to a sudden death using the terminology of a verdict which has yet to be established is indeed curious and indubitably has implications for the management and treatment of road death. If, at the outset road death is assumed to be accidental, it is dealt with under the coroner's system for investigating sudden death, rather than under the criminal justice system for investigating death where assigning blame is a central consideration.

At first sight this may seem a superficial point, but the ramifications of this cultural response to road fatalities are critical in that a verdict of 'accidental death' *becomes the default verdict*. That is, there may be a tacit presupposition that the death was accidental *unless* it can be shown to be otherwise. A report on road death prepared by a Victim Support Working Party noted that, in 1991, of the 4,500 deaths on the road only 416 resulted in prosecution (Victim Support 1994: 3). Even in cases where the driver of the vehicle may appear to be at fault the likelihood of prosecution is relatively slim.

Now let us to consider how the incident is reconstructed during the inquest in such a way as to understand the road fatality as accidental. What impact does this have on the bereaved families?

THE INQUEST

The ritual of the public reconstruction of death takes place at the inquest. (This is not true in Scotland where a different system operates under the office of the Procurator Fiscal: within this system most Fatal Accident Enquiries are held in the privacy of the Procurator Fiscal's office.) In retracing the events that led up to the collision, and in describing its aftermath, the incident is reconstructed in an attempt to uncover all the 'facts' germane to the death. At the inquest the witnesses meet together, each with a narrative focused on the circumstances of death. Two distinct types of witness are called by the coroner – expert and lay – to give evidence which helps to promote an understanding of the death, in terms of the available verdicts. Expert witnesses are relied upon to provide legal and medical evidence; lay witnesses are asked to provide information about the social circumstances surrounding death which might support the medical and legal discourses.

After a lay witness (normally a family member) has first fulfilled the legal requirement of identification, the pathologist's report will provide a medical explanation of death. The case will progress in the light of this report, paying particular attention to how the deceased might have come by their injuries. Further expert witnesses may include the police, paramedics and other emergency service workers, vehicle examiners, and so on. Their testimonies, like those of the pathologist, are based on the narrative of their expert reports – documents which adopt the jargon of their profession and are perceived by the court as inherently *objective*, professional and scientific.

Lay witnesses may be asked to comment on the character of the deceased or of the driver of any vehicle involved in the collision. The discourse here centres around those present at the time of death; those first at the scene; or those with a contribution to make in terms of events leading up to the death, such as the state of mind of the deceased, his or her movements that day, the deceased's relationship with others, and so on. It is the role of the coroner to translate the social discourse of lay witnesses, replete with *subjective* observations and common-sense knowledge, into a knowledge about the death which fits an 'objective' legal verdict.

When the reconstruction is complete – and it is important to recognise that this is reached according to the coroner's interpretation (i.e. it is the coroner who decides which witnesses to call, what evidence to hear, and the significance of that evidence) – the coroner must reach a verdict or, if a jury is sitting, guide the jury to reach a verdict. Official interpretation of the medical, legal and social discourse presented in the courtroom can, however, result in a gulf of understanding between the official purpose of an inquest and the expectations of the bereaved. This conflict of expectation may stem from the fact that the verdicts available to coroners are largely definitive categories which effectively close down routes to prosecution rather than open them up. As is clear from the figures quoted earlier, the possibility of proceeding to prosecution for road fatality is limited.

Consequently, bereaved relatives may be bewildered by the conclusion of the inquest. Nonplussed by the implications of the verdict, they are often left with questions such as, 'Is that all?' or 'What was the point?' As one bereaved woman described: 'Having gone through all that [the inquest] he [the coroner] said it was an accident. And so, that was that. I was shocked. I suppose I expected something more. I couldn't understand how that could be the end of it.' A woman whose child had been killed reported that she 'couldn't believe it. I can't see the point in it – my son's dead and all there is to say is that it was an accident. There's nothing more I can do.' These statements reflect the common expectation on the part of relatives that 'something' will come out of an inquest in the form of an explanation of *social cause* and an assignation of *blame*. As the Brodrick Report (1971: 124) noted when it disclosed the results of a National Opinion Poll conducted in 1970 (i.e. before the abolition of the coroner's power to indict people to trial for unlawful killing): 'Three-quarters of the respondents with knowledge of the coroner suggested that one of his functions should be to discover whether anyone was responsible for the death.'

Although often confused and untutored about the task of the coroner's inquest, families tend to see this legal procedure as part of the criminal justice system rather than as something quite separate. The sister of a road death victim experienced a sense of injustice: 'I don't really think justice was done. I am not sure what I thought would come out of the hearing but it seems to be no one's fault and nothing's being done about it.' If dissatisfaction with the outcome of the inquest derives from a feeling that 'justice has not been done' because no one is being blamed, then this is in large part due to the separation of the coroner's system from the criminal justice system and the consequent loss of its power. In the words of a bereaved mother: 'I know nothing can bring her back but to see him walk out of the courtroom without being prosecuted or anything was terrible. It wasn't right.'

In seeking an explanation which will lead to the apportionment of blame, bereaved families are trying to make sense of sudden death. In modern society, where luck and chance (good or bad) are no longer deemed appropriate levels of explanation for such momentous events, clarification is commonly sought through blame. Given that relatives are rarely present when the death of their loved one occurs, they need a reconstruction to gain some understanding of the tragedy. Indeed, studies have shown that sudden death is particularly difficult for bereaved people to come to terms with – it may well be that this reconstruction of the circumstances surrounding sudden death is important in compensating for the families' lack of preparation. However, having no access to expert reports or lay witness testimonies, they must await the courtroom ritual to expose 'the facts', to hear the witnesses depict the scene of the death, and to reconstruct the incident for themselves. In this respect they have similar motives to the coroner and there is little doubt that many families accept the coroner's interpretation of events and the verdict as pronounced. For a bereaved mother: 'Sitting through the inquest was awful; listening to the accounts of what happened and hearing the pathologist's report. But at least I now know how it happened.' Equally, it is important to acknowledge that many of the friends and relatives of those killed in road fatalities are not satisfied with the way in which death is processed through the coroner's system.

Having noted the differences in expectations of the inquest let us look again at the discourse of the courtroom to see how dissatisfaction may arise.

At the time of investigation, and during the inquest, it is often noticeable – especially in the case of road traffic deaths – that there is a clear sense that all the circumstances come together in such a way as to point unequivocally to an 'accident'. On this understanding, what happened could have been no other way, the accident could not have been avoided. Each movement, each action, all behaviour is focused around the incident of the death, and everything led up to the fatality. Yet from a different perspective, it is one of the purposes of the coroner system to look for factors which might have made it otherwise. In the public interest the coroner is tasked with investigating how a fatal 'accident' might have been avoided: for example, by recommending a change in the speed limit, better street lighting, installing a pedestrian crossing, and so on. At this level, we have an event, leading to the death of an individual, which might not have occurred but for an act of omission or commission. Perhaps culpability might lie with the driver of the vehicle or, more impersonally, at the feet of the local authority or other body or institution.

Whatever or whoever, in the case of death on the road, families may not accept the verdict of 'accidental death' as appropriate. Indeed, they many balk at such a verdict. Groups such as Campaign Against Drink Driving and RoadPeace were created because their members, usually families of road death victims, were angered by what they interpreted as the court's reluctance to acknowledge any culpability in the case of deaths on the road. These organisations argue for greater use of criminal prosecution for such death (unlawful killing, manslaughter) and heavier penalties where death results from careless driving. After all, they argue, this reckless behaviour resulted in death. The results of a Victim Support survey demonstrate the significance of a verdict of 'accidental' death: 'Many families object strongly to the words "accident" and "compensation"; they feel that road crashes, often caused by illegal driving behaviour, are *not* accidents, and certainly nothing can compensate for their loss' (Victim Support 1994: 3). Furthermore, as Green (1992) notes in her discussion of the cultural understanding of the concept of 'accident', the term is used as 'a public affirmation of blamelessness'. In relation to the coroner's court she reminds us that, 'verdicts carry moral meanings' (Green 1992: 384–5).

If the case has not been taken up by the Crown Prosecution Service, or has failed to result in prosecution, in the absence of a public inquiry (which is usually not even considered unless there has been a large-scale loss of life), an inquest is the sole remaining forum for asking questions. And families usually do desire a thorough investigation of the circumstances and cause of death. A woman explained: 'I wanted to go to the inquest because I wanted to know what had happened and I couldn't get anyone to tell me. I think they were protecting me. People don't seem to realise that you need to know.' So, while many coroners have come to view their role in the investigation of sudden death in terms of legal and medical criteria, bereaved people are seeing that role increasingly in terms of discovering the social causes and implications of death. As one particularly vociferous coroner recently observed: 'Relatives may think the inquest will answer their questions and assuage their anxieties.' This coroner, however, was convinced that this was not the purpose of the system and he went on to say: 'There is quite the wrong idea of inquests. That in some way they are provided, as it were, for the delectation of the relatives of the deceased. This is quite wrong in my view.' (Douglas Chambers quoted in *The Times*, 26 April 1994). This disagreement over the purpose of the inquest has led to increasing public demand for a more accountable system. The latest edition of *Jervis* noted:

Public expectations of what the coroner can do run way ahead of what either available resources, or the rules, permit. Current public opinion would have him not merely pick up undetected homicides, and act as a check on the death certification and registration system, but *also* would have him doggedly investigate all hospital, institutional and prison deaths with a view to exposing official indifference, negligence or even worse. If the coroner resists doing so, he is accused by the deceased's family and friends of complicity in a 'cover-up', and more often than not he is subjected to judicial review. If he does *not* resist doing so, he is accused of unwarranted interference by the authorities and (increasingly) the public service unions, and is *also* subjected to judicial review. (Matthews and Foreman 1993: vii)

CONCLUSION

In relation to death, the coroner system began as a way of investigating sudden, violent or other 'non-natural' forms. Following its separation from the criminal justice system the role of coroners developed in response to the demands of systems for measuring and categorising mortality: death registration and certification. Until quite recently the coroner was expected to name persons whom the inquest had found culpable in cases of murder, manslaughter and infanticide. In this way the person was indicted to stand trial in the criminal court; the coroner's inquest was thus a mechanism for bringing to justice those who had committed unlawful killing. Throughout the twentieth century, however, this power, although not formally removed until 1977, has dissipated.

With its gradual disappearance, public perceptions of the inquest have changed and public comprehension of the system has foundered. Forced to participate, and indeed, often demanding an inquiry, bereaved relatives and the public have been somewhat slow to make sense of this separation of justice. Families are obliged to submit to the coroner system if a relative dies in a road traffic incident. They must surrender the body to the coroner's jurisdiction and, if called to do so, be willing to participate in the public ritual of the inquest. Lay witnesses, observers and particularly families, in accounting for this ritual, do so in terms of an expectation that the public discourse of the courtroom will lay bare the 'facts of death', 'get to the bottom of things' and 'discover the cause'. And yet, many are left feeling that it was all a pointless exercise, as recording or registering the medical cause and legal verdict signals completion of the inquiry. Indeed, the social circumstances and their potential implications are often lost.

State agencies and legal systems, however, do not exist in a social and political vacuum. The medical and legal discourse within which the coroner's system functions is supported by a social discourse which is meaningful to the families and to some 'popular' or 'common sense' notion of justice. By submitting to the system, families may not simply become victims of the system; instead, they may interpret the ritual and make it significant for themselves. In an era in which death is medicalised and people encouraged to think of mortality only in terms of individual pathology – whether victims of disease or violence – it is inevitable that when people come into contact with the coroner system (whether through bereavement or via media reports) there is an expectation that death will be explained. They expect that it will be elucidated according to the medical model but, more notably, through the language of *knowledge* and *causation*; a discourse which leads inevitably to blame and ultimately to the criminal justice system. To be confronted with a structure which purports to investigate all the 'facts' of death *without* apportioning blame can appear incomprehensible. A conflict of interests has thus developed between the need for medical and legal knowledge about sudden death and the social expectations of the bereaved and general public. Families and the public at large (as reflected in media coverage) have begun to call for more meaningful inquiries into the social causes of death and for an inquest procedure which might *open up* routes to the criminal justice system rather than *close them off*. In so doing, people are taking state structures which have measured and medicalised death and are demanding that they become more accountable in order to fulfil an additional purpose, that of providing meaning, by identifying causes, apportioning blame and interpreting what seems to be the senseless death of their loved one.

As long as – unreflectingly – we continue to refer to traffic fatalities as 'accidents', road death will continue to be dealt with by the coroner. A system separate from the criminal justice system which is the domain of responsibility and culpability. The argument parallels that of management of deaths at work, usually referred to as 'workplace accidents'. As Slapper (1993) contends, many of these so-called accidents may well have been avoided if companies had been more careful about health and safety, had spent more money, had cut fewer corners, and so on. Yet such deaths automatically go to the coroner's court, and the result is that very few companies are ever charged with corporate manslaughter.

The purpose of the discussion here is not to deny the possibility of accidental death, or to assert that someone is always to blame for a death: such approaches to mortality assume that death can be avoided if only we are careful enough. Yet the social management of sudden death cannot be divorced from the context of its surrounding discourse. If the language we use to explain road fatalities is the language of accident and blamelessness, then death on the road will continue to be constructed and defined as accidental, and hence as an essentially uncontrollable feature of modern living.

Acknowledgements   I am grateful to the British Journal of Sociology and the Nuffield Foundation for funding this research.

Part III

Social consequences, support and intervention

Chapter 13

Preventive psychological intervention for road crash survivors

Michael Hobbs and Gwen Adshead

Road accidents are common, and a major cause of death, injury and permanent physical disability. It is less well recognised that a significant proportion of road crash survivors develop serious, disabling psychiatric problems. Worldwide, one quarter of a million people are killed annually by road 'accidents'. In many cases road crashes are not really accidents, but the result of avoidable error, aggressive driving behaviour, or alcohol and drug misuse. In the countries of the European Union, approximately 50,000 people die and 1.5 million are injured each year, prompting the Director General of the European Union's Transport Division to equate the death toll to the loss of one full jumbo jet, with no survivors, every seventy hours (Gloag 1993). In Britain, although the numbers have fallen in the last year or two, road accidents still cause 5,000 deaths and significant injury to 0.3 million people each year. These statistics, staggering as they are, say nothing about the physical, psychological and social impact of road accidents on those who survive them, and on those others who are affected by them. Relatives and friends, including the bereaved, those who witness the accident, and sometimes the emergency service and frontline hospital staff who care for accident survivors , may be traumatised psychologically by their experience.

The causes of road accidents have been researched extensively. Substantial investments have been made in road engineering and vehicle design in order to reduce the number and destructive physical impact of crashes, with some success (see Chapter 2). No equivalent attention has been given yet to the prevention or amelioration of their psychosocial effects. This chapter reviews the published literature on the prevention of post-accident psychopathology, and reports two recent studies of the efficacy of early psychological interventions in reducing the incidence and severity of psychiatric complications following road accidents.

EPIDEMIOLOGY

The chance of being involved in a road accident is high. A community survey in the United States showed that the annual risk of being involved in an accident sufficiently serious to cause injury or death to one or more people is 2.6 per cent, and the lifetime risk is 23.4 per cent (Norris 1992).

The incidence of post-accident psychiatric problems is also high. In a study of road accident survivors attending a hospital emergency department, Mayou et al. (1993) found that one-quarter experienced psychiatric complications in the year after the accident (see Chapter 3). Of these, 18 per cent displayed an acute stress reaction (ICD-10; acute stress disorder, DSM-IV), a poor prognostic sign which predicts later psychiatric morbidity (Feinstein and Dolan 1991; Koopman et al. 1995). Mayou and colleagues found that long-term psychiatric problems were of three overlapping types: mood disorder (10 per cent), phobic travel anxiety (20 per cent), and post-traumatic stress disorder, PTSD (11 per cent). A high incidence of PTSD (12 per cent) in road accident survivors was demonstrated also in a community survey by Norris (1992), prompting her conclusion that road traffic accidents are 'perhaps the single most significant traumatic event' in view of their combined frequency and destructive impact.

AETIOLOGY

The incidence and severity of post-accident psychiatric problems is not related to the objective seriousness of the accident or threat to life (Feinstein and Dolan 1991). Post-traumatic symptomatology is predicted, however, by the subjective perception of life threat (Malt and Olafsen 1992; Blanchard et al. 1995a), by early horrific memories of the accident (Mayou et al. 1993), and by the severity of physical injuries sustained (Blanchard et al. 1995a). Empirical research suggests also that an early acute stress reaction (Koopman et al. 1995) and the persistence of post-traumatic symptomatology at three months are associated with long-term psychiatric complications.

Pre-accident social difficulties, and a history of neuroticism, severe depression, or previous post-traumatic stress syndromes have been shown to constitute risk factors for post-accident psychopathology (Blanchard et al. 1994b; Breslau and Davis 1992), as have continuing physical complications or disability. These findings are in line with those reported from studies of survivors of other traumatic events.

PREVENTIVE INTERVENTION AFTER ACCIDENTS

Recognition of the high incidence of psychiatric problems in the survivors of road accidents has generated interest, amongst clinicians, in the possibility of preventing the development of post-traumatic psychopathology. A proportion of those who develop psychopathology will suffer long-term problems, including chronic PTSD, mood disorders, and anxiety states. These chronic illnesses are sometimes associated with substance misuse or personality deterioration, and often respond poorly to treatment. Chronic post-traumatic disorders are costly in terms of the patient's reduced capacity to work, the destructive impact on the family, and the demand on health resources. For example, over half of the local psychotherapy budget was used to provide psychological support to the survivors of a recent community disaster (Adshead et al. 1994b).

It has been suggested that early psychological intervention could prevent the development of psychopathology after trauma. This practice originated in military psychiatry, as a means of returning traumatised troops rapidly to active service. Such interventions were named psychological debriefing in order to distinguish them from operational debriefing. Psychological debriefing was then extended to emergency services personnel (Mitchell 1983) and workers involved in the aftermath of disaster (Dyregrov 1989).

Psychological debriefing is a specific psychosocial intervention designed to reduce the incidence and severity of emotional and psychiatric problems following trauma (Dyregrov 1989; Mitchell 1983). Psychological debriefing aims to facilitate emotional and cognitive processing of the traumatic experience, and encourages adaptive coping strategies. As a group intervention, particular emphasis is placed on a collective review of the incident and the promotion of continuing mutual support. Mitchell has described a model of group debriefing in which, during successive stages, an external facilitator encourages group members to describe factually their role in the incident, their immediate thoughts and feelings, and their later physical and emotional reactions. Factual exchange is encouraged in the group, dispelling misperceptions of the event and false assumptions about individual actions or failings. The first session is concluded by the facilitator providing information about common, natural physical and emotional reactions to trauma. The intention is to 'normalise' the participants' experience and to provide advice about adaptive ways of coping with early psycho-physiological symptoms, which otherwise might generate additional fear and maladaptive coping strategies and compound the effects of the initial trauma. There is also recent interest in the preventive value of early psychological intervention for the survivors of disaster, and for individuals traumatised by crime as well as for those bereaved by road crashes (Victim Support 1994).

STUDIES OF PSYCHOLOGICAL INTERVENTION

The aim of any preventive psychological intervention is to assist the survivor in coming to terms with the traumatic experience and prevent the development of psychiatric illness. This is achieved through promotion of emotional and cognitive processing, encouraging healthy coping strategies and the resumption of normal activities. For this purpose an approach strategy is advocated, enabling the survivor to face rather than avoid the trauma.

Combat and other trauma

Early studies of Israeli combat veterans found that psychological debriefing could reduce the rate of subsequent psychiatric illness. More recent studies of psychological debriefing following combat trauma in military personnel (Deahl et al. 1994) suggest that the intervention was welcomed but did not prevent later psychiatric complications. Similar findings have been reported in relation to debriefing emergency personnel (Robinson and Mitchell 1993) and burn victims (Bisson et al. 1996). Only Bisson's study used a randomisation strategy.

Transportation disasters

Following the railway disaster in 1977 at Granville, near Sydney, Australia, counselling was offered to bereaved relatives. At follow-up, 15–18 months after the accident, there was a tendency for those relatives who had received bereavement counselling to show less morbidity on general health measures (Singh and Raphael 1981). Similar findings emerged from a study of child and adult survivors of a cruise ship sinking in Athens harbour in 1988. Those who received higher levels of support after the disaster showed lower levels of post-traumatic symptomatology at a year to 18-month follow-up (Yule et al. 1992).

Interventions after road accidents

In an early study of hospitalised road accident survivors in Australia, Bordow and Porritt (1979) showed that a psychological intervention combining practical support, the mobilisation of social supports, and a psychotherapeutic exploration of the subjects' emotional reactions to the traumatic experience was effective in reducing distress and psychiatric disorder, and in returning the subjects more quickly to normal occupational and social functioning. Their intervention was relatively intensive, however, involving from two to ten hours of contact with the injured patient and relatives.

Stallard and Law (1993), in England, demonstrated that a two-session group intervention for the adolescent survivors of a minibus crash was effective in reducing anxiety, depression, and the intrusive re-experiencing symptoms (but not the avoidance) of post-traumatic stress disorder, even though the intervention was undertaken three months after the accident. In contrast, Brom et al. (1993) found that a three- to six-session intervention had little effect on later psychiatric disorder, although subjects appreciated the intervention which combined practical support, psychotherapeutic examination of the traumatic experience, and 'reality testing'.

In summary, there is a little empirical evidence that psychological debriefing is effective in preventing the development of post-traumatic psychiatric morbidity. Bisson and Deahl (1994) and Raphael et al. (1995) advise caution in its use, and emphasise the need for further randomised controlled trials.

THE LONDON AND OXFORD STUDIES

The studies reported here were prospective randomised controlled trials, and both were designed to test whether a single, early, clinically feasible psychological intervention could reduce the incidence and severity of post-traumatic psychopathology. This is a significant issue for research in view of the potential advantages to the survivors themselves, and the potential savings in health expenditure.

The projects differed in that one studied survivors of road accidents whose injuries were severe enough to require hospitalisation, and the other studied survivors of road accidents and physical assaults with minor injuries. There were similarities, however, in the methodologies, the model of intervention, and the findings.

THE LONDON STUDY

This study was carried out by *K.L.H. Stevens and G. Adshead at St George's Hospital, London*, in 1993. The subjects for this study had attended the Accident and Emergency Department of St George's Hospital following one of three types of injury. They had suffered either a road traffic accident, an assault by a stranger or a dog bite. Subjects excluded from the study were those who were not fluent English speakers, not sufficiently physically fit to be interviewed, medically assessed as in need of immediate psychiatric referral, homeless or intoxicated. Members of the same family involved in one incident were also excluded.

Demographic data were collected consisting of information about age, sex, injury severity, marital status, ethnic group, religion, socio-economic group, home ownership and household membership. Injury severity was recorded using the Injury Severity Score (ISS) which is computed by adding the squares of notional values given to the worst injury in each of the three most injured areas of the body.

Subjects admitted to the study were randomly assigned to 'counselled' or 'uncounselled' groups. Once physical assessment and initial treatment were completed, those randomised to counselling were offered a single standardised interview with an experienced counsellor within 24 hours of attendance. The interview included asking the subject to describe their particular experience in some detail, and about the worst aspect of their experience. Expression of feelings was encouraged in a general sense, but overall there was no directive component to the session. Survivors who became unusually distressed during the interview were excluded from the rest of the study.

Both counselled and uncounselled groups were then seen at one week, one month and three months after their attendance at Accident and Emergency. On each occasion subjects were asked to complete three measures: the Impact of Events Scale (Horowitz et al. 1979), the Beck Depression Inventory (BDI) (Beck et al. 1961) and the Spielberger Self Evaluation Questionnaire (SEQ) (Spielberger 1983). The IES is very commonly used in post-traumatic stress research, with established high validity for PTSD symptomatology. The BDI is a recognised and valid measure of depressed mood, which commonly occurs after trauma. The SEQ is a widely used measure of state anxiety ('how I feel now') and trait anxiety ('how I generally feel'). In addition, at three months there was a follow-up interview. In this interview, further points were expressly covered and spontaneous comments noted. At all follow up interviews, those administering the questionnaires were blind to whether the person had been counselled.

Analysis of data

Forty-four males and nineteen females participated in the study. Twenty-one patients were lost to follow-up; there is no evidence to suggest they significantly differed from those who completed the study. Subjects were principally young, Caucasian, male, white-collar workers who were little injured by the event (ISS, range 1–11; mean = 2.26). Randomisation appeared to generate a skewed population resulting in the counselled group having higher SEQt and BDI scores; they were also older.

The overall score on all questionnaires was computed. The SEQ and BDI were separately scored to give indices of anxiety and depression. The BDI is conventionally scored into grades of depression and these were used in analysis. Those patients whose scores lay in the top 12.5 per cent of the Spielberger score distribution were taken as 'anxious'. The frequency of endorsement of each item of the questionnaires was noted.

The diagnosis of PTSD was made using various items from the different questionnaires, on the basis of the diagnostic criteria then available (DSM III). These were: the IES score; particular items from the SEQ (2, 4, 12, 13) and particular items from the BDI (1, 2, 4, 11, 12, 13, 15, 16, 21). These data were examined only at one and three months since PTSD, by definition, starts at one month. The one week SEQt scores (measure of trait anxiety) were used as a guide to the patient's pre-injury mental state; the one- and three-month scores were used as an outcome measure.

Results of the London study

Analysis of the overall scores showed that despite an initial level of anxiety above the norm as measured by the SEQ, our test population reflected the established working-adult norms by the third month after the incident. The BDI similarly showed the population as a whole to have scores within the normal range. In terms of post-traumatic symptomatology (IES scores), generally all subjects showed a trend towards resolution of symptoms.

Overall, 38 percent of the sample developed PTSD, and 12 per cent developed clinical anxiety or depression. Of those patients who entered the study with high trait anxiety and/or high depression scores, 65 per cent developed PTSD, and 60 per cent developed symptoms of clinical anxiety or depression. A BDI score at any stage was significantly associated with later development of PTSD. There was no significant difference between those patients who were counselled and those who were not in terms of questionnaire measures or development of PTSD. However, in those subjects with high entry SEQt and BDI scores, the counselled group had a significantly better outcome at three months, suggesting a quicker resolution of symptoms in the counselled group.

The patients themselves were asked for their assessment of the usefulness of the counselling session: 66 per cent stated they found it useful, 33 per cent stated that they did not. The latter gave as their reasons that counselling had been offered too early, or that personally they felt they had not needed it.

The contribution to psychiatric disorder of other factors mentioned in the follow-up interview was studied: there were common themes amongst those patients who fared poorly. Most important of these were the degree of expectation of the event and the degree of direct personal vulnerability. Those events in which the person was most directly vulnerable and the agent was human (injured as pedestrian, assaulted) resulted in the worst outcome; a postman bitten by a dog and a driver whose hobby was stock-car racing were little affected by their traumas. Pedestrians fared worse than drivers and survivors of assault worse than other groups. The degree of physical injury suffered did not affect outcome in that the Injury Severity Score was not significantly associated with the scores on psychological test scores.

Table 13.1 London study: Percentage of sample with psychiatric disorder (PTSD or anxiety or depression)

	One month	Three months
Counselled	73%	46%
Non-counselled	56%	56%

THE OXFORD STUDY

This study was carried out by *M. Hobbs, R. Mayou and P. Worlock at Warneford and John Radcliffe Hospitals, Oxford*, in 1993. The research subjects were patients admitted to the John Radcliffe Hospital, Oxford, following injury in road accidents. They were selected according to the following criteria: age 18 to 65 years; residents of Oxfordshire or adjacent districts (to facilitate follow-up); not intoxicated at the time of the accident; and no significant head injury. Those who agreed to participate were allocated randomly to intervention or no-intervention control groups.

Subjects were interviewed by a research assistant within 24 hours of their admission to hospital unless precluded by their physical state, in which case the interview was undertaken as soon as the patient was sufficiently improved. This baseline screening combined a semi-structured interview and two widely used self-report questionnaires, the Impact of Events Scale (IES) (Horowitz et al. 1979), and the Brief Symptom Inventory (BSI), which generates measures of a number of psychiatric symptoms and a global measure of psychological distress, the General Severity Index (GSI), a subscale of the BSI (Derogatis and Melisaratos 1983). The semi-structured interview, which was derived from previous research (Mayou et al. 1993), sought sociodemographic data, information about previous psychiatric problems, outline details of the accident and injuries, and a review of the subject's early psychological reactions to the traumatic experience.

Study participants allocated to the experimental group were offered a debriefing intervention of approximately one hour's duration, comprising a detailed review of the accident, the encouragement of appropriate emotional expression, and initial cognitive appraisal of the traumatic experience. The aim of the intervention was to promote the emotional and cognitive processes which, it is believed, lead eventually to resolution of the trauma.

The intervention was concluded with information about common emotional reactions to traumatic experience, the value of talking about the experience rather than suppressing thoughts and feelings, and the importance of early return to normal road travel. Each subject in the intervention group then received a leaflet which consolidated the information given at interview, encouraged the support of family and friends, and advised consultation with the family doctor if problems persisted. General practitioners were informed of the study and sent a copy of the leaflet.

Regrettably, the experienced clinical nurse specialists and social workers, who were recruited initially to undertake the interventions, found that their primary clinical responsibilities in the emergency psychiatric service prevented their reaching many of the study patients before they were discharged. After the first ten subjects, the interventions were undertaken instead by the research assistant. The intervention therefore immediately followed the screening interview, with which it became merged to some degree, and interviewer 'blindness' was inevitably compromised.

Both experimental and control subjects were offered follow-up contact after four months, again utilising the two self-report questionnaires and a semi-structured interview which identified persisting intrusive and avoidant symptomatology, changes in travel behaviour, and continuing physical problems or disability.

Analysis of data

One hundred and fourteen patients were entered into the study, fifty-nine to the intervention group and fifty-five to the control group (Table 13.2). The intervention group displayed a higher mean injury severity score and mean duration of hospital stay, but there was no significant difference between the two groups in terms of specific post-traumatic or other psychiatric symptomatology at entry to the study. There was no difference between the intervention and the control groups on symptoms acknowledged in interview: 31 per cent (n = 18) of the intervention group acknowledged travel anxiety, compared with 29 per cent (n = 16) of the non-intervention control group. Distressing, intrusive memories were acknowledged by 34 per cent (n = 20) of the intervention group and by 38 per cent (n = 21) of the control group. Fewer people in the intervention group (n = 39) responded to a follow-up appointment or telephone/postal contact than did people in the control group (n = 47): 71 per cent compared with 91 per cent.

Table 13.2 Oxford study subjects

	Intervention group (n = 59)	Non-intervention group (n = 55)
Sex:		
Male	34	37
Female	25	18
Age (mean, range)	36.9 (18–67)	34.6 (17–69)
Driver	51 (86%)	48 (87%)
Passenger	8 (14%)	7 (13%)
Car	38 (64%)	38 (69%)
Motorcycle	16 (27%)	14 (25%)
Lorry/van	5 (8%)	3 (5%)
Injury severity scale (mean)	6.04	4.19
Duration of hospital stay in days (mean)	7.7	3.7

Results of the Oxford study

At follow-up, neither the intervention nor the control groups showed significant reduction in specific post-traumatic symptomatology, mood disorder or travel anxiety. There were no significant differences between the two groups on the main outcome measures, that is, IES, GSI, and interview ratings of intrusive thoughts and avoidant symptomatology, including travel anxiety. Whereas there was a tendency ($p < 0.05$) towards reduction in anxiety and a significant ($p < 0.01$) reduction in somatisation in the control

Table 13.3 Oxford study results: Mean, SD measures at entry and follow-up

		Intervention	Non-intervention control	
Total IES	Baseline	15.13 (14.82)	15.30 (12.35)	n.s.
	Follow-up	15.97 (15.32)	12.87 (14.22)	n.s.
	Difference	+0.85 (13.45)		n.s.
			−2.6 (12.86)	n.s.
GSI	Baseline	0.50 (0.53)	0.42 (0.32)	n.s.
	Follow-up	0.62 (0.78)	0.38 (0.43)	0.087*
	Difference	+0.12 (0.61)		n.s.
			−0.04 (0.32)	n.s.
Anxiety	Baseline	0.57 (0.62)	0.55 (0.54)	n.s.
	Follow-up	0.65 (0.95)	0.39 (0.55)	n.s.
	Difference	+0.08 (0.86)		n.s.
			−0.16 (0.49)	0.34**
Depression	Baseline	0.38 (0.49)	0.40 (0.43)	n.s.
	Follow-up	0.65 (0.91)	0.38 (0.45)	0.090*
	Difference	+0.27 (0.94)		0.076*
			−0.03 (0.42)	n.s.
Somatisation	Baseline	0.76 (0.82)	0.58 (0.58)	n.s.
	Follow-up	0.60 (0.77)	0.34 (0.49)	0.074*
	Difference	−0.15 (0.78)		n.s.
			−0.23 (0.56)	0.007***
Hostility	Baseline	0.37 (0.56)	0.28 (0.37)	n.s.
= irritability	Follow-up	0.63 (0.87)	0.42 (0.57)	n.s.
	Difference	+0.26 (0.63)		0.013**
			+0.14 (0.58)	n.s.
Psychoticism	Baseline	0.23 (0.45)	0.14 (0.22)	n.s.
= alienation	Follow-up	0.49 (0.70)	0.23 (0.39)	0.049**
	Difference	+0.26 (0.66)		0.018**
			+0.10 (0.39)	0.089*

Note: 2-tail sig

*	<0.1
**	<0.05
***	<0.01

group, the intervention group showed trends towards *increased* depression (p<0.1), hostility/irritability (p<0.05), and psychoticism/alienation (p<0.05). Irritability and alienation (a measure of interpersonal detachment or social distancing) are characteristic of post-traumatic states. Other variables (self-report items) designed to measure return to normal functioning and coping showed no significant difference between groups. Despite the aim of the debriefing, indeed, the intervention group actually seemed less likely (p<0.05) to talk to family or friends about their experience.

To quantify long-term outcome a composite 'recovery score' (Murray, personal communication) was constructed, combining change in total Impact of Events Scale (IES), General Severity Index (GSI) scores at follow-up, self-report of 'feeling back to normal', and indices of the problems still experienced in the areas of family relationships, occupational dysfunction, finance, and road travel.

No differences were found between the intervention and control groups, so further data analysis examined the total study population and those with high IES scores. This showed that global recovery was negatively correlated with the severe injury or death of others in the accident (p<0.01), blaming others for the accident (p<0.01), and, for the high IES subgroup, previous psychiatric history (consultation with family doctor for stress, p<0.05; previous psychiatric/psychological treatment, p<0.05). In this subgroup, IES scores remained high at follow-up, indicating vulnerability to long-term psychiatric problems.

A subgroup of intervention subjects (n = 25) and general practitioners (n = 26) were asked to rate the value of the information leaflet. Fifteen of the research subjects remembered reading the leaflet, and the ten who had read it at home as well as in hospital, and the one person who read it at home instead of in hospital, rated it as helpful. Seventeen (65 per cent) of the GPs responded, five of whom did not remember receiving the leaflet. Of those who did, eight thought it was helpful and four did not.

DISCUSSION

The two studies reported here provide no evidence for the preventive effect of an early debriefing intervention after injury in a road accident. In neither study was a significant difference found between the intervention and non-intervention groups in terms of psychological morbidity, as measured by widely accepted instruments. These two negative outcomes replicate the findings of other studies of psychological debriefing. The findings of the London study did suggest a trend towards more rapid resolution of symptoms in the intervention group. However, the results of the Oxford study showed a trend towards symptom deterioration in the intervention group. Significant post-accident psychological morbidity was found in participants in both studies which, without treatment tends to diminish over time. The studies also confirmed the existence of a small group of accident survivors with serious ongoing psychiatric problems which were found throughout the follow-up period.

The London study found that the majority of the intervention group reported that they had found the intervention helpful. This is consistent with the results of studies by Singh and Raphael (1981), Hodgkinson and Stewart (1991), Deahl et al. (1994), and Robinson and Mitchell (1993). Some trauma survivors have reported that they found offers of help intrusive (Hodgkinson and Shepherd 1994), and the significance of this for psychological care must be considered carefully. Worsening symptoms after an intervention, as found in the Oxford study, could imply that the intervention did not focus sufficiently on those psychological factors which facilitate symptom resolution: perhaps too much emphasis on *expression*, at the expense of *processing*. Alternatively, it could imply that the intervention broke through an early protective state of dissociation, and that the intervention was undertaken too early.

From comments made by participants in both studies, it seems likely that the latter explanation is correct, and that the interventions were provided too early. In the immediate aftermath of the accident, patients are often preoccupied with their physical state, and many are emotionally numb. By the end of the first week, most participants (London study) stated that they were more in touch with their feelings and would then have been more responsive to counselling. We would recommend, therefore, that initial assessment and psychological intervention should not be undertaken until one week after the traumatic experience, unless necessitated by an acute psychiatric presentation. For preventive purposes one session may be sufficient, but more severely disturbed or dysfunctional patients may require longer therapeutic intervention.

Our studies might have shown more positive results if patients had been selected for psychological intervention according to specific criteria known to be risk factors. Stress symptoms after trauma resolve spontaneously in most cases, but research findings confirm that some survivors are at greater risk of developing post-traumatic stress disorders and related psychopathology than are others. Preventive psychological interventions may be necessary and of value only for people who manifest specific risk factors, such as a history of neuroticism or previous psychiatric illness (McFarlane 1988; Smith et al. 1990).

It is possible also that the instruments used in these studies were inadequate. They may not have been sufficiently sensitive to measure morbidity in a relatively normal population. Perhaps more importantly, the measures did not identify positive experiences, such as feeling supported, understood or cared for.

Another problem common to both studies was short follow-up. The severity of post-traumatic symptomatology at three or four months may be predictive of more prolonged psychiatric difficulties, but it remains possible that the positive effects of an early psychological intervention might be experienced later than this.

CONCLUSION

These two studies highlight some of the considerable difficulties involved in conducting prospective randomised controlled trials of psychological interventions for traumatised populations. Although the studies were prospective in terms of assessing the subjects early after the accidents, the ideal prospective study would draw on pre-accident data to reduce bias. The ideal study would also assess and allow for the effects of intercurrent life events, such as impact on work capacity, or whether legal action was underway. In both of these studies the period of follow-up was short, and a longer follow-up would have shown the natural course of post-traumatic symptoms in the control populations and may have demonstrated an effect of the intervention in terms of the severity of chronic or delayed PTSD. In both studies it is possible that the non-intervention group obtained benefit from the validation and exploration of their feelings during the screening interview and completion of the questionnaires.

Three questions are raised in relation to further research. First, contemporary public expectation for counselling after traumatic events may lead to the view that random allocation to non-intervention control status is unethical, despite the paucity of evidence for its effectiveness. Second, as has been found in several other studies, participants in the London study reported that they found the intervention helpful in a way that was not reflected in the instrument scores. This may suggest that the instruments are not up to the task of assessing specifically what it is that is helpful about brief interventions. Future studies should aim to evaluate specific components of debriefing to determine which of them have the helpful effect. Finally, simple comparison statistics may not be suitable for assessing complex phenomena. In situations where many variables may be acting in a process which is not static as the experiment progresses, as Altman and Bland (1995) have stated, it may not be safe to conclude that the absence of evidence is evidence of absence.

Chapter 14

Treatment of post-traumatic stress disorder (PTSD) after road accidents

Edward J. Hickling, Warren R. Loos,
Edward B. Blanchard and Ann Taylor

Road accidents are a common experience in the US, as illustrated by the fact of over 3.5 million individuals suffering personal injury in 1992 (National Highway Traffic Safety Administration 1992). In addition to the incidence of personal injury, epidemiological studies have shown that being involved in an accident on the road is one of the leading causes of post-traumatic stress disorder (PTSD). Norris (1992) in her survey of 1,000 adults in four southern US cities, found almost a quarter of the sample had experienced a severe road accident at some time in their life, with 11.5 per cent of the total sample meeting criteria for PTSD secondary to the accident. Breslau et al. (1991) found almost 10 per cent of a sample of 1,007 young urban dwelling adults had suffered a serious road accident, with 11.6 per cent of them subsequently developing PTSD. Mayou et al. (1993), in a study of road accident survivors attending an Accident and Emergency Department found, using the Present State Examination, relatively fewer suffering PTSD in the immediate aftermath (8 per cent), while more (11 per cent) met DSM-III-R criteria for PTSD after one year. Blanchard et al. (1995) examined a sample of road accident survivors who ultimately sought medical treatment. When assessed between one and four months after the accident, almost 40 per cent met DSM-III-R criteria for PTSD, as assessed by the Clinician Administered PTSD Scale (CAPS) (Blake et al. 1990).

The psychological and psychiatric consequences of road accidents have been the subject of much investigation, although research has focused more often on assessment and epidemiology than on treatment efforts. For example, Mayou et al. (1993) found acute, moderately severe emotional distress quite common in a series of 188 consecutive injured road accident survivors. Almost a fifth of this sample suffered an acute stress syndrome characterised by mood disturbance and intrusive memories of the accident. Anxiety and depression were shown to improve for many of the survivors by the end of a year, while several others were found to still have specific post-trauma symptoms, driving phobia or anxiety. Psychiatric symptoms and disorders were found to be frequent and, significantly, to be the result of both major and less severe road accident injuries.

Blanchard et al. (1995c), assessed 158 survivors of car accidents (who sought medical treatment as a consequence) between one and four months after the accident. Sixty-two accident survivors (39 per cent) met the criteria for PTSD (DSM-III-R, as assessed by the CAPS) (Blake et al. 1990). Accident survivors who developed PTSD were also found to be subjectively more distressed and had more impairment in their various roles (e.g. performance at work, school, homemaking, or relationships with family or friends) compared with accident survivors who did not meet criteria for PTSD. This was also found to be true when compared with age and gender-matched controls who had not been in an accident (n = 93). More than half (53 per cent) of the road accident-PTSD group also met the criteria for current severe depression. In this group, a prior history of depression and prior trauma appeared to be risk factors for the development of PTSD.

Given the scope of the problem, it is somewhat surprising that the literature on treatment for PTSD following road accidents is so limited. Brom et al. (1993) in the Netherlands, were able to recruit 151 survivors of serious road accidents within a few weeks of their accident (obtaining this sample from 738 survivors contacted by letter). Half the sample were assigned randomly to brief treatment involving initial assessment and between three and six sessions over a period of two to three months; the other half of the sample were also assessed, but were only provided with brief information on trauma. There was a significant difference found in attrition, with the treatment group showing less attrition (16 per cent) than the controls (24 per cent). However, no significant differences were found between the assessment/treatment group compared with the assessment/information group on the Impact of Events Scale (IES) (Horowitz et al. 1979) completed before and after treatment.

Other studies provide anecdotal evidence of success without a controlled trial. Kuch et al. (1985) describe success using primarily behavioural approaches with ten out of twelve cases of PTSD in road accident survivors. Burstein (1989) reports good results with seventy road accident survivors with PTSD, who were treated with imipramine (a tricyclic antidepressant), behaviour therapy, and/or psychotherapy. Horne (1993) reports the successful treatment of seven road accident survivors, three of whom were diagnosed as having PTSD; McCaffrey and Fairbank (1985) also describe two cases of successful treatment of PTSD following road accident.

COGNITIVE BEHAVIOURAL TREATMENT

We now describe the treatment, using cognitive behavioural methods, of twelve road accident survivors with PTSD. The sample was drawn from a larger National Institute of Mental Health (NIMH) funded research project investigating the psychological effects of motor vehicle accidents: The Motor Vehicle Accident Research Project. Referral to the NIMH project was through a medical professional in the greater Albany, New York area, or by self-referral through reading an advertisement in the local newspaper. Entry criteria, in order to rule out minor accidents ('fender benders'), included their having sought medical treatment after a road accident. Subjects were paid. Systematic data were obtained on 158 road accident survivors as part of the large-scale NIMH assessment study over a period of twelve months: at the time of their recruitment into the study, at six months, and at one year. Thus we were able to obtain a relatively independent assessment of psychological functioning at six-month intervals, during the time when psychological treatment was being conducted. All subjects who were found to have psychological problems were referred for treatment as part of the ethical obligations of the research project.

The present sub-sample of accident survivors (n = 12) included two males (aged 32 and 34 years) and ten females (mean age just under 32 years); all were over 17 years of age. The twelve subjects in this treatment study were seen by two psychologists, both in private practice, and both of whom were also members of the Motor Vehicle Accident Research Project.

Assessment and measures

By participating in the NIMH project, each accident survivor was comprehensively evaluated using a range of measures including: a structured interview detailing the circumstances of the accident, injuries from and reactions to the accident; inquiry into previous traumatic events; assessment of possible post-traumatic stress disorder using the CAPS; current and lifetime DSM-III-R psychiatric diagnosis as assessed by the (Structured Clinical Interview for DSM-III-R (SCID) (Spitzer et al. 1990a); possible personality disorder assessment by use of the SCID-II (Spitzer et al. 1990b); assessment of current and pre-accident psycho-social functioning using the LIFE-Base (Keller et al. 1987); and a general psychosocial history. In addition, each participant underwent a psychophysiological assessment during which they were exposed to audio-taped descriptions of their own accident, and exposed to a standard videotape complete with road accident scenes and sounds (see Blanchard et al. 1994b, for details).

Assessors

The assessors were four licensed, doctoral-level clinical psychologists, all with over five years' experience assessing PTSD in Vietnam veterans. One of the assessors had participated in the development of the CAPS, and so was qualified to train the other three. Two had been trained in the use of the

SCID and SCID-II by personnel from the New York State Psychiatric Institute (NYSPI). They then trained the other two assessors in the instruments also using the NYSPI videotapes. Finally, all four of the assessors received training at Brown University in the use of the LIFE and the LIFE-Base interviews.

Diagnosis of PTSD

PTSD was diagnosed utilising criteria outlined in DSM-III-R (American Psychiatric Association 1987). The diagnosis was reached independently of treatment and was, in fact, the basis of recommending treatment following the initial interview. The interview schedule used for diagnosis was the Clinician Administered PTSD Scale (CAPS) (Blake et al. 1990). As part of the research study, fifteen interview tapes were rescored by an advanced doctoral student in clinical psychology who was uninformed of the initial diagnosis. Reliabilities for total CAPS scores on every symptom ranged from 0.82 to 0.99 with a mean of 0.975 ($p<.001$). Kappa for categorical diagnostic agreement was 0.81, $p<.0005$. The CAPS scores, completed at six-month intervals as part of the subject's participation in the NIMH project were used as the main measure of symptomatic change across treatment.

In addition to the CAPS, psychological tests were obtained from each person at six-month intervals. The Beck Depression Inventory (BDI) (Beck et al. 1961), the State Trait Anxiety Inventory (STAI-state) (Spielberger et al. 1970; Spielberger 1983) to assess current psychological state, while the Impact of Events Scale (IES) (Horowitz et al. 1979) which has been used in many studies of road accident impact, and Keane et al.'s (1984) PTSD scale derived from the MMPI were also used.

TREATMENT

Treatment was designed individually for each person, although the overall approach provided by both psychologists was cognitive behavioural. This allowed comparison of commonalties and differences in treatment across cases with similar initial diagnoses. Table 14.1 describes the sub-sample, the severity of injury, any diagnoses comorbid with post-traumatic stress disorder, and a summary of individualised treatment procedures for particular cases. The Abbreviated Injury Score (Association for the Advancement of Automotive Medicine 1990) was used to assess the severity of each survivor's physical injuries. The AIS was completed by a physician who was given a narrative description of each person's injuries, age and gender. A score of '1' indicates minor injury and '6' the worst possible injury for each of seven areas of the body: the ratings for each area are then summed.

In all twelve cases, cognitive techniques and relaxation were provided

Table 14.1 Subject demographics and diagnoses

Sub #	Age	Sex	AIS	Individualised treatment procedures
102	43	F	4	In vivo and imaginal exposure; EMG biofeedback.
103	32	M	3	Imaginal exposure; driving hierarchy and in vivo.
125	46	F	11	Desensitization; driving hierarchy; in vivo exposure.
129	19	F	4	Imaginal exposure; desensitization.
151	34	M	11	Grief work; treatment for past trauma; anger expression; social skills building; imaginal exposure.
198	31	F	3	Anger management; social skills training; fear of death.
200	24	F	9	In vivo exposure; treatment for past trauma; assertiveness training; fear of death; couples treatment; grief work.
203	24	F	6	Anger management; treatment for past trauma; in vivo exposure.
205	23	F	9	In vivo exposure; fear of death; anger management.
239	57	F	9	Social skills training; assertiveness; anger management.
277	22	F	8	Imaginal and in vivo exposure; driving hierarchy.
278	41	F	5	Past traumatic losses; social skills training.

Note: Co-morbid diagnosis:

Sub #	
103	Major depression, OCD, social phobia
125	Major depression
198	Major depression

using imaginal exposure techniques (encouraging the patient to visualise distressing scenes while in a safe, controlled environment such as the therapist's office), or graded *in vivo* exposure. Treatment for driving reluctance and phobia secondary to the road accident, was found to be a necessary part of the treatment in eleven cases; one person was unable physically to drive (Table 14.2).

Cognitive techniques to help the person understand and cope with the trauma were used effectively in all cases. These techniques included thought stopping, guided self-dialogue (with preparation for the event, confrontation of the situation and management of the event, coping with any feelings of becoming overwhelmed, and self-reinforcement of positive efforts and behaviours, (Meichenbaum 1974). Cognitive restructuring of irrational thinking (Beck et al. 1979) using an A-B-C paradigm (where A is the antecedent event, B is the belief and C is the consequence) was also used. The goal of the model is to help individuals learn to identify distortions of thinking that are thought to result in anxiety, depression or other emotional responses. Modelling and role playing of feared situations were also used. Behavioural techniques to help manage anxiety were thought to be an important component of the overall treatment.

While there were commonalties in treatment, the range of effects of road accidents, and the consequent variety of physical and psychological problems which can develop, necessitate individualised responses within a general treatment model. Some illustrative cases of individualised treatment, and of idiosyncratic responses to the accident are provided (below).

RATIONALE FOR TREATMENT

DSM-III-R and DSM-IV (American Psychiatric Association 1987; 1994) describe three clusters of symptoms comprising PTSD: re-experiencing the traumatic event (Criterion B); persistent avoidance of stimuli associated with the trauma and/or numbing of general responsiveness (Criterion C); and persistent symptoms of increased arousal not present prior to the trauma (Criterion D). Because survivors of road accidents do not all present

Table 14.2 Driving reluctance

	Yes	No	N/A
Currently driving	10	2	—
Avoid accident area	3	7	2*
Reluctant to ride	6	6	—
Restrict speed	7	3	2*
Drives only local roads	5	5	2*
Avoid pleasure trips	2	8	2*

Note: * One subject driving phobic, one physically unable to drive identically (Kuch et al. 1985; Blanchard et al. 1994a) we believe it might be more useful to consider PTSD after road accident as comprising *four* interrelated sets of symptoms and clinical problems (symptoms associated with re-experiencing; avoidance; psychic numbing; and hyperarousal) since each might require somewhat different treatment interventions.

Re-experiencing

A major symptom of PTSD is the presence of intrusive thoughts, recollections and dreams about the accident, perhaps most graphically demonstrated by dissociative flashback experiences, or distress when exposed to situations resembling the accident or some particular aspect of it. Road accident survivors in our culture frequently are faced with many evocative situations, including driving or riding in a car, watching the news on television or reading descriptions of local road accidents. Or, as some of our patients have reported, going home and seeing their own accident on the news. Each exposure can lead to distress.

Given our current understanding from research and clinical reports, vicarious exposure and encouraged re-experiencing of the trauma, coupled with education and cognitive therapy to re-interpret the event and its sequelae, are indicated. This follows, in part, from conceptualising the memory of trauma and the re-experiencing of symptoms in terms of emotion processing (Foa and Kozak 1986). A focus of treatment is to help the survivor understand that re-experiencing symptoms is a normal part of a reaction to trauma, and to help them to gain access to and confront as many parts of the cognitive network of difficult memories as possible. This reduces avoidance and makes memories more conscious and salient. Through the patient describing the accident and their emotional reaction to it orally or in writing, vicarious exposure takes place. This is carried out in a supportive therapeutic environment, with the negative consequences acknowledged although reinterpreted in as positive a way as possible.

Avoidance

There is considerable evidence (e.g. Foa et al. 1989; Horne 1993; Burstein 1989) that avoidance symptoms can be approached through education about how trauma reactions develop, using Mowrer's (1947) Two Factor Theory, and Keane's et al.'s (1995) recent formulation. Avoidance symptoms can also be approached using graded exposure homework, applied relaxation to assist in coping with the negative arousal which symptoms may elicit, and cognitive techniques to aid in the reinterpretation of the experiences. Existing behavioural treatments for PTSD have used graded exposure (Munjack 1984), while cognitive therapy is well recognised as effective in managing phobic avoidance (Meichenbaum 1977).

A very important and related psychological consequence of a road accident is its subsequent impact upon the person's willingness to drive or be a passenger in a car. In our studies, we use a rather narrow definition of *driving phobia* to mean the situation in which an individual avoids all driving, or only endures essential driving with a great deal of subjective discomfort. We also use the concept of *driving reluctance*, to mean a less powerful form of avoidance, where the individual avoids all or most discretionary driving, such as pleasure trips, avoids the accident area or driving circumstances related to their accident (e.g. rainy weather or high speeds), drives only on local roads, or is reluctant to ride in cars. Relatives, friends or partners of the accident survivor may be enlisted to assist the therapist with the exposure tasks. This can be especially important in treating driving phobia or driving reluctance as some accident survivors prefer to drive themselves for the sense of control this affords. Managing perceived loss of control as a passenger often requires exposure-based treatment at some point in the therapy and, in this, a significant other can be of central importance in carrying out the task. Treatment for this centres on a cognitive behavioural intervention related to the cognitive schema surrounding the particular accident circumstances, using systematic exposure through graded *in vivo* and imaginal exposure tasks. Relaxation is often applied to assist the patient to deal with any heightened arousal that exposure may bring about (Hickling et al. 1986)

Psychic numbing and social estrangement

As Litz (1992) has commented, the symptoms of psychic numbing and estrangement are the least well studied and understood symptoms comprising PTSD, proposing that they represent 'a selective emotional processing deficit'. Keane et al. (1985) sees emotional numbing as avoidance representing an attempt to suppress all strong affect since it is a reminder of the trauma and, hence, is viewed as dangerous. We conceptualise this cluster of symptoms as closely resembling depression and amenable to behavioural techniques such as pleasant events scheduling, increased activity within the limits of any physical injury, and greater involvement with people with whom the survivor had been close before the accident but from whom they now feel distanced. Depressive schema and irrational beliefs can be challenged as appropriate through the use of cognitive techniques.

Hyperarousal

Patients with PTSD present with symptoms of hyperarousal, both in general and for specific cues reminiscent of their accident. Relaxation has been shown to be an effective technique in helping to counter such symptoms in a Vietnam veteran, and in a road accident population (Hickling et al. 1986).

In individuals who require it, biofeedback techniques can be used to facilitate relaxation training. In addition, monitoring of cognitions during exposure tasks is suggested, to deal with any self-defeating or catastrophic thoughts which may be contributing to the elicitation or continuation of anxiety symptoms, and subsequent avoidance.

CHANGES IN PTSD SYMPTOMS, PSYCHOLOGICAL SYMPTOMS AND SOCIAL FUNCTIONING DURING TREATMENT

Table 14.3 shows changes in PTSD symptoms (as measured by the CAPS) for each case across a twelve-month period, and the total number of treatment sessions. The change in symptom clusters for each case is also shown. A drop in CAPS scores reflects a reduction in symptoms on an average for total scores and across symptom clusters.

Table 14.4 shows changes in psychological test scores over twelve months. One person had dropped out by the twelve-month assessment (no. 103), so follow-up data for this person are available only at the six-month assessment. Two individuals (nos. 205 and 277) showed a worsening of symptoms, one of whom (no. 277) had an extremely high initial score. All others showed an improvement over the treatment period. Psychological inventories, in general, reflected change consistent with change in the CAPS scores.

Table 14.5 shows change in psychosocial functioning. Improvement in psychosocial functioning is reflected in an overall increase in the DSM-III-R's GAS scores (a mean of 51.6 at initial rating to a mean of 69.7 at the end of one year), with nine subjects showing improvement, although three remained unchanged or worsened over the course of treatment. Higher scores reflect a greater level of impairment, with a range of 0 to 6 being found across subjects. Scores derived from the LIFE showed a corresponding change over the course of treatment for ratings of relationships with family and friends, in general, consistent with an overall improvement (or worsening) in psychological function.

ILLUSTRATIVE CASES

The following cases are included to illustrate our approach. Successful outcome depends on commonalties in treatment coupled with treatment specifically designed for individual patients focusing on idiosyncratic aspects of their response to the accident. Some required help for past traumas in addition to treatment for the impact of the road accident; other variations of treatment required that partners or significant others should be involved; some required anger management. In some cases, specific stimuli were associated with individual memories and emotional responses. As an

Table 14.3 Change in CAPS scores and symptom clusters across six-month intervals

Sub #	Total CAPS scores					Symptom cluster B Re-experiencing			Symptom cluster C Avoidance and numbing			Symptom cluster D Arousal		
	Total CAPS initial	Number of treatment sessions between initial & 6-months	Total CAPS 6-months	Number of treatment sessions between 6-months & 12-months	Total CAPS 12-months	Initial	6-months	12-months	Initial	6-months	12-months	Initial	6-months	12-months
102	41	7	35	2	4	8	10	0	12	9	0	21	16	4
103	87	7	37	11	DO	20	10	DO	34	0	DO	33	27	DO
125	99	10	34	0	12	28	8	3	39	10	2	32	16	8
129	32	1	9	0	10	6	3	0	15	6	6	11	0	4
151	38	8	0	0	0	16	0	0	15	0	0	7	0	0
198	29	11	18	16	13	5	3	2	12	12	9	12	3	2
200	54	16	23	15	35	23	7	7	16	13	11	15	3	17
203	29	4	7	15	13	11	2	3	11	0	0	7	5	10
205	35	17	38	22	56	17	10	14	4	15	25	14	13	17
239	57	12	44	18	31	6	5	6	35	30	19	16	9	6
277	104	17	90	8	128	28	25	32	45	32	53	31	33	43
278	57	24	15	0	23	25	0	7	29	8	10	3	7	6
Mean	55.17	11.17	29.17	8.92	32.20	16.08	6.92	6.73	22.25	11.25	12.27	16.83	11.00	10.64

Note: DO = Dropout from assessment study.

Table 14.4 Change in psychological test scores across six-month time intervals

Sub #	Impact of events scale			Beck depression inventory			STAI-state			STAI-trait			PTDS subscale		
	Initial	6-months	12-months	Initial	6-months	12-months	Initial	6-months	12-months	Initial	6-months	12-months	Initial	6-months	12-months
102	3	28	*	8	18	*	44	94	*	38	68	*	0	14	*
103	58	45	DO	24	13	DO	86	65	DO	69	66	DO	33	30	DO
125	59	*	42	17	*	*	100	*	57	44	*	62	*	*	4
129	29	*	7	7	*	20	73	*	62	66	*	61	14	*	18
151	27	7	7	8	8	2	73	52	59	58	52	48	1	3	0
198	7	18	7	17	15	26	43	73	53	63	62	74	12	20	16
200	47	41	32	12	21	25	38	72	98	31	84	86	9	19	23
203	39	9	16	6	1	4	57	47	42	45	45	43	0	2	5
205	29	42	43	10	8	13	64	61	55	45	59	69	9	14	13
239	37	*	28	22	*	20	95	*	96	80	*	80	23	*	20
277	51	59	70	33	39	50	85	79	91	77	83	105	30	39	44
278	8	38	20	13	11	16	45	58	45	66	62	62	25	16	22
Mean	32.8	31.9	22.4	12.3	14.9	15.8	66.9	66.7	63.0	56.8	64.5	65.0	14.2	17.4	13.4

Note: DO = Dropout from assessment study.
* Subjects failed to return instruments.

Table 14.5 Change in psychosocial functioning across six-month time intervals

Sub #	GAS			Work/school			Family			Friends		
	Initial	6-months	12-months	Initial	6-months	12-months	Initial	6-months	12-months	Initial	6-months	12-months
102	61	75	85	2.5	0.0	0.0	1.00	2.00	1.33	1.0	1.0	2.0
103	45	65	DO	2.5	3.0	DO	2.83	2.00	DO	4.0	3.0	DO
125	41	60	61	2.5	2.0	1.0	3.00	1.00	1.00	5.0	1.0	1.0
129	60	70	71	1.0	1.0	1.0	1.50	1.67	1.67	2.0	1.0	1.0
151	50	91	95	0.0	1.0	1.0	1.00	1.00	1.00	1.0	1.0	1.0
198	60	51	50	2.0	3.0	6.0	1.50	2.50	2.50	3.0	2.0	2.0
200	51	55	61	1.0	2.0	2.0	2.20	2.00	2.00	2.0	3.0	3.0
203	55	50	75	0.0	0.0	0.0	1.00	1.50	1.00	1.0	1.0	1.0
205	60	55	40	1.5	3.0	2.0	1.00	2.40	2.00	1.0	2.0	4.0
239	50	59	50	1.5	2.0	1.0	3.00	2.50	3.25	1.0	3.0	3.0
277	40	40	40	2.5	0.0	4.0	2.00	2.00	2.50	1.0	3.0	2.0
278	41	60	50	1.0	2.0	3.0	1.00	1.00	2.00	1.0	2.0	4.0
Mean	51.6	61.0	69.7									

Note: DO = Dropout from assessment study.

example, if an accident took place in a rainstorm, or during the autumn, particular environmental cues to do with rain or autumn subsequently provoked powerful emotional memories. If specific cues are ignored or not responded to – for example, seemingly innocuous environmental stimuli such as trees or particular weather conditions – their impact can be overlooked and the treatment rendered ineffective. Careful behavioural assessment and exploration of underlying cognitive schema are also essential if each individual is to have the best opportunity for improvement. These points are illustrated in the following cases.

Ms A   In this case, the impact of previous traumas, the loss of her home in a fire, sexual assault as an adolescent, witnessing a suicide from a bridge which was similar to the scene of her accident, all had to be dealt with as part of the treatment. Fear associated with these earlier traumas was related to worsening of the pain due to soft tissue damage in the shoulder and chest area caused by a seat belt in a rear-end collision. The accident had been caused by a male driver and the subsequent injuries limited her ability to draw and write. This led to feelings of anger toward the male assailants in her past and resulted in her current feelings of vulnerability. Physical examination of her shoulder injury and the proximity of the examination to her breast was associated by the patient with memories of sexual abuse. These anxiety-provoking memories were addressed with coping strategies, and methods to deal assertively with her own safety, which she saw as having been compromised by the male driver.

Ms B   Treatment began with the patient being instructed in the normal course of the development of PTSD symptoms according to the Two Factor Theory (Mowrer 1947). She was asked to describe the accident in detail and this material subsequently was used to help her to visualise the accident in subsequent sessions in which the emotionally laden words and images she had provided were emphasised. Cognitive techniques were employed. These included cessation of negative self-talk (e.g. 'I can't drive again'; 'I might be killed this time'), which was challenged and changed to more positive statements (e.g. 'I can drive again'; 'I am a good driver'; 'While driving is somewhat risky I can minimise the risk and use my skills to increase my chances to survive'). The thought of possible death was challenged and perspective given by challenging the certainty of it (e.g. 'It is unlikely that you will be killed, most people survive daily driving'). The thought that the accident increased the likelihood of death was changed by such statements as, 'One close call does not put me at any greater risk'. Substitution of statement mastery (e.g. 'I can use my relaxation skills to cope with any anxiety I might face, and I am able to succeed in breaking down the challenges into manageable steps which I have accomplished in the past') as well as challenging irrational and catastrophic thinking were used to counter the negative affect brought on by her accident. In her accident she was trapped in her car overnight, off the road, believing she would bleed to death or die from shock before being discovered. She was taught relaxation methods to be used to reduce physiological discomfort brought on by the desensitisation sessions in which she was encouraged to visualise the accident, and during other anxiety provoking moments. She was taught to challenge the anxiety by examining the cognitions which provoked the anxiety, and to substitute more rational alternatives. An important component of her presenting symptoms was her focus on her own mortality, which had resulted from the intense fear she had felt before being discovered by the highway patrol. In a recent paper, Blanchard et al. (1995a) report that the extent of physical injury and a fear of dying in an accident independently predicted PTSD in a sample of ninety-eight road accident survivors. This case provides an example of the significance of such experiences and perceptions at the time of the accident.

Ms C   This patient was seen on only two occasions because of an extended vacation out of the country. Due to the very limited time before her scheduled departure, a modified, cued desensitisation technique was developed. Details of the patient's accident were presented, reviewed, and discussed in order to determine which images provoked the greatest distress. Both her subjective discomfort and pain perception were assessed at various points throughout her narration. She was instructed in diaphragmatic breathing and imaginal exposure techniques for relaxation during which her subjective discomfort and pain perception were assessed. A desensitisation procedure designed for use at home was introduced, including home practice and exposure, with reported reduction in distress demonstrated by measures on rating sheets mailed over the time outside of treatment, and assessed by telephone contact.

Ms D   A woman who had done well in treatment made subsequent contact because her feelings of distress had returned. Cues reminding her of the same weather conditions as prevailed at the time of her accident in late autumn, such as cooler temperatures and barren trees, had apparently resulted in a return of intrusive thoughts and feelings about the accident. In the psychologist's office during relaxation, she was encouraged to visualise tree branches against an evening sky, and winter scenes reminiscent of the accident scene. In addition, she was fearful of having another car accident, which was associated with a fear of her own death. In turn, this appeared to be related to memories of her mother's death and the impact of this event on her. To counter anxiety caused by fear of her own death, an 'implosive strategy' was employed (in which the patient is encouraged to stay for a protracted period of time with highly anxiety-provoking images –

for example, the scene of her own death – while they are presented), paired with deep relaxation and cognitive restructuring. She was subsequently able to understand that she had 'lived well' following her mother's death, and so could 'live well' following her accident. Her anxiety reduced significantly at this point in her treatment. *In vivo* exposure then followed, utilising cognitive techniques such as coping and statement mastery and decatastrophising the memory when confronted with contemporaneous events.

DISCUSSION

This study has demonstrated that a significant portion of the distress associated with road accidents, including PTSD, can be treated with a cognitive behavioural approach and that certain treatment modalities can be applied to all road accident survivors. There is a need, however, to recognise the powerful impact on recovery which the patient's idiosyncratic reactions to the accident can have, and the possible associations with past traumas the accident might have for the patient. Attention to the commonalties and differences in treatment modalities affords a flexible, yet theoretically coherent, treatment intervention for each individual.

By using a range of measures, it is possible to assess the degree to which each symptom cluster changes, and to design specific interventions in an efficient and theoretically sound way. The CAPS is useful as a method of chronicling change in PTSD overall, as well as for evaluating change in one or more symptom cluster, and such information could lead to change in treatment strategy. Psychological tests measure mood and state functions associated with general improvement, while the psychophysiological measures allow improvements in hyperarousal to be assessed objectively. In clinical practice, a heart rate measure could provide similar information of use to practising psychologists. Measures of psychosocial functioning allow another important indication of overall impairment and allow an indirect measure of estrangement and emotional numbing (along with the BDI).

The number of treatment sessions varied greatly between individuals in the study, which is not surprising given the myriad of possible factors thought to contribute to the continuation of PTSD. It is also consistent with research by Burstein (1989), which showed that while a significant number of road accident survivors improved in less than three months, a large number required prolonged treatment of more than one year.

One strength of this study is that while the treatment was conducted with the flexibility of practising clinicians, the evaluation of outcome was done with the rigour of independent researchers. The clinicians functioned under a generally consistent theoretical framework conceptualising PTSD and methods of change, yet as with most practitioners, used the sessions flexibly in an effort to the meet the patients' needs at the time. The researchers completed their assessment independently and unaware of the what was occurring in treatment, focusing solely in the measures of change for each person. This availablity of sensitive, independent measures of change is thought to be a unique feature of this treatment study.

The incidence of psychological distress following road accidents, and the consequent disturbance in social relationships and driving behaviour clearly are all important areas for further study. The findings of the present study, and other past studies underline the need for a large-scale, controlled study in the very near future. In the meantime, the treatment rationale described here appears to hold merit as one guide to providing psychological treatment to this group of trauma survivors.

Acknowledgements   The authors thank the National Institute of Mental Health (MH-48476) for funding the research reported in this chapter.

Chapter 15

Treatment of pain, fear and loss following a road accident

A case study

David J. de L. Horne

It was a terrible day – raining, and foggy and cold, and the road was very slippery and visibility was very poor. I was driving along and all of a sudden three visible lanes became one, so I swerved to the left as fast as I could and with the side of the road now being muddy all over, the tyres touched the mud and the car went out of control. There was nothing I could do to stop it. The car kept going for a while by itself until it crashed and turned upside down, then hitting a tree and stopping with a hard bang. The windscreen shattered in front of my eyes and I was waiting for the car to crash in on us. Nick was screaming. I was worried just in case the car was going to catch on fire and really panicked. We were hanging upside down from the seat belts. Then I moved across and helped Nick by pressing his seat belt button and he fell on top of the roof. I'll never forget the feeling of being underneath the crashed car with the shattered glass in front of me and I couldn't breathe and I was terrified. I tend to get that claustrophobic feeling every time I'm in a small closed room or elevator. I was afraid that I would die with Nick in it. Then two cars stopped to come to help us and two men got us out of the badly smashed car. I was badly shaking, they helped us to get on the road and asked if we wanted to ring my husband to come over. And they asked if we wanted to go to hospital but decided that it was a lot closer to go to a nearby clinic, which was five minutes away. One of the men was from the Royal Automobile Club and called a tow truck, because there was no way we could move the car. Then my husband came rushing and was pale and worried and hugged us and he drove us to the clinic. We saw a lady doctor. She checked us and said that I had a bad whiplash and she prescribed tablets because I was shaking and told us to see her in three days. That night at home I was full of sobs and pains and could hardly move. And every time I tried to rest and close my eyes I could see the car rolling and rolling over and over again. I was shaking all over, very tense and frightened, and every time I closed my eyes it felt as if I was getting an electric shock.

I was very sick for about four weeks. I could hardly eat anything. I had lost a stone. I used to have horrible nightmares, mainly of cars, smashing and crashing. From that time on everything bad changed and I haven't been the same again. I felt that I had lost my confidence, couldn't make decisions, was very depressed, jumped at the slightest sound. I hated the phone when it rang. I hated to receive letters. I couldn't stand bright light and the sound of water dripping really irritated me; I felt like a 90-year-old woman without energy or strength; it didn't feel like me at all. It felt as if some one else had taken my place. I hated myself – I felt really empty inside, and I cried most of the time.

This is the account of a road accident and its immediate consequences experienced four years previously by a 39-year-old woman (Jane), on her initial presentation for assessment and treatment.

Jane's marriage was intact and she had succeeded in returning to her part-time job so, in terms of the more gross indices, an acceptable degree of recovery had been achieved. But debilitating chronic pain, a complex hierarchy of fears, and low self-esteem, along with post-trauma avoidance and intrusion, significantly compromised her enjoyment of life. It is striking that Jane was reliving the accident scene daily as if it had just happened and her feelings of self-worth, and the quality of her life at home and at work, were significantly impaired. It is important to question why, four years later, this chronic situation was continuing and it speaks of the overall lack of attention that is often paid to the survivors of road accidents who appear in relative terms to have 'recovered' after a life-threatening incident.

The letter from her general medical practitioner reflects the chronicity of Jane's situation and describes the series of treatment modalities which had been attempted previously, to little effect. The letter is unedited other than to conceal identities; the pharmaceuticals are a combination of antidepressant and anti-anxiety drugs:

> Thank you for seeing this patient who has significant post-traumatic stress disorder following an MVA in 1989. She has been unsuccessfully managed by a psychiatrist, and a psychologist. She still has flashbacks and sleeplessness +, of course, pain. She is on Xanax, (Alprozolam), Rivotril (clonazepam), Tolvon (Mianserin hydrochloride) +/- Amitriptyline. Please help her.

While some guidelines on how to manage and treat civilian trauma have emerged from the research (Brende 1993), most studies of appropriate treatment for psychological stress reactions concern veterans of the Vietnam War or other wars, survivors of torture, or survivors of large scale disaster. Research specifically on road trauma has described the incidence, prevalence and nature of stress reactions to this most common source of trauma (Blanchard et al. 1994b; Green et al. 1993; Mayou 1992), with rather less emphasis on treatment, although this situation is changing (Horne 1993; also see Chapters 13 and 14).

Various taxonomies to classify a disaster have been developed according to its scale and its geographical or political impact (e.g. Murray Parkes 1990). Thus the Lockerbie air disaster, which resulted directly in the deaths of 259 people from twenty-one different countries, is large and international. By contrast, a 'routine' car crash is small and local. In terms of the resources mobilised, and the practical and emotional support provided, it may be 'better' for a survivor's psychological health to be involved in a large-scale disaster. The survivors of road accidents are often left to fend for themselves, once the physical injuries are treated. The experience for the individual and their immediate family can be as significant as it is for those involved in larger-scale disasters. This theme of 'hidden distress' is reflected throughout this volume.

A road traffic accident is a common event, and because of this, people may become inured or desensitised to them. Wrecked cars on the roadside are a common sight and the sound of emergency vehicles is a frequent fact of urban living, as are the detours imposed on our daily journeys by emergency vehicles attending to an accident. Just as people in war-torn countries may become habituated to the sights and sounds of war, and go about their daily business with a surprising normality, so it also appears to be with road accidents. Perhaps the effects of road accidents are the 'battle scars' of a society dependent on cars, although travelling in the much beloved car is a daily risky activity for a large percentage of the population (Bureau of Transport and Communication Economics, Australia, 1992). The study of the psychological consequences of road accidents and the recognition that significant psychological disorder can be associated with them, is a relatively recent focus of research attention (Pilowsky 1985; Horne 1993). That it has taken so long to accept that road accidents can produce adverse emotional and psychological reactions could be explained by their being commonplace. This topic is itself worthy of study.

There is evidence that mild anxiety disorders, such as phobias, are the most common emotional problems experienced after a car accident, and fully developed PTSD is not uncommon (Green et al. 1993; Horne 1993). Green et al. (1993: 533) found that one-third of their sample of accident survivors 'at follow-up had clinically significant symptoms. Their disorder had not been diagnosed or treated in any way despite the fact that their symptoms had been readily apparent from direct questioning during the initial hospitalisation.' This is untenable when both post-accident phobic anxiety and PTSD can be treated effectively using cognitive behavioural therapies (Horne 1993).

JANE

The focus in this chapter will be the person whose accident story was presented at the beginning of the chapter; her symptoms, from the author's clinical experience with road accident survivors, and his research on the sequelae of road accidents, are quite typical.

At her first consultation with the author (almost four years after the accident) Jane walked very slowly into the office, with a stooped posture. She sat on the edge of the chair and spoke very quietly. However, she was alert and able to give a lucid account of her accident, her history, her complaints and previous treatments. She was born in Europe and came to Australia at the age of 13. She had three years of schooling in Australia, leaving at 16 and marrying at 18. She had two sons, one aged 16 and one aged 9. The younger one, Nick, was with her in the car at the time of the accident. Because of her symptoms and slow recovery, she was very dependent on her husband, her children and her mother for help with domestic duties. Some improvement in her physical state had allowed her to resume her former work for four hours a day at a local supermarket.

She neither drank alcohol nor smoked. Her pre-morbid history was of a well-adjusted, happily married woman who enjoyed her family, her work and her social life. Her son, Nick, was not injured in the accident, but he was very jumpy, still having night terrors, and was fearful of car travel, although he was doing well socially and at school.

Jane had been diagnosed variously as having PTSD, whiplash injury and chronic pain from a neck injury. Previous treatments had included 'talk therapy' with a psychiatrist, relaxation education from a psychologist, medication (described in the referring physician's letter), and self-administration of analgesics such as Codral and Panadol. None of these interventions had produced significant improvements. On the basis of clinical examination, she met the criteria for PTSD, obtaining maximum scores for both intrusion and avoidance on the Impact of Event Scale (IES) (Horowitz et al. 1979).

TREATMENT PLAN

A cognitive behavioural approach to therapy was adopted, concentrating on three interrelated domains: pain management, dealing with her fears, and managing her loss and grief. The treatment plan centred on a functional analysis of the relationship between her physical symptoms of pain and tension, and her emotional status, and the effect that these had on her daily thoughts, feelings and activities. She was asked to keep a daily record of these in a self-monitoring diary. Mutually agreed treatment aims were set at the end of the second one-hour session. These were to monitor analgesic use, to receive relaxation training, to identify and think about one pleasant thing a day, to construct a fear hierarchy as a basis for systematically reducing her fears through therapy, to visit the site of the accident, and during therapy sessions to work through coping with her sense of loss.

PAIN MANAGEMENT

The nature of chronic pain and its potential influence on the way she felt, thought and behaved was explained to her in terms of learning theory. Peck's (1985) formulation of the 'traps' of chronic pain such as the 'take it easy trap' or the 'medication trap' was discussed with her. The aim of this part of the treatment was to improve Jane's ability to cope with chronic pain so that her life was less impaired by it. Jane was taught to self-monitor her levels of pain, using an analogue rating of '0' for 'no pain', to '100' for 'almost unbearable pain'. The goal of breaking the nexus between analgesic self-medication and the experience of severe pain was established. Before treatment started, Jane would take analgesics whenever the pain became severe, but during therapy she was encouraged to take one or two analgesics before the pain built up rather than waiting until it became severe.

Jane was also taught relaxation coupled with guided imagery using a code word: for example, 'delta' was her code word to connote 'lying on the beach in the warm sun listening to the sound of the waves'. She was also encouraged to use very short relaxation periods any time she needed to, particularly during her working day (from 10 a.m. to 2 p.m.), by ceasing what she was doing if she noticed tension or pain developing, and taking a very short break of 30 to 120 seconds. During these short pauses she was encouraged to use her relaxation code word, and check her whole body for tension while gradually letting her breathing slow down and the tension slip away.

Her pain management showed progressive improvement, accompanied by increased relaxation and decreased use of analgesics. In summary: *Session 4*: Panadol (1–2 per day) on a time rather than a pain schedule. In this session she reported that keeping the self-monitoring diary 'nearly drove me mad'. Nevertheless, she found that instead of feeling overwhelmed by pain she could tell herself, 'I can control the pain rather than let it control me'. *Session 8*: She had built in rest pauses at work and had reduced her Panadol use to ten tablets a week. Her pain rating was 55–75 on the analogue scale and she noticed the pain fluctuating according to what else was going on in her life; for example, when she had flu the pain became worse (90+). *Session 11*: Her pain was still rated at 55–75 although she noticed variation in the actual sensation of pain ranging from a dull ache to an acute burning sensation. *Session 13*: The pain was less at weekends (maximum rating 65), although at work it was still rated at 77–79. She also noticed that her behaviour and mood was less controlled by pain, and that the relationship with her husband had improved. *Session 16*: Her pain rating at home was on occasion down to 5, although still around 50 at work. *Session 18*: By this final session she reported that she was no longer thinking so much about her pain, although it was still there but controlled by the occasional Panadol. Jane had practised the relaxation strategies assiduously throughout treatment and became adept at using the relaxation code word 'delta'. She also continued to use brief relaxation pauses to manage day-to-day pain and anxiety symptoms. When seen at a follow-up session nine months after starting therapy, she reported using no medication of any kind and rated her pain at a maximum of 10.

DEALING WITH HER FEARS

By recording her fears in the self-monitoring diary Jane could identify and rank order them, using a subjective unit of distress (SUD) analogue scale, where '0' would mean 'no anxiety at all', and '100' would mean 'panic'. These ratings were used to lay the groundwork for systematic desensitisation and to monitor progress. Table 15.1 shows the striking number and complexity of fears she experienced, which had continued unabated since the accident, four years previously. The aim of this part of treatment was to assist Jane to manage her fears using a treatment approach combining imagined and *in vivo* exposure with relaxation, sometimes assisted by her husband.

A continuing source of concern she expressed early on in treatment was her fear that members of her family would be injured. Jane was unable to prevent her mind racing over all the bad things that could possibly happen and to counter this she tried to control everywhere they went. This was the case particularly with Nick, her younger son, who had been with her in the accident. It emerged that she was overprotective of him. She would not allow him to ride his bicycle to school, to cross the road by himself, or to play with friends at their homes, preferring his friends to come to his house. These worries continued despite his being 9 years old, and the school being very close by.

Jane had resumed driving her car before commencing therapy with the author, primarily in order to keep her part-time job. The journey to work involved passing the site of the accident, which she was able to do, although only by avoiding thinking about the accident and by attempting to drive past the site in as calm a way as possible. It is remarkable that even after four years of repeated exposure, the fear listed as 'Driving by the road where the accident happened', was given a subjective distress score of 89.

Two months after starting treatment, and around the fourth anniversary of the accident, it was planned that Jane would visit the accident site and stop there. It will be recalled that the accident happened on a wet foggy day and so it was agreed that her first deliberate visit to the accident site should

Table 15.1 Patient's worst fears post-accident with initial subjective unit of distress (SUD) ratings

Fears related to driving/travel/family

SUD	Fear
98	Driving a car.
95	Seeing a car accident.
92	Transport accident warning, advertisements on TV.
90	Nightmares (e.g. falling off a cliff in a car).
90	Son driving with L-plates on.
89	Driving by the road where the accident happened.
89	Car breaking down.
88	Nick (son) disappearing from home all of a sudden.
87	Elder son or husband coming home late.
75	Nick (son) crossing the road by himself.
70	Tram ride.
70	Being a passenger while husband driving.

Other fears

SUD	Fear
98	Fears of the unknown.
97	Fear that something horrible is just about to happen to family.
85	Receiving mail, especially from insurance company.
82	Answering the telephone and expecting bad news.
82	Darkness, night time.
80	Rainy, foggy, bad weather.
80	Loud noises and screaming.
75	Elevator
75	Lightning and thunder.
65	Spiders
60	Looking out of window at home at rainy or foggy weather.
40	Noise inside house (e.g. a bang).

Note: In follow-up driving a car, the fear that something horrible is just about to happen to family, seeing a car accident and the elder son or husband coming home late, still held a residual amount of fear, whilst any fear diminished in all other categories.

be on a sunny day. She did so three days after the anniversary on a bright day. Jane went to the site on her own, and sat for half an hour by the tree her car had crashed into. She reported having cried continuously. She also found pieces of her car still scattered around. During this *in vivo* visit she noted her feelings of distress, using the subjective unit of distress analogue scale, on arrival and at departure; these were 95 and 80. She said of this visit: 'It feels as if part of you is just there; as if you're buried there.'

Her subsequent distress when passing the site daily remained at 80 until, ten weeks later, on another sunny day, she stopped at the accident site again. She reported crying much of the time, although on this occasion she took flowers with her and placed them under the tree her car had crashed into. While she did this she noticed three wild rose bushes growing nearby and was able to remark to herself, 'How lovely they are'. On this occasion she found she was unable to generate a distress rating at all but was able to recognise her fear and desire to run away. However, she stayed until she felt inwardly calm and peaceful, and only when this had been achieved did she get into her car to drive away.

She continued to stop for brief visits at the accident site until her subjective distress reduced entirely. At the final consultation, she stated: 'It (the accident site) doesn't bother me at all now. I feel I should go there just to go, because something of me is still there.' At nine months she no longer experienced intrusive thoughts about cars, but still occasionally would go to sit under the tree at the accident site. By this stage she felt her life had returned to normal, she had resumed her social activities and interests and was involved enthusiastically in her family affairs. Phobic anxiety had stopped and there was no evidence of depressive feelings or thoughts. Concurrently, her nightmares (such as those about her being in a car falling off a cliff) decreased in frequency and intensity.

DEALING WITH HER FEELINGS OF LOSS AND GRIEF

At presentation, Jane had said: 'I feel so old and sore and full of aches and pains', and, 'I can't accept everything that has happened. I'm just a totally different person since the accident. I feel so empty inside.' The grief and sense of loss she felt surrounding the physical site of the accident (crying, the laying of flowers, the sense of 'part' of herself being at the site) provides a graphic and poignant illustration of these symptoms. As Jane's fearfulness and avoidance behaviours decreased, issues over loss and grief became more salient, involving processes of grieving over a lost past and reorienting her life to the present and future. She had expressed some suicidal thoughts, although she was certain she would not make a suicide attempt.

The aim of this component of the therapy was to encourage her to detect thinking that was maladaptive and negative, and even irrational, and to help her to restructure her thinking towards positive coping and improved self-esteem. DSM-IV (American Psychiatric Association 1994) identifies such symptoms, especially in terms of feelings of detachment or estrangement from others; restricted range of affect, such as, being unable to have loving feelings; and a sense of foreshortened future, such as not expecting a career, marriage or children, or a long life.

Expressions of affection and intimacy between Jane and her husband had been impaired, as would be expected in a person experiencing chronic pain and post-trauma symptoms. Gradually affection and intimacy returned, so that nine months following the commencement of treatment, Jane reported feeling 'warm inside' instead of the previous black and empty feeling. She and her husband agreed that their being together and enjoying intimate touching were back and as enjoyable and frequent as they had been before the accident. Based on clinical experience with accident survivors, particularly young adults, successful grieving over these concomitant feelings of lost youthfulness and vitality is often important before the person can pick up the threads of their life.

Jane's ability to manage her feelings of loss and grief showed progressive improvement during therapy. In summary: *Session 3*: Mood definitely improved; was now interested in enjoyable activities but many fears were still present, as were nightmares (although these were less terrifying). *Session 4*: She had identified some positive thoughts and feelings, although was continuing to have difficulties with concentration. *Session 11*: Smiling and alert and less self-absorbed. Intrusive thoughts had decreased. Socialising much better. She was able to counter negative thoughts with more positive ones. For example, it was a big step ahead for her to be able to think, when Nick rode his bicycle to school or played away from home, that 'if an accident happens, it happens' but such an eventuality is most unlikely. *Session 17*: Jane was bright and animated and said 'that horrible feeling has gone'. At follow-up nine months after starting treatment she said: 'I can see myself like I used to, whereas before everything was so black.' Her sense of humour had returned, and her relationship with her husband and her sons was greatly improved.

DISCUSSION

Single case histories of road accident survivors cannot prove the effectiveness of therapeutic interventions, but they are useful to describe common reactions to road accidents and to describe the assessment and treatment of accident survivors. Case histories can also detail the procedures used and the complexities involved in assessing and treating particular clinical problems. This patient undoubtedly had chronic pain coupled with PTSD. Detailed functional analysis of her symptoms and the implications this analysis had for planning psychological intervention was greatly helped by the use of the self-monitoring diary and a cognitive behavioural framework. This emphasises the importance of the relationship between detailed diagnosis and treatment, a point also discussed by Hickling and colleagues in Chapter 14. The self-monitoring diary she maintained throughout treatment provided useful information and feedback to both herself and the therapist. Monitoring actual behaviour provides valuable information about progress, for example, in overcoming avoidance of specific fears. Simple analogue measures are easily understood and completed, and provide robust information (McCormack et al. 1988). Self-monitoring by the patient, using simple analogue scales and simple behavioural measures, should probably be part of the repertoire of all clinicians.

Would it have been better to treat this patient with intensive therapy, perhaps as an in-patient, or is it better to spread therapy over a period of time? There is no clear answer to this question and little available research. Whatever the approach, therapy requires the provision of specialist centres or clinics which are rare and expensive to provide. This case study reflects therapy provided over an extended period of time and there are some arguments why this might be an effective approach, particularly for chronic conditions which persist long after the accident. Therapy over time allows the person to practice what has been learned in therapy between treatment sessions and to monitor their own reactions and progress. In this way, the person is actively involved in both the cognitive and the behavioural elements of therapy. Therapy conducted over time also facilitates the person's reintegration back into normal family, work and social life. In this case, Jane's husband played an important role and usefully supplemented Jane's own self-monitoring. On occasion, he accompanied her to therapy and so could be included in discussions about treatment alternatives, and about ways in which he could help.

Several important issues cannot be addressed by considering a single case. Amongst these are whether early intervention could have prevented the development of chronic pain and post-accident phobic anxiety. It seems likely that had Jane started self-monitoring soon after injury, the extent and severity of her problems may well have been detected and so treated much earlier. In addition, the role of medication is not addressed in this case although it is clear that the considerable medication she had been taking before coming to therapy had been of little use. No psychotropic medication was used during therapy.

The role of compensation and legal procedures in maintaining disability deserve some mention. Towards the end of therapy Jane rather suddenly was confronted with the decision whether to be compensated by a one payment settlement, albeit a limited one, or to continue legal proceedings. She opted for the former course. The only observable impact of compensation proceedings was the period of confusion and mild depression she went though at the time of deciding which course to follow. What is certain is that in Jane's case considerable clinical improvement had been achieved while compensation issues remained unresolved; their sudden resolution certainly did not hinder her recovery. There is a paucity of research on the effects of compensation and legal proceedings on both the course and recovery from car accident-induced post-traumatic stress reactions. In the author's clinical experience of assessing and treating car accident survivors, pursuing a compensation claim definitely is not a motivating force for continuing disability. Rather, resolution of claims removes a major source of anxiety; concepts such as 'compensation neurosis' probably are a great deal too simplistic. The author has discussed these complex issues in greater detail elsewhere (Horne 1994, 1995).

Green et al. (1993) have shown that failure to detect those at risk of psychological distress after a road accident is a serious problem. It is hoped the detailed analysis of the case presented here will add to medico-legal professionals' awareness of the need to detect psychological disorder in accident survivors as early as possible, and so ensure that appropriate treatment is implemented, also as soon as possible. Road accidents are such a common event and evidence is accumulating that a significant percentage of survivors do suffer from identifiable post-trauma stress reactions. There is also evidence that some post-trauma symptoms respond well to appropriate psychological interventions (Horne 1993). If early recognition of symptoms and intervention were a matter of course following road accidents, perhaps the unnecessary suffering in the community, psychological distress and the damage to quality of life resulting from road accidents could be reduced.

It could also be argued that if survivors of accidents were more aware of likely reactions to having experienced a road accident, then they might feel less isolated, 'crazy' and distressed and so be in a better position to insist on appropriate treatment for their psychological problems.

Chapter 16

Road accidents
The impact on everyday life

Bridget Bryant

Road accidents can have wide-ranging effects on quality of life, even when injuries are medically relatively minor. These effects have generally been underestimated by doctors and lawyers concerned with physical recovery and return to work of injured survivors. While impairment is likely to be greatest and most obvious in those suffering serious physical injury, studies of representative groups of survivors show that the relationship between physical injury and social impairment is not a simple one, that psychological factors are also important, and that accidents involving minor injury, or even no injury, can have considerable effects (Mayou et al. 1993; Mayou and Bryant 1994; see also Chapter 3). In our current series of 1,100 consecutive survivors attending an Accident and Emergency department over a one-year period, preliminary analysis of the first six months' data indicate that about one in six who were not injured were having difficulty one year later with work and/or daily tasks, and one in five rated the quality of their life as worse than before the accident (Bryant et al. (unpublished)).

The aim of this chapter is to give a flavour of these difficulties and what they meant to the individuals concerned, and to draw out some common themes from their descriptions of their experiences. It will draw mainly on interviews with a subgroup from our current study, the first fifty vehicle occupants admitted to hospital, thirty of whom were injured, and a further twenty who were uninjured or whose injuries were very slight but who were admitted for observation because of the combined speed of the impact.

WORK

Being unable to work and the associated financial hardship were, as would be expected, the most devasting effects on daily life mentioned by injured survivors. One year after the accident, five manual workers were still unable to work and had lost large sums of money and incurred debts. Another two had been unable to take up jobs they had been offered just before the accident and were still unemployed. However, other factors were also important for both injured and uninjured individuals. Loss of the use of a car, whether through not being able to afford to replace it or through a driving ban, could have serious effects on getting to work and doing the job once there, and also caused stress for them and their families. One man lost his job because there was no public transport from his village and he could not get to work on time. Another felt his job was under threat because his dependence on public transport meant he could not put in the long hours expected of him. Five people were banned from driving, three of whom needed to drive to do their job. One of them ran a small delivery business with his wife who had to take over all the driving, and they had lost several important contracts because she felt so tired and stressed.

Psychological factors such as mood disturbance and anxiety about travel were more frequently, but not exclusively, mentioned by the uninjured, resulting in loss of job satisfaction, switching jobs or even giving up work. A computer operator was suffering from mild depression and severe headaches since the accident, and was having difficulty concentrating at work: 'I keep taking more and more pills and making more and more mistakes; I don't enjoy it any more.' A secretary had switched to a job in the city centre served by a bus because she could not face driving past the end of her road where the accident happened; she was enjoying this job much less and felt very angry. A police dog handler had become very anxious about high-speed driving to emergencies, and was considering giving up his job. (His dog, which was in the car at the time of the accident, also appeared to be suffering from travel anxiety!) A woman who was driving with her six-week-old baby in her car when she was hit by an oncoming car overtaking another, felt psychologically unable to return to her £20,000 job as a sales office manager at the end of her maternity leave. Breast feeding became disrupted after the accident, confirmed by the baby's weight chart which showed an immediate drop in weight gain, and the mother became very anxious about the baby and about driving. At one year she was very bitter about having to stop work: 'I feel the accident has destroyed my plans to continue a career.'

LEISURE ACTIVITIES AND SOCIAL LIFE

As with work, injury in a road accident can have direct and obvious consequences for those whose leisure pursuits require physical fitness. Four in the injured group had leisure lives that centred on sports which they were unable to do one year after the accident, with loss not just of a valued activity, but also of the associated social life. Some continued to go as spectators, but said the sense of camaraderie was lost and their enjoyment was spoilt. Another seven in this group mentioned considerable limitation or inability in acitivies such as walking, dancing, gardening, DIY, housework and playing football with their children. The need to economise to make up for financial losses from the accident also restricted leisure activities, and people reported going out less, and putting off taking holidays and buying things for their children and home.

Anxiety about travel was a very significant source of limitation in leisure and social life, especially in the uninjured survivors, nearly a third of whom reported effects. For example, a 42-year-old man who used to take his wife and children out on trips most week-ends was now very reluctant: 'I avoid outings by car unless it's something very specific, like if the wife has organised a trip to Alton Towers and bought tickets. We never just jump in the car and go somewhere now.' He was also very anxious about his children going on school trips: 'On one occasion I insisted on driving them to the school rugby match myself.' Avoidance was often quite specifically connected with the circumstances of the accident. Two young women returning from a nightclub in a taxi that was involved in an accident in which the other driver was killed were both avoiding going out at night one year after. A woman with three young children had stopped taking her children swimming, something they had all enoyed, because the accident had happened driving away from the pool. Another young woman, who used to enjoy shopping expeditions with her friends, could no longer go into crowded shops because of panic attacks. A couple who drove most weekends to York to see his parents now travelled all the way on side roads because his girlfriend refused to go on the motorway where the accident had happened.

These sorts of anxieties created frequent hassle and irritation for survivors and their families and friends. Some people refused to travel in the same position in the car as in the accident, making others move to the front or back seat. Others could not travel in cars of the same make or colour as the accident, and one woman had stopped going out with a friend whose car was red like her own.

Sometimes these effects became quite tortuous. A mother described how she had refused all year to go on a family holiday, but had reluctantly agreed to go to Wales. Since they could not all go in one car, her older daughter travelled with her grandmother: 'I gave strict instructions that they were to go first and to phone to say they had arrived safely, before I would leave the house with the rest of the family. I spent the whole morning by the telephone waiting for the call.'

Unpleasant feelings associated with passing the accident spot were common, and in four instances resulted in people regularly taking quite long detours to avoid it. One woman whose accident happened on the way to work was able to keep to her usual route on the way home, but added several miles to her journey each morning to avoid the spot. Another always approached her own home using the bypass, an extra two miles, in order to avoid a right turn (where the accident had happened) across the traffic into her street. Both felt this was an added burden on their daily lives, but preferred to do it.

Leisure and social life were also affected by depression. Six in the injured group and two in the uninjured group reported feeling depressed during the year after the accident, with loss of interest in activites and not wanting to go out or to see people. Two of them were also convicted of a driving offence, and in both cases the onset of the depression occurred after they learned they were to be prosecuted: 'That's when it all started, when the letter from the police arrived.'

A few people mentioned self-consciousness about scars making them not want to go out so much. A young man who had lost the tip of one finger had stopped going out to the pub with his mates, his main leisure activity, because: 'they take the mickey, so I feel I don't want to take my hand out of my pocket, so I can't join in the fighting!'

RELATIONSHIPS

About a fifth of those interviewed reported a deterioration in relationships over the year after the accident, with daily life often being lived in an atmosphere of tension and anger. Five of them attributed much of this to their own mood changes. For example, one girl said: 'I'm less patient with everyone, fly off the handle ever so quickly. Dad doesn't understand anything – he makes stupid remarks about the crash which upset me.' The strain caused by financial and legal worries created enormous feelings of guilt for survivors responsible for the accident, and anger and resentment in their relatives. The couple already quoted who were running their own delivery business and where the husband had been banned for a drink-driving offence were near to breaking up at one year. As well as losing a lot of money he had been incorrectly insured and his insurance company had refused to accept liability, so he was being sued by others injured and they stood to lose their house as well. He said: 'The stress caused has been enormous, far worse than the physical [a fractured wrist and severed tendon]; I've been very lucky physically. She is worn out and has no time to herself and is very angry.' His wife confirmed this: 'My whole way of life has changed as I have to do my husband's job as he can't drive. My family and home are neglected and I am rushing about at weekends trying to fit everything in.' Their sex life had also been affected as she was no longer interested Altogether eight people said their sex lives had deteriorated. Two couples had split up at one year follow-up; in both cases, the husband had become depressed after the accident.

Loss of independence as a result of the accident also made people frustrated and irritable and contributed to relationships deteriorating. Physical dependence while in plaster casts or other appliances could last for some months but was eventually resolved, but dependence on others for money or transport were often more long-lasting. A wife who had previously had her own income and company car said: 'I feel totally dependent now . . . I hate not having my own money . . . I feel I have to ask to borrow the car . . . it's a bad atmosphere and we are having more rows.' Young people living with their parents became very irritated by what they saw as their parents' overprotectiveness, and reported rows about being allowed to borrow the car or having to telephone to tell their parents where they were.

SELF-ESTEEM AND SELF-IMAGE

Several people talked about how the accident had changed the way they saw themselves, and how this had affected the quality of their lives for the worse. The most obvious was bodily change. Even very minor scarring left two or three people feeling damaged. As one woman who was left with a tiny patch of reddening on one cheek put it: 'I feel I'm not the same person I was – every time I look in the mirror I feel this, even though I know it's silly. I can't really get my mind round it – it makes me feel unsure of myself, where I'm going.'

Other changes seemed to centre round failure in particular social roles, especially as a parent. An accountant in his fifties who had been convicted of dangerous driving described how before the accident he had always seen himself as: 'a good family man, a good father, but that's all gone now . . . I don't feel I can ever get that back.' In his case he had been at fault and none of his family had been involved in the accident, but three women who had all been driving with their children expressed similar feelings, even though one was definitely not at fault and the others probably not. The mother already quoted who had decided not to go back to work because of worries about her baby said: 'I felt good in myself before about being a good mother and a good career woman; now I don't feel I'm either.' Another said: 'I feel a bad mother . . . that's why the liability issue was so very important to me, that it wasn't my fault . . . I don't feel in control of my life any more, it has all been spoilt.'

The feeling of having lost control of one's life, that plans could be shattered in an instant by one's own or someone else's stupidity on the road, and the unpleasant sense of vulnerability this engendered, were mentioned by quite a few people. 'It makes you realise you are not invincible' was a typical remark. Often it evoked considerable anger. One couple with debts of over £6,000 one year after the accident said: 'It's not that we were well off, but we were both working and had planned our money and felt we could manage the mortgage, but this has all been shattered. It's not us running our lives now . . . we both feel very angry and bitter . . . it's there all the time, this feeling.'

CONCLUSION

The great majority of road accident survivors return to a full normal life after a road accident, and a few even see it is as a positive experience that makes them more appreciative of life and family. About 6 per cent of the current six-month series rated the quality of their lives as better one year after the accident. For a sizeable minority, however, the adverse effects of road accidents on daily life can be much more wide-ranging and persisting than many health workers or the survivors themselves anticipate, and can touch on every aspect of people's lives. These effects have been considered here under separate 'domains' of work, leisure, social life and family, but in practice these are interrelated, and effects in one domain can have consequences for all the others.

It has been implied throughout this chapter that the relationship between accident and social impairment is a simple one of cause and effect, but there is often a complicated interaction between pre-existing life circumstances, the accident, injury and post-accident intervening factors. Those who work in manual occupations, live in rural areas, are less affluent, have family responsibilities, are heavy drinkers, are psychologically vulnerable, or whose lives and relationships are already stressful, are likely to be more at risk of practical and psychological difficulties following a road accident. Drinking behaviour and stress may be contributory factors in accidents occurring. It is probable that much of the limitation of activities which was not attributable to physical disability would not have occurred without the onset of psychiatric symptoms.

Many of the effects which road accidents have on everyday life are similar to those following any serious illness, or indeed following many types of threatening life events. However, there were very important effects specific to road accidents which accounted for much of the limitation described by this and other series of survivors, and in particular, anxiety about travel, which was both persistent and distressing. Only one person had had any form of counselling for this, and there is clearly a need for psychological interventions to help people deal with these fears.

Chapter 17

Voluntary organisations and their role in providing support in the aftermath of accidents

Sue Jeavons

It is the purpose of this chapter to consider the role of voluntary community groups in provision of support to people affected by road trauma. While it is recognised that emergency service workers are also affected (see Chapter 9), it is argued here that many of these services have more or less well-developed informal peer support networks, and some have formal psychological debriefings and one-to-one support which can be utilised (Robinson and Mitchell 1993). Others affected by road trauma do not.

Statistics give the annual figures for death and serious injury on the roads, but cannot convey the extent of personal suffering experienced by everyone involved. The emotional needs of road accident survivors, witnesses and their families and friends often are not met by existing professional agencies. Self-help and voluntary groups therefore offer other avenues of support to people suffering emotionally after accidents. This chapter outlines the structure and function of these groups and later gives a detailed description of the development of one such group in Australia, the Road Trauma Support Team (RTST).

SELF-HELP GROUPS

Self-help groups are a growing force in several communities, providing support for many forms of health conditions, disabilities, socially isolated people or people who are required to cope with the emotional after-effects of many kinds of stressors. In Chapter 12, Howarth speaks of the dissatisfaction which bereaved families often feel at the way road death is managed in the justice system. Some of the more minor but still extremely debilitating effects of, for instance, minor head injury or driving phobia may not be well managed by medical and social services once acute care is concluded. The rise of 'consumerism' and dissatisfaction with institutions intended to care for those with medical, psychological or social difficulties has led to an increase in 'self-help'. In accordance with the theme of this volume, the commonplace nature of road traffic accidents, and their frequency forces them into the community. Self-help groups can be thought of as being that community's response to the serious problem of the devastation caused by road accidents, which does not get the attention it deserves. Most often a person whose life has been damaged by a particular injury or disease will make it a cause to raise awareness, and to provide support to those similarly affected. A self-help group may be defined as:

> An association of people with common or similar problems working to overcome the practical obstacles caused by their problems and attempting to change community attitudes by education and example. Self help groups provide that one essential support that the major systems, by their very nature, cannot: Emotional support. This is not to say that this is all they provide and all they can do for the community. Self-help groups determine their own affairs when working in association with, but not under direction from, the professional health and welfare fields. (Association of Self Help Organisations and Groups (ASHOG) 1977)

Characteristics of self-help groups include: acknowledging a common need and recognising the benefits of collective support and action; setting up of the group by those with needs which are not met by existing organisations; reliance on members to provide mutual help; active involvement of members in policy and programme decisions; and development of an identity for members through identification with the common values and shared attitudes of the group (Tenenbaum 1979). Typical activities of self-help organisations can be thought of as: the provision of emotional and social mutual support among the membership through meetings, discussions, telephone contact, visiting, and participating in recreational and social activities. They also provide information and advice on practical techniques for dealing with particular situations, and perform an educational function for professionals and the public through seminars, publicity material, personal networking and use of the media.

Self-help groups both challenge and complement health and legal services by lobbying for change, advocating on behalf of consumers, and pushing for alternative models of care. Members of self-help groups who recognise gaps in the health care system and lobby for change must also recognise that they are dependent on health and other professionals and that they need to work with them. The strengthening of links between self-help groups and professional bodies, however, can result in increasing pressure on groups to expand their role and services, including perhaps social advocacy and research, aiming to influence the public as well as professional and legislative bodies (Tenenbaum 1979; Kearney 1991). The activities of self-help groups may be based on quite different philosophies and approaches than those of conventional agencies, and have a democratic rather than a bureaucratic structure. The support which is provided for its members is action oriented, often practical, readily accessible and will continue as long as it is required. Help is predicated on shared experience and is seen as being mutually helpful to all involved, which is a very different model that the 'top down' or one-way traditional notion of the relationship between the helper and the helped. Groups encourage a normalisation of the needs expressed by members rather than labelling them as problems.

Self-help groups have obvious limitations in that they often receive only minimal funding, while at the same ti me attempting to operate in an environment of ever-increasing government cutbacks and rising costs. While they may achieve great success despite limited resources, it is obvious that they have limited effectiveness in solving underlying social problems and cannot be considered to be an alternative to social action by governments – as can sometimes be the case. The informal structures of self-help groups can make them vulnerable to domination by particular individuals or interests that may not always be shared by the rest of the group. Tenenbaum (1979) has also pointed out that groups also need to be cautious that their lobbying does not alienate them from the professionals who might be instrumental to them in pursuit of their goals. This can be a considerable challenge to members of self-help groups, many of whom have turned to this mode of assistance, or created it, because of frustration they may have experienced in their dealings with medical, legal or political bodies.

Other groups may be run by volunteers who often obtain great satisfaction from participating in community activities and addressing human and social needs in this active and direct way (Volunteer Centre of Victoria 1994). In contrast to self-help groups, it is often the case that volunteers who work in such groups will not have experienced or suffered the issue which is the focus of the group. This can restrict mutual self-help because of survivors' often strong feelings that only those who have been through a traumatic experience, or people similarly touched by tragedy, can understand the needs and emotional reactions. Within such a structure, more of a distinction between the helpers and the helped can emerge compared with a group in which all its members share similar experience.

Overall, apart from the obvious advantages in providing services not available from other agencies, financial savings, and empathy from shared experience, self-help groups and voluntary organisations may appeal to survivors for other reasons. One reason may be that such groups have less formal procedures, and in particular, less formal requirements for those who wish to join the group and participate. Also, because they are community based, volunteer groups are probably less threatening to users who might fear potential stigmatisation in attending agencies such as psychiatric services, where their needs and problems might be labelled in pejorative ways. The mutuality involved in the ethos of self-help groups may also appeal to some people. They may find something satisfying in being able to help others, construed as empowering, while at the same time being helped themselves; this could well be helpful to them in their own recovery. Furthermore, the assistance offered within self-help groups, again because it is based within the community and run by *ordinary* people rather than by professionals, may be seen as more practical.

ROAD TRAUMA: NEEDS AND SERVICES

The psychological sequelae of road accidents have been discussed in previous chapters. They can include acute stress reactions, emotional distress such as anxiety and depression, post-traumatic symptoms such as post-traumatic stress disorder or phobic travel anxiety, organic mental disorder, or alcohol or substance abuse. Reduced quality of life as a consequence of physical, emotional and cognitive sequelae of road accidents is also a pervasive difficulty. In the wider context, the family and friends of survivors can also experience significant difficulties in coping with the loss of a person killed in a road accident, or coping with physical disability or head injury of a family member involved in an accident. These can have a critical impact on family life which has been well documented elsewhere.

It has been argued throughout that witnesses and helpers at the scene of an accident can also experience considerable psychological distress (see Chapter 9). Particularly when a witness to a road accident is not a member of the emergency services, they can become a 'hidden' casualty, having no avenues available to them through which debriefing could be offered. Nor are they covered by transport accident insurance. At the accident scene, most attention is taken up dealing with victims and assisting survivors, and often no one is available to help other witnesses involved more remotely. An example of the potentially devastating impact on witnesses comes from the author's research: a man who stopped to assist at an accident with a double fatality was unable to return to his employment for almost a year because of an acute post-traumatic stress reaction.

VOLUNTARY AGENCIES FOR ROAD TRAUMA SURVIVORS

A number of existing voluntary community organisations offer services to road accident survivors in the UK, the USA, and elsewhere. Examples in Australia are Headway (which provides advocacy and support for head-injured people); Solace (support following death of a partner) and Compassionate Friends (support following death of a child), as well as the Road Trauma Support Team (RTST) described below. All of these organisations are represented in the UK. A working party commissioned by the UK Victim Support organisation (Victim Support 1994) looked at voluntary and self-help groups and agencies which provide support for families of road death victims internationally. The report cited Cruse, Samaritans, Victim Support, Campaign Against Drinking and Driving, Compassionate Friends and Road Peace in Britain; the National Organisation for Victim Support in the Netherlands; the European Federation of Road Crash Victims; and the Road Trauma Support Team in Tasmania.

Volunteers may also be used in conjunction with a health care agency. For instance the Hartford Hospital in the USA developed a Trauma Support Team which has a multidisciplinary group of health professionals, as well as volunteers to meet the needs of traumatised families, available on a 24-hour basis. Members assist bereaved families at the hospital by providing both practical and emotional support and the hospital also runs an After Care Program staffed by volunteers who follow up families in which a family member has died suddenly and traumatically (Coolican et al. 1989). A group for trauma survivors, called Trauma Survivors Anonymous has adapted the well-known Alcoholics Anonymous (AA) 'twelve step programme', developing a model which sees recovery as continuous, and a spiritual dimension is at the core of the programme. Group leadership and attendance at meetings is emphasised, along with acknowledgement of symptoms, sharing, hope and education (Brende 1993).

Other examples of self-help groups for bereaved people were reported by Hopmeyer and Werk (1994: 245), who summarised the benefits as: 'commonality, normality, solidarity, reciprocity and control'. Preliminary data from the groups in their study suggest that members may not realise the help that they are giving others and may feel that they receive more than they give. In this way they share the opportunity to complete the process of bereavement.

THE AUSTRALIAN CONTEXT

It is estimated that annually in Australia there are half-a-million road crashes. In financial terms, the cost to the community is in the region of $A6 billion (£3 billion), which include lost earnings of survivors and families, vehicle damage, pain and suffering, and insurance administration, as well as the cost of hospital, medical and rehabilitation treatment, legal costs, ambulance, travel delay and crash investigation (Bureau of Transport and Communication Economics 1994). In the state of Victoria, Australia (population 4 million), in 1994, there were 378 people killed in road crashes and 5,338 people seriously injured (Vic Roads 1995). This represents a large number of people who are directly affected by road trauma, especially when all those others likely to be affected in each person's family and social networks are included. It is also noteworthy that these statistics do not include people less seriously injured, those who were not injured but were shocked by the accident, or those who assisted at or witnessed accidents.

The pain and suffering costs for survivors of road accidents and their family and friends are the most difficult to value. Available estimates relate only to direct victims and do not include family and friends, and published estimates tend to be based on court awards (Bureau of Transport and Communications Economics 1992). They too exclude the pain and suffering of 'indirect victims', people affected by accidents which are not reported, or minor injuries which may nevertheless have great impact on the survivors (e.g. through a phobic anxiety state that seriously restricts their own or their family's lives). For 'direct victims' of the accident, transport injury insurance may reimburse lost wages or provide compensation in cases of long-term disability. In Australia, these benefits and the insurance system vary from state to state. In Victoria there is a single compulsory motor vehicle transport injury insurer, the Transport Accident Commission (TAC) and premiums are paid as part of three million vehicle registrations each year. This covers every person involved in an accident, regardless of who was at fault, for hospital, medical and rehabilitation costs, and loss of earnings or death benefits. If injuries remain serious for more than 18 months, additional benefits, paid by the TAC, may be claimed by common-law action against a driver at fault. Drivers at fault may have benefits reduced if convicted of a serious offence, such as drink-driving.

Services available to those with psychological sequelae of road trauma can include medical, psychiatric, psychological and community social workers. The TAC will pay for counselling of direct victims of accidents and for family counselling in the case of a person killed in an accident. No counselling is funded by the TAC for accident helpers or witnesses or families or friends of those injured. Also, each person not admitted to hospital must pay the first $A407 of medical costs. To many people, this can represent a lot of money, especially if more than one member of a family requires treatment or counselling. The provision of services is hampered by non-detection of psychological trauma. Once patients leave a hospital casualty department, there is no follow-up. Unless symptoms become florid, or a close friend or family member recognises a post-traumatic reaction, lower-level but distressing symptoms can continue for years.

THE ROAD TRAUMA SUPPORT TEAM (RTST) IN TASMANIA

The following section describes the Road Trauma Support Team and, as such, may act as a model for other community-based groups. Voluntary organisations cannot replace professional counselling for people with post-traumatic and other psychiatric and psychological conditions following accidents. However, there is a definite place for their operation to complement existing services. The 'ripple effect' when someone is killed or injured in an accident means that there are many 'indirect victims' who may have few services. There is also a great need for support which can be provided by trained volunteers who are available outside normal working hours for accident survivors. The previously discussed advantages of self-help and voluntary groups are all relevant to road trauma. There is also a need for public education about road trauma. One person who joined the Road Trauma Support Team describes her experience as follows:

> The Road Trauma Support Team has helped me a lot over the last twelve months or so since I first decided to go along and find out what it was all about. I was involved in two car accidents within seven months of each other in 1993. These caused major changes and adjustments to my lifestyle and meant that I would probably never be able to go back to my chosen career. I was angry and confused and didn't cope well. My husband and three sons just didn't understand what was going on. By going along to the support group I have realised that I was not the only one going through these experiences and feelings. It was great to be able to say how I felt and know that other people there had been through it all too. By talking about these experiences with other people we have been able to share ideas and strategies on coping with our problems. Family members of road trauma victims are most welcome, as they are often left without support to cope with difficult situations. I was amazed at how much just sharing with others has helped me to accept what has happened and to get on with my life.

This was written by a member of a support group, Road Trauma Support Team, created by a road accident survivor in Tasmania, whose teaching career was cut short by a whiplash injury following road accident. Over a number of years, seven members of her family, including her mother, have been killed in road accidents and no group existed to comfort, to share the burden of grief, to support or to help by providing information. She observed that most people were left to get on with their lives as best they could, and for some, this was a long, slow process. Some suffered relationship breakdown or difficulty working. Some also had feelings of guilt, confusion, anger or resentment for a long time. While the structure and operation of the support team are described in detail later, some background to the concept of self-help or voluntary organisations will help to place this particular initiative in context.

The Road Trauma Support Team Ltd (RTST) was founded in Launceston, Tasmania, in 1989 by Colleen Hall, who felt that the emotional needs of road accident victims, their family and friends, and witnesses to accidents were not being met. The RTST is a non-profit organisation providing counselling, support and befriending to direct and indirect victims of road accidents. Referrals can be from any source. Having personal experience of accidents and the loss of family members, she started work on the group after two multiple fatality accidents of young Tasmanians. She called a meeting at the local hospital (the Launceston General) with representatives of police, ambulance, hospital, Community Welfare, Motor Accident Insurance Board, Transport Tasmania, Lifelink / Samaritans telephone befriending, Headway (a voluntary organisation for head-injured people), psychologists, and social workers (Igoe 1992). Following acceptance of the idea that a support team was needed, a public meeting was held, a steering committee formed and the Team's constitution established. Meanwhile, Colleen Hall continued to seek information and support within Australia and overseas. The Launceston General Hospital and the Tasmanian Health Department awarded seeding grants. In late 1991, the Tasmanian Health Department funded a part time co-ordinator, while the hospital provided a room adjacent to Accident and Emergency for easy access by relatives and staff after accidents.

The administrative structure of RTST is evolving as the organisation grows. Currently RTST groups exist in Tasmania and Victoria with proposals to start teams in Sydney and Canberra. Lack of resources prevents the establishment of other teams at present, despite interest from other states. As each new team is formed, it becomes incorporated and in taking on the name RTST agrees to accept the aims and structure of the organisation. Representatives from local teams have formed state committees, which are concerned with dissemination of information, fund raising, and dealing with issues such as insurance and representation to government as needed. Representatives from each state will eventually form a national committee.

Not all teams provide the same service or have the same resources or needs in the community, and therefore, information presented here may not apply to every team. This review aims to provide an overview of the organisation and the services that it can provide. Support may be offered in a number of ways. A paid co-ordinator provides one-to-one counselling. Volunteer health professionals may provide some backup if there is no co-ordinator. After hours there is a team of 'crisis carers' who are professional counsellors and who come in to the hospital at short notice, or offer support in people's homes following police notification of an accident. These carers are paid sessional rates and work with families and friends of people injured in serious accidents. They may also assist with a driver at fault if other relatives are expressing anger towards him or her. Volunteer 'befrienders' provide ongoing support in adjusting to life with disability or loss of a family member. This support may vary in its nature and encompasses social contact, practical help (filling out forms, shopping or leisure activities), personal support in potentially stressful situations (attendance at inquests or court cases) or telephone calls at significant times (settlement of court cases, anniversaries of the accident, birthdays or Christmas).

A support group for anyone affected by road trauma enables sharing of support and mutual self-help by people who can truly understand one another's feelings and experience. A professional counsellor may facilitate the group initially, but as members feel more comfortable with the group and work through their own emotional issues after the accident, they can take over the leadership. In one region, the support group meeting takes place in the informal setting of a café.

Two other functions of the RTST involve public education. Teams have organised public lectures by people with expertise in medical, psychological or legal areas for other professionals, victims of accidents, their family and friends or the general public. One of the functions of such public lectures is the 'normalisation' of post-traumatic reactions after accidents. Many victims fear that they are going crazy when they experience symptoms after an accident. To hear these described as 'normal' may be a great relief as well as providing hope for recovery and information about treatment options. Public meetings can be a source of new members for steering committees or support groups as well as help with fund raising. They also increase public awareness of the impact of road trauma and the availability of help. The production of pamphlets about the RTST and common reactions of grief or trauma is also part of the public education role. Early education experts and a psychologist are writing a children's book, following a number of interviews with child RTST clients. It will be used in conjunction with nursing, education or counselling work during the recovery process or deprivation of parental contact due to injury or death (Igoe 1992).

As the basis of the RTST is its volunteers, the selection and training of befrienders is very important. While strict guidelines for suitability criteria have not been documented, volunteers must not have experienced a recent traumatic event in their own lives and may have a security check for criminal record. Screening volunteers occurs during training. Unsuitable volunteers may undertake later training after resolving whatever issue may have prevented their entry at that point. Training programmes vary from team to team. Where possible, established training programmes are used, but some teams have developed a specific programme to suit their needs. For instance, in one team the befriender training starts with a small group session at which the volunteer role is discussed in detail. The second stage involves an interview to assess suitability of the befriender, and finally, 30 hours of training over two weekends also acts as a further screening. The training encompasses areas such as support skills, loss and grief, reactions to trauma, volunteer rights, information on transport insurance, and when to refer on to professionals. Ongoing monthly training provides backup, debriefing and skills development. Befrienders can also telephone the co-ordinator for backup if needed.

Referrals to befrienders can be from any source and may be direct victims, family and friends, co-workers, school friends, witnesses or those who face police charges following an accident. Befrienders and clients are matched according to such factors as age, gender, geographical location, and interests before a contract for contact is arranged. This can be reviewed monthly. The original Launceston team is the only one currently offering support to acute hospital patients. One team is using trainee psychologists to befriend drivers seen to be at fault in accidents. Teams without a paid co-ordinator can use a roster of volunteers to clear calls for the service on a message-bank telephone system.

RTST has attempted to utilise resources from the community, in the form of sponsorship, involvement of university academics and students and research grants, in furthering the aims of the organisation. For example, business students have written a business plan, and occupational therapy students are preparing a brochure for general practitioners outlining the post-traumatic symptoms that can be experienced after accidents. The Honda Foundation provided a vehicle for two years and North Ltd has provided paper for use by the RTST. Local service clubs have also pro-vided sponsorship. Government grants have also been obtained. RTST is using these for the planning and documentation of a befriender training programme and the development of a rural trauma support programme. Another proposal aims to develop peer support teams in secondary and tertiary education institutions for helping other young people injured in accidents.

Unfortunately, as the RTST is a relatively new organisation with mini-mal financial resources, there has been limited recording of detailed sta-tistics or evaluation. This is an area targeted for improvement. A computer record-keeping system has been devised and an evaluation of the Launces-ton team is underway.

CHALLENGES FOR ROAD TRAUMA SUPPORT TEAMS

As with any new voluntary organisation the RTST has faced challenges, and it is due largely to the vision, persistence and ongoing work of the founder and the members that so much has been achieved. In the current economic climate where government agencies have cut back staff and services, the demand for volunteers is high and some teams have had difficulty gaining and maintaining adequate membership to provide the desired service. Some members joined teams initially with a strong desire to be directly involved in providing support to accident victims and lost interest as initial groundwork had to be done in setting up administrative structures and procedures. This resulted in frustration and their leaving the team. Other teams have had difficulties with members who had some expertise in the area of road trauma but had personal agendas to control the direction of the group or use it as a source of referrals for their own practice. Many volunteers are very busy people, and despite their best intentions have not always been able to do things that they promised, resulting in frustration for others. Fortunately these have been relatively rare occurrences and are far outweighed by the positive contribution of professionals and communities.

Fund raising has been a continuing challenge. There is an increasing demand for funds by community groups and many members dislike fund raising or do not feel they have expertise beyond cake stalls and selling raffle tickets. Lack of money limits the service of some teams. In view of this, RTSTs need to make decisions about practical priorities and direction, find suitable venues for committee or support group meetings, deal with matters such as legal incorporation and insurance cover, and publicise the team's existence and its service and network with local medical, allied health and emergency services personnel, accident insurers, community support groups, and transport and road safety authorities. Limited availability of members' time has also restricted travel to state committee meetings. Teleconferences are being considered as an alternative. If there is no paid co-ordinator to organise volunteers, a roster of contact people to facilitate the matching of volunteers and clients on an after hours basis may also be complex, especially if there are minimal funds for telephone redirection or message banks. Each team must decide on its priorities and procedures within the context of its own and community resources.

The RTST lies somewhere between a self-help group and a voluntary organisation. Though founded by a road accident victim, some volunteers have not been in accidents. They may nevertheless have a great deal to offer and find their involvement a rewarding experience. The success of the RTST is difficult to measure objectively at present, but anecdotal feedback has been very positive. In the first three years of operation the part-time counsellor in Launceston, a regional city (population 68,000), saw over 1,000 clients. While voluntary support and self-help groups cannot replace professional counselling, they are able to benefit many people who are ineligible for transport insurance, cannot afford private counsellors or who would prefer less 'official' health care systems. The RTST also has 24-hour availability in the hospital in Launceston for relatives of seriously injured people, a service normally not available. As the service becomes more widespread and more widely recognised, the greater public awareness of symptoms of road trauma may lead to earlier detection and treatment. The breadth of service offered by RTSTs in one-to-one counselling, befrienders, crisis carers, support groups, public education and research and training renders RTST a valuable resource for anyone needing emotional support following an accident. This was reflected in the award to RTST of an *Advance Australia Award for Community Service* in 1994.

This chapter has outlined the organisation and purposes of a typical, and successful, self-help group, which also depends on volunteer support. The benefits of self-help groups and the challenges that they face are outlined and can be used to guide the formation of other such groups. This chapter also provides an insight for other professionals as to the potential value of such groups. In conclusion, people with similar experience have something very significant to offer fellow-survivors, and the quality of that support may be quite different from that available from professionals, or from people who have not had that experience. A phrase which can make a survivor feel extremely isolated is the well-intentioned 'I know how you feel', when perhaps the speaker doesn't: A main benefit of self-help groups is their shared experience. As Moore (1991: 89) recounts:

> In all these things my experiences were somewhat different. And yet beneath it all I felt a bond of understanding with the most basic feelings of that huge number of Australians whose bodies have been damaged and whose emotions have been torn on the roads. I knew in my heart my experience was united with theirs.

Chapter 18

Psychological services for road accident victims and their relatives

Gwen Adshead

One purpose of this book is to remind the reader that road traffic accidents are disasters for those involved. This chapter will examine the psychological services provided for the victims of large-scale disasters, and attempt to place services for the survivors of road traffic accidents and their relatives in that context. Although large-scale transport disasters remain comparatively rare events, the last decade has seen an increase in the number of major incidents affecting the UK. Alth ough there is as yet no definitive evidence that post-traumatic psychological interventions prevent the onset of psychological morbidity (see Chapter 13), there is ample evidence that survivors of small and large-scale disasters find such interventions helpful. Where trauma victims do develop post-traumatic psychiatric illness, there is good evidence that such illness is treatable, especially if the disorder is not allowed to become chronic. There is thus a rationale for providing some sort of psychological support to survivors of disasters.

BACKGROUND

The impact of large-scale disasters is now well recognised. Such disasters cause an enormous range of psychosocial morbidity, whose impact on mental health services and the community has been recognised increasingly over the last fifty years. The disorders caused by severe traumas include anxiety, phobic states, depression and post-traumatic stress disorder (PTSD). There have been no British epidemiological studies researching the level of PTSD within the community, but an American study has shown a lifetime prevalence of 1.3 per cent for the disorder (Davidson et al. 1991). However, there is general evidence available which shows that between 40 and 70 per cent of of those directly involved in a catastrophe will experience psychological distress and impairment during the first month following the incident (Raphael 1986). After one year, this will have dropped to between 25 and 40 per cent, although between 15 and 20 per cent will experience chronic levels of anxiety which will remain high for periods of longer than two years. Six months following the release of hostages just prior to the Gulf war in 1991, 25 per cent of male subjects studied required further help for continued psychological disturbance (Easton and Turner 1991). Populations particularly at risk are the poor, minority groups, children and the elderly.

There is evidence that post-traumatic disorder may persist in a minority of survivors. A twelve-year follow-up of survivors of the Buffalo Creek disaster showed that the level of PTSD fell from 44 per cent in 1974 to 28 per cent in 1986 (Green et al. 1990a). Three-quarters of the population improved while less than 10 per cent worsened. This latter group developed PTSD and other disorders during the follow-up period, suggesting that post-traumatic stress can have delayed onset. There is also evidence that professionals fail to recognise and diagnose post-traumatic disorders (Davidson and Smith 1990).

Most research has focused on survivors of large-scale disasters, and the literature on the post-traumatic psychological sequelae of road accidents is comparatively small. The research is reviewed elsewhere in this volume by Mayou and others (see Chapter 3). One point of interest which is relevant here is the definition of the stressor (Criterion A). In DSM-III-R, Criterion A stated that a diagnosis of PTSD could not be made *unless* the person had suffered a trauma 'outside the range of usual human experience' (American Psychiatric Association 1987). This definition caused some debate (e.g. Breslau and Davies 1987) because the research on the psychological sequelae of accidents made it clear that even quite common events could produce severe psychological morbidity. Criterion A has now changed to take account of this (American Psychiatric Association 1994). However, it would be fair to say that there remains a public perception that road accidents are less troubling than large-scale transport accidents, and barely qualifying for the term 'disaster'.

DEFINITIONS OF DISASTERS

This public perception of road accidents as minor trauma may be detected in organisational plans for dealing with disasters. Within the UK there is no acceptable definition of a disaster, with variations even between government departments (Home Office 1992). In fact there are more than forty different definitions of disaster in the literature (Korver 1987). To add to the problem, there is insufficient research data available to evaluate differing responses to different types of disaster. However, it has been suggested that man-made trauma, such as war, crime, terrorism or mechanical failure, is likely to produce more psychological shock in man than a natural disaster and so increase the likelihood of psychological sequelae (Fisher and Reason 1988). Road traffic accidents may be large or small in scale, varying from two cars in a minor collision to a major pile-up on a motorway, resulting in many fatalities. Current emergency planning might only be activated in certain circumstances, after the ambulance services has declared a major incident. However, Accident and Emergency staff report that they frequently deal with serious road accidents, involving at least one death or serious injury, which would not qualify as a major incident. In such circumstances, it is possible for the psychological needs of the survivor and relatives to be overlooked, especially if the survivor requires intensive or long-term physical treatment. Even if the accident is defined as a major incident, it still may not be viewed as a 'psychological' disaster, in the same way as the Lockerbie bombing or the Clapham rail disaster.

THE TRAUMATIC STRESS PROJECT STUDY

In England, health authority major incident plans contain the organisational structure for providing medical care after a major incident. The Traumatic Stress Project carried out a study for the Department of Health through the Department of Forensic Psychiatry at the Institute of Psychiatry, under the directorship of Professor John Gunn (Adshead et al. 1994a) which was aimed at examining the extent to which English regional health authorities had made provision for *psychological* needs in their post-disaster planning. We anticipated that, despite a wealth of published research on the prevalence and likely severity of post-disaster psychiatric morbidity, there would be little evidence of planning for the provision of psychological support and care. Such planning might be highly relevant to the care of survivors and families affected by road accidents.

Under this project, a letter was sent to what were then the English Regional Public Health Departments, asking for information about the psychological care element within their major incident plans. All these requests were passed to the relevant Regional Health Emergency Planning Officers, and if the response provided inadequate or no information, personal contact was made. In addition, semi-structured interviews were carried out with professionals in the field, such as psychiatrists, psychologists and social workers. Interviews were also held with senior police officers, fire and rescue personnel and local authority emergency planning officers. The researchers were also invited to attend planning meetings in two regions as observers.

The study found that the provision for psychosocial care following a disaster in England is extremely variable, and although there are undoubtedly local areas of interest and expertise, it appears that there is, in reality, no provision in some regions. Where there was evidence of planning, the scope is often limited, and there may be no evidence of planning for the implied costs (such as training of staff). Our conclusions were that firm and centralised clinical and organisational guidelines need to be set in this area, and we argued for the provision of regional units which could provide clinical service for survivors and families of victims of large- and small-scale disasters, train volunteers and professionals, and also facilitate research.

IMPLICATIONS

The traditional focus of the major incident plans has been the physical needs of disaster victims, and psychological needs have traditionally been almost ignored. This raises the question of the quality and scope of major incident health plans. Confusion may arise between health authority major incident planning and local authority post-disaster planning. Local authority plans typically focus on the provision of amenities, but some also plan to offer support to survivors, their relatives and the community. There is therefore scope for some confusion between health authority plans (which may fail to address the needs of those victims who do not use health services) and local authority plans (which may miss those survivors and their families who are admitted to hospital). In addition, local authorities and health authorities may have different expectations of what psychological support should be offered, based on their differing experiences of different client groups. Finally, psychological support after disasters may be provided by other groups, such as religious bodies and voluntary agencies, all of whom may have their own equivalents of major incident plans. The existence of multiple sources of support may help to explain why psychological support after disasters may be fragmented and uneven in application.

In 1990, the Department of Health (1990) convened a working party looking at the optimal provision of psychological support after disasters, which published its report, *Disasters: Coping for a Caring Response* (Allen 1991). This made several recommendations for improving psychological supports, including placing the responsibility for the organisation and co-ordination of social and psychological support with each local authority Director of Social Services. However, if services are mainly provided by local authority social services, there is danger that those with chronic psychological disability who may need specialist service will be overlooked. Such plans may also overlook the needs of those who live outside the borough boundaries and cannot easily gain access to help provided by the borough in which the disaster occurs. For example, many of the survivors of the Clapham disaster did not live in the relevant social services borough. Local authority plans may not address the need for staff debriefing which staff value, even though its efficacy remains unproved (Dyregrov 1989).

Concepts of clinical standards are intermeshed with practice issues. Disasters are high-profile events which can confer organisations with political and therapeutic power. This 'power' can be reinforced by a failure to disseminate skills and information between organisations. At meetings attended by the researchers, there was evidence of this interagency failure in communication. This is particularly problematic for the care of the psychological needs of disaster survivors, who may present a range of needs, not all of which can be met by one agency. For example, after a serious road accident, a psychological support plan would need to provide for hospitalised survivors, non-injured survivors, bereaved relatives, non-bereaved relatives, emergency personnel and Accident and Emergen cy staff. Some of these needs might be best dealt with by social services, some by health care workers, and some by community agencies such as medical general practitiners or clergy.

In Britain, the complexities of providing psychological support after a disaster needs also to be seen within the recent reforms within the National Health Service. 'GP fund holders' are able to purchase outpatient mental health services, but are unlikely to do so for road accident survivors unless they are aware of the need. Although, in theory, general psychiatric and psychological services should be able to provide such care, in practice many general psychiatric services are comparatively ignorant about the treatment of post-traumatic disorders. There are some specialist clinics for the treatment of PTSD, but only two are NHS services. Psychiatric services may also be inappropriate for patients, especially as psychiatric outpatient services are dominated by the needs of psychotic patients.

Another financial issue is the costs involved in providing psychological care after a major incident, and the drain of these resources from more frequent but smaller incidents. For instance, the cost to the local authority of running the *Herald Assistance Unit* for fifteen months following the *Herald of Free Enterprise* sinking at Zeebrugge in 1987 was £320,000 (Hodgkinson and Stewart 1991). In a health context, one-quarter of the psychotherapy budget was used in treating survivors after the Hungerford massacre (an incident in which a 27-year-old man shot and killed fifteen people), two years after the incident (Jane Knowles, head of West Berkshire Psychotherapy Service, personal communication).

THE ROLE OF MENTAL HEALTH CARE PROFESSIONALS

The role of mental health services and social services in relation to road accident survivors and victims' families should be to provide a flexible comprehensive service which can be augmented at fairly short notice after both 'minor' and 'major' disaster. Psychological interventions may be classified at four levels. *Primary* interventions are those aimed at preventing future morbidity: for example, critical incident debriefing, crisis intervention, staff debriefing. They will be *secondary* when responses are provided by existing services for established need: for example, supportive therapy and medication from GPs, referral to general psychiatry and psychology, support from the voluntary sector such as CRUSE. Interventions will be *tertiary* when specialist services are required because the patient has special needs, or because secondary services lack the training and skills to provide for victims.

There may also be groups who have special needs. Children who have been exposed to traumatic stress may need specialised services, which liaise with schools (Yule 1992). Survivors with head injury, permanent disability or cosmetic injuries (such as burns) may require extended care tailored to their special needs. The needs of staff and emergency personnel also have to be considered. There can be difficulties for staff in obtaining services, which are sometimes related to a 'macho' culture within the uniformed services and sometimes to problems of ease of access. In such circumstances, it may be important to involve uniformed personnel in the delivery of support and care.

Different types of work can be done by different health care staff. Consultants need to be informed about the organisation of the psychosocial response in their area, and it should be part of the major incident plan. Awareness of the psychological needs of road accident survivors should be increased in Accident and Emergency departments, and it may be helpful if there are one or two identified nursing staff whose job it is to address the psychological needs of both patients and staff. Junior medical and nursing staff can be taught to enquire about past histories of psychiatric illness – a factor which has been shown to be a risk factor for PTSD (Smith et al. 1990).

RESEARCH AND TRAINING

There is an urgent need for both research and training in these activities, which cannot be organised properly while psychological support is seen only in terms of responses to major large-scale public disasters. Social workers, health care professionals and lawyers need to be educated about post-traumatic stress, its natural history and prognosis. Health care managers also need to be educated about the cost of providing appropriate services, given the frequency of road accidents, and the potential use of psychological services that could be made.

Research requirements are most obvious in relation to chronicity and long-term health needs following road accidents. However, there is also an urgent need for research into protective factors after trauma, as well as evaluation of therapeutic interventions. The cost to the community and the health service of post-traumatic stress after road accidents can only be guessed at, but it must be considerable, given that serious road accidents are common, and traumatic stress not only gives rise to formal psychiatric syndromes such as depression and PTSD, but also causes increases in substance abuse, interpersonal violence and sick leave. Research is especially required into the efficacy of proactive interventions in preventing these types of problems.

It appears that the general level of knowledge about post-traumatic psychological disorders could be improved. Psychiatry and psychology have a role to play in the teaching of staff, including GPs. It is likely that GPs will see the majority of people who suffer from post-traumatic stress, and how they are handled at GP level may well affect their recovery (Mitchell 1993). Early adequate intervention at GP level may prevent repeated psychiatric clinic visits later, and more work is needed to evaluate this. Most road accident survivors and their families can be managed by community services, and probably only a minority will have to seek specialist help from psychiatry or psychology. For those who do, it would be easier to provide specialist services if there were existing specialist clinics which co-ordinate local responses to a disaster, and which could offer experience in dealing with acute and chronic traumatic stress.

Acknowledgements   This chapter is based on previous work carried out by the Traumatic Stress Project, Institute of Psychiatry.

Chapter 19

Social psychological aspects of motorcycling safety

Derek Rutter

In 1993, the most recent year for which official statistics are available at the time of writing, more than 3,800 people were killed on British roads. More than 1,750 of them were car drivers and their passengers (46 per cent), against 'only' 427 motorcyclists and their passengers (11 per cent), yet the number of cars registered in Great Britain was over thirty times the number of motorcycles. When average distance travelled is taken into account, motorcycles were more than six times more likely than cars to be involved in an accident and motorcyclists were over thirty-six times more likely to be killed or seriously injured than car drivers. In collisions between a motorcycle and a car, the probability of death or serious injury was over forty times greater for those on the motorcycle than those in the car. Almost 40 per cent of deaths and serious injuries among motorcyclists were to riders aged 24 or less (Department of Transport 1994).

In this chapter we ask whether social psychology can contribute to a theoretical understanding of motorcycling accidents and safety. Two main approaches are identified in the existing literature (Chesham et al. 1993). The first, prevalent in the 1970s, was based on accident analysis, and the main objective was to identify and control factors that contribute to the *severity* of motorcycling accidents. The main concerns were to reduce head and brain injuries through safety helmets, to reduce multivehicle collisions through daytime use of headlamps, and to reduce drink-riding. The second approach, which dominated the 1980s, focused on what might be called 'riding analysis', that is, analysis of the *process* of motorcycle riding. Particular attention was paid to skills testing, training evaluation, and perceived risk. More recently, a third approach is developing, with a new emphasis on the rider as 'active agent'. Theoretical models from *social* psychology are being applied, based on beliefs and attitudes, and an attempt is being made to predict riding behaviour and so accident involvement. It is to this latest tradition that our own research belongs, and we shall draw extensively from our findings in the remainder of the chapter. Three main issues will be addressed: do riders' beliefs about motorcycling safety predict accident-related behaviour; is the high rate of casualties among young riders the product of youth or inexperience; and do our findings have implications for policy and practice?

The new tradition of research, the rider as active agent, is not yet well developed and little has been published so far (Rutter et al. 1993). Moreover, there are two main weaknesses in the existing literature. First, no attempt has been made to examine the issues systematically, by means of established theoretical models or accepted ways of conceptualising beliefs and attitudes; and second, none of the research has been prospective, which means that, since beliefs and behaviour have been measured at the same time, it is impossible either to make genuine *predictions* of behaviour or to avoid the contamination of beliefs by behaviour.

The purpose of our own research, which is based on a national survey of motorcyclists, has been to address both issues. First, the design was *prospective*: the principal dependent measure, accident-related behaviour, was predicted from beliefs and attitudes measured twelve months earlier. Second, the structure of our measures and analyses was guided by established theoretical models: the Theory of Reasoned Action (Fishbein and Ajzen 1975) and its extension, the Theory of Planned Behaviour (Ajzen 1988); and the Health Belief Model (Rosenstock 1966; Janz and Becker 1984). Both approaches have already been used with some success in understanding road user behaviour: wearing seat belts (Wittenbraker et al. 1983; Budd et al. 1984; Nelson and Moffit 1988; Sutton and Hallett 1989; Stasson and Fishbein, 1990), using car seats and restraints for children (Webb et al. 1988; Gielen et al. 1984), avoiding drink-driving (Åberg 1994), and wearing cycle helmets (Arnold and Quine 1994).

PREDICTING ACCIDENT-RELATED BEHAVIOUR

The first stage of our research, an analysis of accident-related behaviour, was reported in Rutter et al. (1993, 1995). Some 4,000 riders from a random sample of registered motorcycle keepers in Great Britain were asked to complete two postal questionnaires a year apart. The first measured their beliefs about safe riding and elicited details of current behaviour and past accidents. There were five sections: 'Safe Riding', which examined beliefs; 'You and Your Bike', covering the characteristics of the machine, the respondent's riding career, and current behaviour; 'Spills and Accidents', asking for details of mishaps on the road in the preceding twelve months; 'Bikes and Biking', a test of knowledge about riding and the road; and 'Some Details about You', a set of demographic questions about age, education, and other social inputs. For half the subjects the belief questions were based on the Theory of Reasoned Action, and for the other half they were based on the Health Belief Model. The Reasoned Action items covered behavioural beliefs and normative beliefs about safe riding, while the Health Beliefs items were concerned with perceived vulnerability to accidents, the perceived severity of their likely consequences, and the perceived benefits and barriers associated with safe riding.

A year later, the second questionnaire was sent out, this time the same for both groups of respondents, and it asked about two main factors: current behaviour; and spills and accidents in the twelve months since the first questionnaire. At Time 1, completed questionnaires were received from 64 per cent of respondents and 7 per cent who were no longer riding, a total of 71 per cent. A year later, 62 per cent of subjects who had replied at Time 1 completed the Time 2 questionnaire, and 24 per cent who were no longer riding, producing a total of 86 per cent.

In the twelve months to Time 2, 13.6 per cent of the sample had at least one spill or accident, and the first issue that concerned us was whether they differed demographically from respondents who were accident free. Table 19.1 presents the results. Young, inexperienced, trained riders were more likely to have had accidents than those who were older, more experienced, and untrained, while riders with formal educational qualifications were more likely to have had accidents than those without – probably reflecting age and experience and perhaps training too. There were no effects for sex of rider or size of machine. The second question we addressed was whether accident involvement might be associated with particular behaviours. Mean values for the twelve behaviours we included,

Table 19.1 Accidents in twelve months to Time 2 by demography

		% reporting accident	chi^2
Age at Time 1	Up to 19	32.6	30.4***
	20 – 29	13.4	
	30 – 59	12.3	
	60 plus	9.2	
Experience at Time 1	Up to 2 years	25.4	28.4***
	3 years	29.1	
	4 years	14.3	
	5 – 9 years	12.7	
	10 years plus	11.5	
Training	Trained	18.1	8.2**
	Untrained	12.1	
Education	No qualifications	10.0	13.3**
	Up to O level	16.9	
	A level	9.9	
	Technical	16.7	
	Degree	13.5	

Note: N = 1,466, of whom 197 (13.6%) reported one or more accidents or spills. There were no effects for sex or machine size.
**p < 0.01;   ***p < 0.001.

Table 19.2 Accidents in twelve months to Time 2 by mean behaviour

	Time 1 Behaviour			Time 2 Behaviour		
	Accidents	No accidents	t	Accidents	No accidents	t
Maintenance	3.7	3.7	0.7	4.0	4.0	0.1
Speeding	2.8	2.4	4.0 ***	2.9	2.5	4.4 ***
Wearing helmet	5.0	4.9	1.3	5.0	5.0	0.1
Drink-riding	1.3	1.2	1.0	1.3	1.2	0.6
Breaking traffic laws	2.3	2.0	3.8 ***	2.4	2.0	4.3 ***
Using daytime headlamp	3.5	3.3	1.9	3.7	3.5	2.2 *
Doing as taught	3.3	3.4	0.3	3.8	3.8	0.5
Breaking Highway Code	2.3	2.1	3.1 **	2.3	2.1	2.0
Wearing bright clothing	2.7	2.8	0.7	2.6	2.8	1.7
Riding too close	2.1	1.8	4.5 ***	2.1	1.9	2.7 **
Showing consideration	4.1	4.2	0.6	4.2	4.3	1.3
Losing concentration	1.9	1.8	2.6 **	2.0	1.8	2.8 **

Note: * $p < 0.05$;   ** $p < 0.01$;   *** $p < 0.001$.

and their relationship with accident history, are shown in Table 19.2. Time 1 speeding, breaking traffic laws, breaking the Highway Code, riding too close, and losing concentration all revealed significant differences between riders who reported accidents and those who did not, and the pattern was much the same for Time 2 behaviour. Principal components analysis at Time 1 confirmed that the behaviours belonged together in one factor, which we named Breaking Law and Rules. Breaking Law and Rules proved to be much the best behavioural predictor of accident involvement, and the remainder of our analyses therefore went on to examine whether it could itself be predicted, from demographic variables and from beliefs.

The most useful way to present the findings is through path analysis, and the results are given in Figures 19.1 and 19.2. In the Reasoned Action data, both age and sex led directly to behaviour and were also mediated, age by beliefs about obeying the law and rules of safe riding, sex by beliefs about taking care: young people were more likely to have negative beliefs about obeying the law and rules of safe riding, and women were more likely to have positive beliefs about taking care. Education also led indirectly to behaviour, through beliefs about taking care. In the Health Beliefs data, age and sex again produced both direct and mediated paths, while experience and training led to behaviour directly. What the findings thus demonstrated was that beliefs did lead to accident-related behaviour, but that their main role was to *mediate* demographic inputs such as age, education and sex. That is, much of the effect of age and the other demographic variables occurred *through* beliefs, so that older people had different beliefs from younger people, for example, and it was those differences in beliefs that in large part produced the differences in behaviour.

From the first stage of our work we were able to draw the following

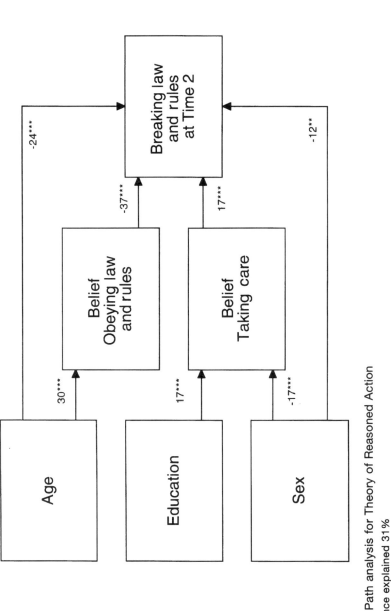

Figure 19.1 Path analysis for Theory of Reasoned Action

Notes: Variance explained 31%
Standardised beta weights are shown without decimal points
** p < 0.01
*** p < 0.001

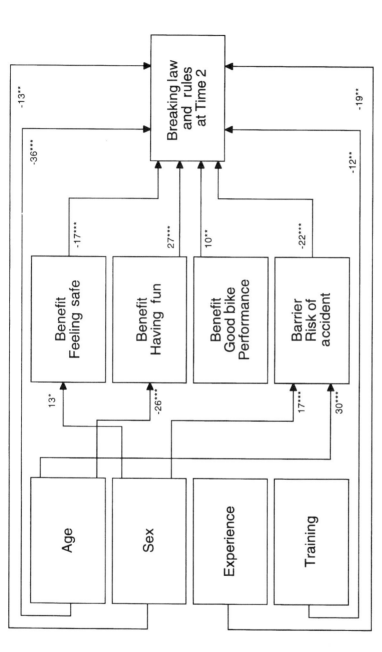

Figure 19.2 Path analysis for Health Belief Model

Notes: Variance explained 44%
    Standardised beta weights are shown without decimal points
    * p < 0.05
    ** p < 0.01
    *** p < 0.001

conclusions. The main predictor of accident involvement was a behavioural factor we named Breaking Law and Rules, and beliefs predicted it successfully, whether conceptualised according to the Theory of Reasoned Action or according to the Health Belief Model. All the significant predictors were expectancy-value beliefs – behavioural beliefs in the Theory of Reasoned Action, and perceived benefits and barriers in the Health Belief Model. Normative beliefs played no part; and perceived vulnerability, which did predict behaviour when beliefs were examined alone, dropped out when demographic measures were added, indicating that its effect was absorbed by one or other of the demographic variables. The most important beliefs were to do with behavioural 'violations' rather than 'errors or lapses', as Parker et al. (1992 a, b) and Reason et al. (1990) have found in their work on car driving. Accidents were predicted by behaviour, behaviour was predicted by beliefs, and beliefs were predicted by demography. The main role of beliefs was to mediate the link between demography and outcome.

AGE AND EXPERIENCE

The objective of the second stage of our work was to consider whether the apparent effects of age in the accident statistics, and in our own analysis of accident-related behaviour, are genuinely attributable to age or whether they may be the product of inexperience. Although young riders sometimes have experience off road, for the majority of motorcyclists, age and experience are confounded. Despite the theoretical and practical significance of the issue, little if any attempt has been made in past research to disaggregate the variables. What was needed was a further examination of the data we had collected for the first stage of the project.

Our first new analysis examined whether accidents at Time 2 were associated with age and experience at Time 1. Riders' ages were broken down into three categories – up to 19, 20 to 24, and 25 and over; and so was experience – up to 2 years, 3 years, and 4 years or more. The youngest group had consistently high rates of accidents, averaging 32.8 per cent, against 16.9 per cent for riders aged 20 to 24 and 11.7 per cent for riders aged 25 or over. In all three experience categories, as Table 19.3 shows, the youngest group had higher rates of accidents than the oldest group, and the clearest pattern of all emerged for the experienced group: accidents were three times more common in the youngest group than the oldest group, with the intermediate group close to the oldest. The association between age and casualty rates therefore appears *not* to be an effect of experience: young people have accidents because they are young, not because they lack experience. The question then was why.

The first part of the answer came from our analysis of behaviour. For all twelve of the behaviours we had identified in the first part of our work, analyses of variance were carried out, with three levels of age and three

Table 19.3 Accidents in twelve months to Time 2 by age and experience at Time 1

	Up to 19		20-24		25 plus		chi²
	N	%	N	%	N	%	
Up to 2 years' experience							
Accidents	9	30.0	2	22.2	1	8.3	
No accidents	21	70.0	7	77.7	11	91.7	2.2
3 years' experience							
Accidents	8	34.8	7	36.8	4	16.0	
No accidents	15	65.2	12	63.2	21	84.0	3.0
4 years' or more experience							
Accidents	7	35.0	13	12.7	123	11.5	
No accidents	13	65.0	89	87.3	943	88.5	10.3**

Note: ** $p < 0.01$

levels of experience. The results are given in Table 19.4, and there are three points to note: all but four of the measures revealed a significant difference between age groups, and the four that belonged to Breaking Law and Rules were the most reliable; there was only one effect of experience; and four of the measures produced significant interactions between age and experience, though with no clear pattern. Overwhelmingly, therefore, age was the major source of variance, and the very behaviours we knew were associated with accidents were the most reliable discriminators between the groups. In general, the young and intermediate groups were similar and reported frequent 'unsafe' behaviours, while the group aged 25 and over reported a much higher frequency of 'safe' behaviours.

The second part of the answer to why youth is associated with accidents came from the path analyses presented earlier. In the Reasoned Action data, age led directly to behaviour, but was also mediated – by beliefs about obeying the law and rules of safe riding. Thus younger riders behaved less safely than older riders, through both a direct effect and a negative belief about obeying the law and rules of safe riding. In the Health Beliefs data, age again produced both direct and mediated paths, mediation this time occurring through three factors: belief in the benefits of feeling safe and having fun, but also in the costs of risking an accident. There was thus good evidence from both models that the relationships between age and experience on the one hand and unsafe behaviour on the other were mediated by beliefs, as the first stage of our work had indicated, though direct effects were revealed too. Youth brings particular beliefs, which lead to a willingness to break the law and violate the rules of safe riding, which in turn produces accidents.

Table 19.4 Time 2 behaviours by Time 1 age and experience

	Age			Experience			Age F Ratio	Experience F Ratio	Age x Experience F Ratio
	Up to 19 Mean	20 to 24 Mean	25 plus Mean	Up to 2 yrs Mean	3 yrs Mean	4 yrs plus Mean			
Maintenance	4.0	4.1	4.0	3.9	4.1	4.0	0.6	0.6	2.5*
Speeding	3.5	3.4	2.6	3.0	3.2	2.7	42.5***	1.3	4.1**
Wearing helmet	5.0	5.0	5.0	4.9	5.0	5.0	0.1	0.6	2.6*
Drink-riding	1.3	1.3	1.3	1.2	1.3	1.3	0.1	0.7	1.5
Breaking traffic laws	2.7	2.7	2.1	2.5	2.5	2.1	22.9***	0.2	0.8
Using daytime headlamp	4.1	3.8	3.5	4.0	3.9	3.5	3.8*	0.3	1.3
Doing as taught	3.6	3.5	3.8	3.8	3.6	3.8	3.2*	0.2	0.8
Breaking Highway Code	2.7	2.6	2.2	2.5	2.6	2.2	14.6***	0.8	1.3
Wearing bright clothing	2.1	2.3	2.8	2.8	2.4	2.7	14.2***	4.2*	0.9
Riding too close	2.3	2.3	1.9	2.1	2.1	2.0	12.8***	0.5	1.5
Showing consideration	4.1	4.2	4.3	4.3	4.1	4.3	4.4*	1.1	2.7*
Losing concentration	1.8	1.9	1.8	2.0	1.9	1.8	0.6	1.0	1.8

Note: * p < 0.05 ** p < 0.01 *** p < 0.001 .

IMPLICATIONS FOR POLICY AND PRACTICE: TRAINING

From the second stage of our work we were able to conclude that youth played a much greater role than inexperience in accident involvement. Moreover, the accident-related behaviour we had identified already was particularly common among young riders and was underpinned by beliefs. What mattered to us now was to explore the implications of the findings for policy and practice, and the most immediate appeared to us to concern training. In the United Kingdom, as in many other countries, government-accredited training is mandatory for new motorcyclists, the majority of whom are young. Typically, however, training programmes are skills based, and little attention is paid to what might be called the 'cognitive underpinnings' of those skills: *why* particular behaviours are important, what are the likely *consequences* of unsafe riding, *why* training matters, and so on. It is well known that casualty rates among formally trained riders are higher than among those who are untrained (Jonah and Dawson 1979; Jonah et al. 1981, 1982; Mortimer 1984, 1988; McDavid et al. 1989; Rutter et al. 1993), and our findings suggest that the failure of courses to teach what is needed may well be one explanation (Chesham et al. 1992, 1993). Only when a proper set of underpinning beliefs and perceptions is provided for behaviour will skills be turned into safety.

The objective of the third and final stage of our work was to design a programme of training that would be based on the findings and arguments we have outlined in the previous sections of the chapter. To guide the programme, we made use of one of the 'dual process' models of persuasion (Eagly 1992; Eagly and Chaiken 1993), the Elaboration Likelihood Model (Petty and Cacioppo 1986a and 1986b). According to Petty and Cacioppo, there are two routes to persuasion, the 'peripheral' route and the 'central' route. To steer people into the peripheral route it is necessary only to excite their interest briefly, perhaps by a short emotional appeal. There will be an immediate and measurable impact on beliefs and even behaviour, but probably no longer-term effect. For effects that last, people must be steered into the 'central' route, in which they will be encouraged to *think* about the information they are given and to *elaborate* the arguments for themselves. Typically, the arguments will be presented as personally relevant, and every attempt will be made to involve the recipients and encourage them to participate in the debate. The procedure takes longer than 'peripheral' persuasion – and will not succeed if the recipients of the message lack the ability or motivation to process information systematically – but we reasoned that it would offer the greater likelihood of building the cognitive underpinnings we sought.

From the earlier stages of our work we knew that the key beliefs we should attack were those that led to the behavioural violations we had called Breaking Law and Rules: particularly beliefs about speeding, close following, and breaking traffic laws. In the first phase of our training programme, novice riders attending their first session are asked to 'list as many reasons as you can think of why some motorcyclists always . . . keep to the speed limit', and so on. For each belief item they are then shown a short video recording to illustrate the significance of the behaviour. For example, for the item about speeding, they see a rider travelling at different speeds, and they are shown how long it takes to stop. They then discuss the reasons they first produced for keeping to the speed limit, and after the discussion they list as many 'issue relevant' thoughts as they can for each of the arguments they have considered. The number and quality of the thoughts are taken to indicate the effect the procedure has had on the subject's cognitive structure.

Our preliminary results are promising. We have been able to demonstrate that most people *are* able to process relevant information systematically and that the training procedure *does* produce an increase in listed thoughts in a way that is consistent with developing cognitive structure. As yet, however, we do not know how long the effects will last, nor whether they will produce a significant impact on behaviour and safety. For that, we must await further data.

References

Åberg, L. (1994) Relations among variables influencing drivers' intentions to drive after drinking, in D.R. Rutter and L. Quine (eds.), *Social Psychology and Health: European Perspectives*, Aldershot: Avebury, 89–100.

Adams, J.H. (1992) Head injury, in J.H. Adams and L.W. Duchen (eds), *Greenfield's Neuropathology* (5th edn), London: Edward Arnold, 106–152.

—— Graham, D.I., Gennarelli, T.A., and Maxwell, W.L. (1991) Diffuse axonal injury in non-missile head injury, *Journal of Neurology, Neurosurgery, and Psychiatry*, 54: 481–483

Adshead, G. (1994) Psycho-social aspects of disaster: planning for the future. Conference at the Institute of Psychiatry, de Crespigny Park, London. February.

—— Canterbury, R. and Rose, S. (1994a) *Current Provision for the Management of Psycho-Social Morbidity Following Disaster in England*, London: The Institute of Psychiatry Traumatic Stress Project.

—— —— —— (1994b) Current provision and recommendations for the management of psychosocial morbidity following disaster in England, *Criminal Behaviour and Mental Health*, 4: 181–208.

Ajzen, I. (1988) *Attitudes, Personality and Behaviour*, Milton Keynes: Open University Press.

Allen, A.J. (1991) *Disasters: Coping for a Caring Response*, London: HMSO.

Altman, D.G. and Bland, J.M. (1995) Absence of evidence is not evidence of absence, *British Medical Journal*, 311: 485.

Alves, W.M., Colohan, A.R., O'Leary, T.J., Rimel, R.W., and Jane, J.A. (1986) Understanding post-traumatic symptoms after minor head injury, *Journal of Head Trauma Rehabilitation*, 1: 1–12.

—— Macciocchi, S.N., and Barth, J.T. (1993) Postconcussive symptoms after uncomplicated mild head injury, *Journal of Head Trauma Rehabilitation*, 8: 48–59.

American Psychiatric Association (1980) *Diagnostic and Statistical Manual of Mental Disorders* (DSM-III), Washington, DC: American Psychiatric Press.

—— (1987) *Diagnostic and Statistical Manual of Mental Disorders* (DSM-IIIR), Washington, DC: American Psychiatric Press.

—— (1994) *Diagnostic and Statistical Manual of Mental Disorders* (DSM-IV), Washington, DC: American Psychiatric Press.

Andreasen, N. (1995) Posttraumatic stress disorder: psychology, biology and the Manichaean warfare between false dichotomies, *American Journal of Psychiatry*, 152 (7): 963–965.

Arnold, L. and Quine, L. (1994) Predicting helmet use among schoolboy cyclists: an application of the Health Belief Model, in D.R. Rutter and L. Quine (eds),

Social Psychology and Health: European Perspectives, Aldershot: Avebury, 101–130.

ASHOG (1977) *Association of Self Help Organisations and Groups: An Outline*, Sydney: New South Wales Council of Social Service.

Association for the Advancement of Automotive Medicine (1990) *The Abbreviated Injury Scale*, Des Plaines, IL: AAAM.

Auerbach, A.H., Schefflen, N.A., and Scholz, C.K. (1967) A questionnaire survey of the posttraumatic syndrome, *Diseases of the Nervous System*, 28: 110–112.

Baker, S.P., O'Neill, B., Haddon, W. and Long, W.B. (1974) The injury severity score: a method for describing patients with multiple injuries and evaluating emergency care, *Journal of Trauma*, 14: 187–196.

Balla, J. I. (1982) The late whiplash syndrome: a study of an illness in Australia and Singapore, *Cultural Medicine and Psychiatry*, 6: 191–210.

Barth, J.T., Alves, W.M., Ryan, T.V., Macciocchi, S.N., Rimel, R.W., Jane, J.A. and Nelson, W.E. (1989) Mild head injury in sports: neuropsychological sequelae and recovery of function, in H.S. Levin, H.M. Eisenberg and A.L. Benton (eds), *Mild Head Injury*, New York: Oxford University Press, 257–275.

Bartone, P.T., Ursano, R.J., Wright, K.M. and Ingraham, L.H. (1989) The impact of a military air disaster on the health of assistance workers, *J. Nervous and Mental Disease*, 177: 317–328.

Beck, A., Ward, C., Mendelson, M., Mock, J., and Erbaugh, J., (1961). An inventory for measuring depression, *Archives of General Psychiatry*, 4: 561–571.

—— Rush, A. J., Shaw, B. F., and Emery, G. (1979) *Cognitive Therapy of Depression*, New York: Guilford Press.

Berry, D.T.R., Wetter, M.W., Baer, R.A., Youngjohn, J.R., Gass, C.S., Lamb, D.G., Franzen, M.D., MacInnes, W.D. and Buchholz, D. (1995) Overreporting of closed-head injury symptoms on the MMPI-2, *Psychological Assessment*, 7: 517–523.

Binder, L.M. (1986) Persisting symptoms after mild head injury: a review of the postconcussive syndrome, *Journal of Clinical and Experimental Neuropsychology*, 8: 323–346.

—— (1990) Malingering following minor head trauma, *The Clinical Neuropsychologist*, 4: 25–36.

—— (1992) Malingering detected by forced choice testing of memory and tactile sensation: a case report, *Archives of Clinical Neuropsychology*, 7: 155–163.

—— (1993) Assessment of malingering after mild head trauma with the Portland Digit Recognition Test, *Journal of Clinical and Experimental Neuropsychology*, 15: 170–182.

—— (1994) Psychogenic mechanisms of prolonged autobiographical retrograde amnesia, *The Clinical Neuropsychologist*, 8: 439–450.

—— and Rohling, M.L. (in press). Money matters: A meta-analytic review of the effects of financial incentives on recovery after closed head injury, *American Journal of Psychiatry*.

—— and Willis, S.C. (1991) Assessment of motivation after financially compensable minor head trauma, *Psychological Assessment: A Journal of Consulting and Clinical Psychology*, 3: 175–181.

Birleson, P. (1981) The validity of depressive disorder in children and the development of a self-rating scale for depressive disorder in childhood (Depression Self-rating Scale), *Journal of Child Psychology and Psychiatry*, 21: 83–88.

Bisson, J.I. and Deahl, M.P. (1994) Psychological debriefing and prevention of post-traumatic stress: more research is needed, *British Journal of Psychiatry*, 165: 717–720.

—— Jenkins, P.L. and Bannister, C. (1996) A randomised controlled trial of psychological debriefing for victims of acute burn trauma, *Psychosomatic Medicine*.

Blake, D., Weathers, F., Nagy, L., Kaloupek, D., Klauminzere, G., Charney, D. and Keane, T. (1990) *Clinician Administered PTSD Scale* (CAPS), Boston, MA: National Center for Post-Traumatic Stress Disorder, Behavioral Science Division.

Blanchard, E.B., Hickling, E.J., Taylor, A.E., Loos, W.R. and Gerardi, R. J. (1994a) Psychological morbidity associated with motor vehicle accidents, *Behaviour Research and Therapy*, 32 (3): 283–290.

—— —— —— —— (1994b) The psychophysiology of motor vehicle related post-traumatic stress disorder, *Behavior Therapy*, 25: 453–467.

—— —— Mitnick, N., Taylor, A.E., Loos, W.R. and Buckley, T.C. (1995a) The impact of severity of physical injury and perception of life threat in the development of post-traumatic stress disorder in motor vehicle accident victims, *Behaviour Research and Therapy*, 33: 529–534.

—— —— Taylor, A. E., and Loos, W. R. (1995b) Psychiatric morbidity associated with motor vehicle accidents, *Journal of Nervous and Mental Disease*, 183: 495–504.

—— —— Taylor, A.E., Loos, W.R., Forneris, C.A. and Jaccard, J. (in press) Who develops PTSD from motor vehicle accidents? *Behavioural Research Therapy*.

—— —— Vollmer, A.J., Loos, W.R., Buckley, T.C. and Jaccard, J. (1995) Short-term follow-up of post-traumatic stress symptoms in motor vehicle accident victims, *Behaviour Research and Therapy*, 33 (3): 369–377.

Blumbergs, P.C., Scott, G., Manavis, J., Wainwright, H., Simpson, D.A. and Mclean, A.J. (1994) Staining of amyloid precursor protein to study axonal damage in mild head-injury, *Lancet*, 344: 1055–1056.

Bordow, S. and Porritt, D. (1979) An experimental evaluation of crisis intervention, *Social Science and Medicine*, 13: 251–256.

Brende, O.B. (1993) A 12-step recovery program for victims of traumatic events, in J.P. Wilson and B. Raphael (eds), *International Handbook of Traumatic Stress Syndromes*, New York: Plenum Press, 867–877.

Breslau, N. and Davies, G. (1987) PTSD: The stressor criterion, *Journal of Nervous and Mental Disease,* 175: 255–264.

—— and Davis, G.C. (1992) Post-traumatic stress disorder in an urban population of young adults: risk factors for chronicity, *American Journal of Psychiatry*, 149: 671–675.

—— Davis, G.C., Andreski, P. and Peterson, E. (1991) Traumatic events and post-traumatic stress disorder in an urban population of young adults, *Archives of General Psychiatry*, 48: 216–222.

Brewer, R.D., Morris, P.D., Cole, T.B., Watkins, S., Patetta, M.J. and Popkin, C. (1994) The risk of dying in alcohol-related automobile crashes among habitual drunk drivers, *New England Journal of Medicine*, 331 (8): 513–517.

Broadbent, D.E., Cooper, P.F., FitzGerald, P. and Parkes, K.R. (1982) The cognitive failures questionnaire (CFQ) and its correlates, *British Journal of Clinical Psychology*, 21: 1–16.

Brodrick Committee (1971) *Report of the Committee on Death Certification and Coroners*, Cmnd. 4810, London: HMSO.

Brom, D., Kleber, R.J. and Hofman, M.C. (1993) Victims of traffic accidents: Incidence and prevention of post-traumatic stress disorder, *Journal of Clinical Psychology*, 49 (2): 131–140.

Broughton, J. (1990) *Trends in drink / driving revealed by recent road accident data*, Transport and Road Research Laboratory Research Report 266, Crowthorne, Berkshire, England.

Bryant, B., Mayou, R. and Lloyd-Bostock, S. (in press) Compensation claims following road accidents: a six-year follow-up study, *Medicine, Science and the Law*.

Bryant, R.A. and Harvey, A.G. (1995a) Acute stress-response: a comparison of head-injured and non-head injured patients, *Psychological Medicine*, 25: 869–873.

—— —— (1995b) Avoidant coping style and post-traumatic stress following motor vehicle accidents, *Behavioural Research Therapy*, 33 (6): 631–635.

Budd, R.J., North, D. and Spencer, C. (1984) Understanding seat belt use: a test of Bentler and Speckart's extension of the 'theory of reasoned action', *European Journal of Social Psychology*, 14: 69–78.

Bull, J.P. (1985) Disabilities caused by road traffic accidents and their relation to severity scores, *Accident Analysis and Prevention*, 17: 387–397.

Bureau of Transport and Communications Economics, (1992) *Social Cost of Transport Accidents in Australia*, Canberra: Australian Government Publishing Service, ch. 3.

—— (1994) *Costs of road crashes in Australia–1993*, Information Sheet 4, Canberra: Australian Government Publishing Service.

Burke, J.M., Imhoff, C.L. and Kerrigan, J.M. (1990) MMPI correlates among post-acute TBI patients, *Brain Injury*, 4: 223–231.

Burman, S.B., Genn, H.G. and Lyons, J. (1977) Pilot study of the use of legal services by victims of accidents in the home, *Modern Law Review*, 40: 47.

Burstein, A. (1989) Post-traumatic stress disorder in victims of motor vehicle accidents, *Hospital and Community Psychiatry*, 40: 295.

Butcher, J.N., Dahlstrom, W.G., Graham, J.R., Tellegen, A. and Kaemmer, B. (1989) *Manual for Administration and Scoring the Minnesota Multiphasic Personality Inventory–2*, Minneapolis: University of Minnesota Press.

Cane, P. (1987) *Atiyah's Accidents Compensation and the Law*, London: Weidenfeld and Nicolson.

Canterbury, R., Yule, W. and Glucksman, E. (1993) PTSD in child survivors of road traffic accidents. Paper presented to the Third European Conference on Traumatic Stress, Bergen.

Cardena, E., Classen, C. and Speigel, D. (1991) *Stanford Acute Stress Questionnaire*, Stanford, CA: Department of Psychiatry and Behavioural Sciences, Stanford University.

Chesham, D.J., Rutter, D.R. and Quine, L. (1992) From theory to practice in the design of safety training: promoting habitual accident avoidance by novice motorcyclists, In G.B. Grayson (ed.), *Behavioural Research in Road Safety II*, Crowthorne, Berkshire: Transport and Road Research Laboratory, 108–116.

—— —— —— (1993) Motor cycling safety research: a review of the social and behavioural literature, *Social Science and Medicine*, 373: 419–429.

Cicerone, K.D. and Kalmar, K. (1995) Persistent post-concussive syndrome: structure of subjective complaints after mild traumatic brain injury, *Journal of Head Trauma Rehabilitation*, 10: 1–18.

Coolican, M., Vassar, E., and Grogan, J. (1989) Helping survivors survive, *Nursing*, August, 52–57.

Creamer, M., Burgess, P., Buckingham, W. and Pattison, P. (1989) *The psychological aftermath of the Queen Street shootings*, Technical Report, Department of Psychology, University of Melbourne, Australia.

Davidson, J. and Smith R. (1990) Traumatic experiences in psychiatric outpatients, *Journal of Traumatic Stress*, 3: 459–474.

——— Hughes D., Blazer D. and George L. (1991) Post-traumatic stress disorder in the community: An epidemiological study, *Psychological Medicine*, 21: 713–721.

Deahl, M.P., Gillham, A.B., Thomas, J., Searle, M.M. and Srinivasan, M. (1994) Psychological sequelae following the Gulf war: factors associated with subsequent morbidity and the effectiveness of psychological debriefing, *British Journal of Psychiatry*, 165: 60–65.

Deans, G.T., Magalliard, J. N., Kerr, M. and Rutherford, W.H. (1987) Neck sprain – a major cause of disability following car accidents', *Injury*, 18: 10–12.

Demi, A.S. and Miles, M.S. (1983) Understanding psychological reactions to disaster, *Journal of Emergency Nursing*, 9: 11–16.

Department of Health (1990) *Emergency Planning in the NHS: Health Services Arrangements for Dealing with Major Incidents*, HC (90) NHS, London: HMSO.

Department of Transport (1994) *Road Accidents Great Britain 1993: The Casualty Report*, London: HMSO.

Derogatis, L.R. and Melisaratos, N. (1983) The Brief Symptom Inventory: an introductory report, *Psychological Medicine*,13: 595–605.

Dickenson, D. and Johnson, M. (1993) *Death, Dying and Bereavement*, London: Sage.

Dikmen, S.S., McLean, A. and Temkin, N.R. (1986) Neuropsychological and psychosocial consequences of minor head injury, *Journal of Neurology, Neurosurgery, and Psychiatry*, 49: 1227–1232.

——— Ross, B.L., Machammer, J.E. and Temkin, N.R. (1995) One year psychosocial outcome in head injury, *Journal of the International Neuropsychological Society*, 1: 67–77.

Duckworth, D.H. (1990) *The Nature and Effects of Incidents which Induce Trauma in Police Officers*, London: Police Research Group, Home Office.

Dunning, C. (1990) Mitigating the impact of work trauma: administrative issues concerning intervention, in J.T. Reese, J.M. Horn and C. Dunning (eds), *Critical Incidents in Policing*, Washington, DC: FBI.

Dyregrov, A. (1989) Caring for helpers in disaster situations: psychological debriefing, *Disaster Management*, 2 (1): 25–30.

Eagly, A.H. (1992) Uneven progress: social psychology and the study of attitudes, *Journal of Personality and Social Psychology*, 63: 693–710.

——— and Chaiken, S. (1993) *The Psychology of Attitudes*, New York: Harcourt, Brace and Jovanovich.

Easterbrook, J.A. (1959) The effect of emotion on cue utilisation and the organisation of behaviour, *Psychological Review*, 66: 183–201.

Eaton, J.A. and Turner, S.W. (1991) Detention of British citizens as hostages in the Gulf – health, psychological consequences, *British Medical Journal* 303: 1231–1234.

Edwards, J.G. (1995) Depression, antidepressants and accidents. Pharmacological concerns need epidemiological elucidation, *British Medical Journal*, 311: 887–888.

Ehrenzweig, A. (1953) A Psychoanalysis of Negligence, *Northwestern University Law Review*, 40: 855.

Eisenberg, H.M. and Levin, H.S. (1989) Computed tomography and magnetic resonance imaging in mild to moderate head injury, in H.S. Levin, H.M. Eisenberg and A.L. Benton (eds), *Mild Head Injury*, New York: Oxford University Press, 133–141.

Fahrenberg, J., Hampel, R. and Selg, H. (1984) *Das Freiburger Persönlichkeitsinventar (FPI)*, Göttingen: Dr. C.J. Hogrefe.

Farbman, A.A. (1973) Neck sprain: associated factors, *Journal of American Medical Association*, 223: 1010–1015.

Faust, E., Hart, K., Guilmette, T.J. and Arkes, H.R. (1988a) Neuropsychologists' capacity to detect adolescent malingerers, *Professional Psychology: Research and Practice*, 14: 508–545.

—— —— —— (1988b) Pediatric malingering: the capacity of children to fake believable deficits on neuropsychological testing, *Journal of Consulting and Clinical Psychology*, 56: 578–582.

Fee, C.R.A. and Rutherford, W.H. (1988) A study of the effect of legal settlement on post-concussion symptoms, *Archives of Emergency Medicine*, 5: 12–17.

Feinstein, A. (1993) A prospective study of victims of physical trauma, in Raphael, R. and Wilson, J. (eds.), *The International Handbook of Traumatic Stress Syndromes*, New York: Plenum Press.

—— and Dolan, R. (1991) Predictors of post-traumatic stress disorder following physical trauma: an examination of the stressor criterion, *Psychological Medicine*, 21: 85–91.

Fishbein, M. and Ajzen, I. (1975) *Belief, Attitude, Intention and Behaviour: An Introduction to Theory and Research*, Reading, MA: Addison-Wesley.

Fisher, S. and Reason, J. (1988) *Handbook of Life Stress Cognition and Health*, New York: Wiley.

Foa, E.B. and Kozak, N.J. (1986) Emotional processing of fear: exposure to corrected information, *Psychological Bulletin*, 99: 20–35.

—— Riggs, D.S. and Gershuny, B.S. (1995) Arousal, numbing and intrusion: symptom structure of PTSD following assault, *American Journal of Psychiatry*, 152: 116–120.

—— Steketee, G. and Rothbaum, B.O. (1989) Behavioral/cognitive conceptualizations of post-traumatic stress disorder, *Behavior Therapy*, 20: 155–176.

Fordyce, D.J., Roueche, J.R. and Prigatano, G.P. (1983) Enhanced emotional reactions in chronic head trauma patients, *Journal of Neurology, Neurosurgery, and Psychiatry*, 146: 620–624.

Fox, D.D. (1994) Normative problems for the Wechsler Memory Scale-Revised Logical Memory Test when used in litigation, *Archives of Clinical Neuropsychology*, 9: 211–214.

—— Lees-Haley, P.R., Earnest, K. and Dolezal-Wood, S. (1995) Base rates of post-concussive symptoms in health maintenance organization patients, *Neuropsychology*, 9: 427–434.

Foy, D.W., Carroll, E.M. and Donahoe, C.P. (1987) Etiological factors in the development of PTSD in clinical samples of Vietnam combat veterans, *Journal of Clinical Psychology*, 43 (1): 17–27.

Frankowski, R.F. (1986) The demography of head injury in the United States, in M.E. Miner and K.A. Wagner (eds), *Neurotrauma: Treatment, Rehabilitation, and Related Issues,* Boston: Butterworths.

Frederick, C.J. and Pynoos, R.S. (1988) *The Child Post-Traumatic Stress Disorder (PTSD) Reaction Index,* University of California: Los Angeles.

Galanter, M. (1974) Why the haves come out ahead: speculation on the limits of legal change, *Law and Society Review*, 9.

Gass, C.S. and Russell, E.W. (1991) MMPI profiles of closed head trauma patients: impact of neurologic complaints, *Journal of Clinical Psychology*, 47: 253–260.

Genn, H. (1987) Hard bargaining: out of court settlement, in *Personal Injury Action,* Milton Keynes: Open University Press.

Genn, H. (1994) Personal injury compensation: how much is enough? A study of the compensation experiences of victims of personal injury, Law Commission Report No. 225, London: HMSO.

Gersons, B.P.R. and Carlier, I.V.E. (1990) *PTSD and the police: Scope of the issue*. Paper presented at the Second European Conference on PTSD, Utrecht, Holland.

Gibbs, H.M. (1989) Factors in the victim that mediate between disaster and psychopathology: a review, *Journal of Traumatic Stress*, 2: 489–514.

Gielen, A.C., Ericksen, M.P., Daltoy, L.H. and Rost, K. (1984) Factors associated with the use of child restraint devices, *Health Education Quarterly*, 11: 195–206.

Gloag, D. (1993) Europe needs more road safety, *British Medical Journal*, 306, 165.

Gordon, R. and Wraith, R. (1993) Responses of children and adolescents to disaster, in J.P. Wilson and B. Raphael (eds), *International Handbook of Traumatic Stress Syndromes,* New York: Plenum Press, 561–575.

Gouvier, W.D., Uddo-Crane, M., and Brown, L.M. (1988) Base rates of post-concussional symptoms, *Archives of Clinical Neuropsychology*, 3: 273–278.

Green, B.L. Grace, M.C. and Glesser, G.C. (1985) Identifying survivors at risk, *Journal of Consulting and Clinical Psychology*, 53: 672–678.

—— —— and Lindy, J.D. (1990a) Buffalo-Creek survivors in the second decade: stability of symptoms stress, *American Journal of Orthopsychiatry 1990*, 60: 43–54.

—— —— —— Glesser, G.C. and Leonard, A. (1990b) Risk factors for PTSD and other diagnoses in a general sample of Vietnam veterans, *American Journal of Psychiatry*, 147 (6): 729–733.

Green, J. (1992) The medico-legal production of fatal accidents, *Sociology of Health and Illness*, 14 (3): 373–389.

Green, M.M., McFarlane, A.C., Hunter, C.E., and Griggs, W.M. (1993) Undiagnosed post-traumatic stess disorder following motor vehicle accidents, *Medical Journal of Australia*, 159: 529–534.

Greiffenstein, M.F., Baker, J. and Gola, T. (1994) Validation of malingered amnesia measures with a large clinical sample, *Psychological Assessment*, 6: 218–224.

—— —— —— (1995) MMPI–2 validity scales versus domain specific measures in detection of factitious traumatic brain injury, *The Clinical Neuropsychologist*, 9: 230–240.

Gronwall, D. (1977) Paced Auditory Serial Addition Task: a measure of recovery from concussion, *Perceptual and Motor Skills*, 4: 367–373.

—— and Wrightson, P. (1974) Delayed recovery of intellectual function after minor head injury, *Lancet*, 2: 605–609.

—— —— and Waddell, P. (1990) *Head Injury: The Facts*, Oxford: Oxford University Press.

Guilmette, T.J., Hart, K.J. and Giuliano, A.J. (1993) Malingering detection: the use of a forced-choice method in identifying organic versus stimulated memory impairment, *The Clinical Neuropsychologist*, 7: 59–69.

Harris, D.R., Maclean, M., Genn, H., Lloyd-Bostock, S., Fenn, P., Corfield, P. and Brittan, Y. (1984) *Compensation and Support for Illness and Injury*, Oxford: Oxford University Press.

Hathaway, S.R., and McKinley, J.C. (1989) *The Minnesota Multiphasic Personality Inventory–2*. Minneapolis: University of Minnesota Press.

Heaton, R.K., Smith, H.H., Lehman, R. and Vogt, A.T. (1978) Prospects of faking believable deficits on neuropsychological testing, *Journal of Consulting and Clinical Psychology*, 46: 892–900.

Heptinstall, E. (1996) *Healing the Hidden Hurt*, London: Child Accident Prevention Trust.

Hetherington, A. (1992) *Human resource management in times of stress*, London: Home Office, Police Research Group.

—— (1993) Traumatic stress on the roads, *Journal of Social Behavior and Personality*, 8 (5): 369–378.

—— (1994) Stress and hardiness in accident and emergency personnel and road traffic patrol officers, unpublished PhD, Cranfield University.

Hickling, E.J. and Blanchard, E.B. (1992) Post-traumatic stress disorder and motor vehicle accidents, *Journal of Anxiety Disorders*, 6: 285–291.

—— Sison, G.F.P. and Vanderploeg, K.D. (1986) The treatment of post-traumatic stess disorder with biofeedback and relaxation training, *Biofeedback and Self-Regulation*, 11: 125–134.

Hirsch, S.A., Hirsh, P.J., Hiramoto, H. and Weiss, A. (1988) Whiplash syndrome: fact or fiction? *Orthopaedic Clinic of North America* 19: 791–795.

Hodge, J.R. (1971) Whiplash neurosis, *Psychosomatics*, 12: 245–249.

Hodgkinson, P.E. and Stewart, M. (1991) *Coping With Catastrophe: A Handbook of Disaster Management*, London: Routledge.

Hodgkinson, P.E. and Shepherd, M.A. (1994) The impact of disaster support work, *Journal of Traumatic Stress*, 7: 587–600.

Holmes, D. 91993) Breaking bad news, *Police Magazine*, November, 22.

Home Office (1992) *Dealing With Disaster,* London: HMSO.

Hopmeyer, E. and Werk, A. (1994) A comparative study of family bereavement groups, *Death Studies*, 18 (3): 243–256.

Horne, D.J. de L. (1993) Traumatic stress reactions to motor vehicle accidents, in J.P. Wilson and B. Raphael (eds), *The International Handbook of Traumatic Stress Syndromes*, New York: Plenum Press, 499–506.

—— (1994) The psychology of working with victims of traumatic accidents, in R. Watts and D.J. de L. Horne (eds), *Coping with Trauma: The Victim and the Helper*, Brisbane, Australia: Australian Academic Press, 85–99.

—— (1995) Detection and assessment of PTSD by health and legal professions, *Psychiatry, Psychology and the Law*, 2: 65–73.

Horne, J.A. and Reyner, L.A. (1995) Sleep related vehicle accidents, *British Medical Journal*, 310: 565–567.

Horowitz, M.J. (1976) *Stress Response Syndromes*, New York: Jason Aronson.

—— Wilmer, N. and Alvarez, N.W. (1979) Impact of events scale: a measure of subjective stress, *Psychosomatic Medicine*, 41: 209–218.

—— —— Kaltreider, N. and Alvarez, N.W. (1980) Signs and symptons of post traumatic stress disorder, *Archives of General Psychiatry*, 37: 85–92.

Howarth, G. (1996) *Last Rites: The Work of the Modern Funeral Director*, Amityville, NY: Baywood.

Hugenholtz, H., Stuss, D.T. Stethem, L.L. and Richard, M.T. (1988) How long does it take to recover from a mild concussion? *Neurosurgery*, 22: 853–858.

Igoe, P. (1992) The work of the road trauma support team. Paper delivered at the Australian Critical Incident Stress Association Conference, Sydney.

Illingworth, C.M. (1979) 227 road accidents to children, *Acta Paediatrica Scandinavia*, 68: 869–873.

Jacobson, R.R. (1995) The post-concussional syndrome: physiogenesis, psychogenesis and malingering: an integrative model, *Journal of Psychosomatic Research*, 39: 675–693.

Janz, N.K. and Becker, M.H. (1984) The Health Belief Model: a decade later, *Health Education Quarterly*, 11: 1–47.

Jaworowski, S. (1992) Traffic accident injuries of children: the need for prospective studies of psychiatric sequelae, *Israeli Journal of Psychiatry and Related Sciences*, 29 (3): 174–184.

Jennett, B. and Bond, M.R. (1975) Assessment of outcome after severe brain damage: a practical scale, *Lancet*, 2: 81–84.

Jonah, B.A. and Dawson, N.E. (1979) Validation of the motorcycle operator skill test, *Accident Analysis and Prevention*, 11: 163–171.

—— —— and Bragg, B.W.E. (1981) Predicting accident involvement with the motorcycle operator skill test, *Accident Analysis and Prevention*, 13: 307–318.

—— —— —— (1982) Are formally trained motorcyclists safer? *Accident Analysis and Prevention*, 14: 247–55.

Kay, T. (1992) Neuropsychological diagnosis: disentangling the multiple determinants of functional disability after mild traumatic brain injury, in L.J. Horn and N.D. Zasler (eds), *Rehabilitation of Post-Concussive Disorders*, Philadelphia: Hanely and Belfus, 109–128.

Keane, T.N., Malloy, P.F. and Fairbank, J.A. (1984) Empirical development of an MMPI sub-scale for the assessment of combat related post-traumatic stress disorder, *Journal of Consulting and Clinical Psychology*, 52: 888–889.

—— Zimering, R.T. and Caddell, J.N. (1985) A behavioral formulation of post-traumatic stress disorder in Vietnam veterans, *The Behavior Therapist*, 8: 9–12.

Kearney, J. (1991) The role of self help groups: challenging the system and complementing professionals, *Health Issues*, 28 September, 29–31.

Keller, M.B., Lavori, P.W., Friedman, B., Nielsen, E., Endicott, J., McDonald-Scott, P. and Andreasen, N.C. (1987) A longitudinal interval follow-up evaluation: a comprehensive method for assessing outcome and prospective longitudinal studies, *Archives of General Psychiatry*, 44: 540–548.

Kellner, R. and Sheffield, B.F. (1973) The one-week prevalence of symptoms in neurotic patients and normals, *American Journal of Psychiatry*, 130: 102–105.

Kessler, R.C., Sonnega, A., Bromet, E., and Nelson, C.B. (in press) Posttraumatic stress disorder in the National Comorbidity Survey.

Kobasa, S.C. (1979) Stressful life events, personality and health: an inquiry into hardiness, *Journal of Personality and Social Psychology*, 37: 1–11.

Koopman, C., Classen, C., Cardena, E. and Spiegel, D. (1995) When disaster strikes, acute stress disorder may follow, *Journal of Traumatic Stress*, 8: 29–46.

Korver, A.J.H. (1987) What is a Disaster? *Hospital and Disaster Medicine*, 2: 152–153.

Kroes, W.H. (1976) *Society's Victim – the Policeman – an Analysis of Job Stress in Policing*, Springfield, IL: Charles C. Thomas.

Kuch, K., Swinson, R.P. and Kirby, M. (1985) Post-traumatic stress disorder after car accidents, *Canadian Journal of Psychiatry*, 30: 426–427.

—— Cox, B.J., Evans, R. and Shulman, I. (1994) Phobias, panic and pain in fifty five survivors of road vehicle accidents, *Journal of Anxiety Disorders*, 8 (2): 181–187.

Lees-Haley, P.R. (1992) Efficacy of MMPI-2 validity scales and MCMI-II modifier scales for detecting spurious PTSD claims: F, F-K, Fake-Bad Scale, Ego Strength, Subtle-Obvious subscales, DIS, and DEB, *Journal of Clinical Psychology*, 48: 681–688.

—— and Brown, R.S. (1993) Neuropsychological complaint base rates of 170 personal injury claimants, *Archives of Clinical Neuropsychology*, 8: 203–209.

Leininger, B.E. and Kreutzer, J.S. (1992) Neuropsychological outcome of adults with mild traumatic brain injury: implications for clinical practice and research, in L.J. Horn and N.D. Zasler (eds), *Rehabilitation of post-concussive disorders*, Philadelphia: Hanely and Belfus, 169–182.

—— —— and Hill, M.R. (1991) Comparison of minor and severe head injury emotional sequelae using the MMPI, *Brain Injury*, 5: 199–205.

Leiter, M. (1991) Coping patterns as predictors of burnout: the function of control and escapist coping patterns, *Journal of Organisational Behaviour*, 12: 123–144.

Levin, H.S., Mattis, S., Ruff, R.M., Eisenberg, H.M., Marshall, L.F., Tabaddor, K., High, W.M. and Frankowski, R.F. (1987) Neurobehavioral outcome following minor head injury: a three-center study, *Journal of Neurosurgery*, 66: 234–243.

Lewis, R. (1993) The merits of a structured settlement: the plaintiff's perspective, *Oxford Journal of Legal Studies*, 13: 530.

Lezak, M.D. (1983) *Neuropsychological Assessment* (2nd edn), New York: Oxford University Press.

Linden, A.M. (1977) *Canadian Negligence Law*, vol. 2, Toronto: Butterworth.

Lindemann, E. (1944) Symptomatology and management of acute grief, *American Journal of Psychiatry*, 101: 141–148.

Linet, M.S., Stewart, W.F., Celentano, D.D., Ziegler, D. and Sprecher, M. (1989) An epidemiologic study of headache among adolescents and young adults, *Journal of American Medical Association*, 261: 2211–2216.

Lishman, W.A. (1988) Physiogenesis and psychogenesis in the 'post-concussional syndrome', *British Journal of Psychiatry*, 153: 460–469.

Litz, B.T. (1992) Emotional numbing in combat-related post-traumatic stress disorder: a critical review and reformulation, *Clinical Psychology Review*, 12: 417–432.

Lloyd-Bostock, S. (1979a) Commonsense morality and accident compensation, in D.P. Farrington, K. Hawkins and S. Lloyd-Bostock (eds), *Psychology, Law and Legal Processes*, London: Macmillan.

—— (1979b) The ordinary man and the psychology of attributing cause and responsibility, *Modern Law Review*, 2: 143–168.

—— (1991) Propensity to sue in England and the United States of America: the role of attribution processes, a comment on Kritzer, *Journal of Law and Society*, 18 (4): 429–430.

McCaffrey, R.J. and Fairbank, J.A. (1985) Behavioural assessment and treatment of accident-related postraumatic stress disorder: two case studies, *Behavior Therapy*, 16: 406–416.

McCann, I.L. and Pearlman, L. (1990) *Psychological Trauma and the Adult Survivor: Theory, Therapy and Transformation*, New York: Brunner/Mazel.

McCormack, H.M., Horne, D.J. de L. and Sheather, S. (1988) Clinical applications of visual analogue scales: a critical review, *Psychological Medicine*, 18: 1007–1019.

McDavid, J.C. Lohrmann, B.A. and Lohrmann, G. (1989) Does motorcycle training reduce accidents? Evidence from a longitudinal quasi-experimental study, *Journal of Safety Research*, 20: 61–72.

McFarlane, A.C. (1988) The longitudinal course of PTSD: the range of outcomes and predictors, *Journal of Nervous and Mental Disease*, 176: 30–90.

McKinlay, W.W. and Gray, J. (1992) Assessment of the severely head injured, in J.R. Crawford, D.M. Parker and W.W. McKinlay (eds), *A Handbook of Neuropsychological Assessment*, Hove: Lawrence Erlbaum, 363–378.

—— Brooks, D.N., Bond, M.R., Martinage, D.P. and Marshall, M. (1981) The short-term outcome of severe blunt head injury as reported by relatives of the injured persons, *Journal of Neurology, Neurosurgery, and Psychiatry*, 44: 527–533.

McMillan, T.M. (1991) Post-traumatic stress disorder and severe head injury, *British Journal of Psychiatry*, 159: 431–433.

McMordie, W.R. (1988) Twenty-year follow-up of the prevailing opinion on the posttraumatic or postconcussional syndrome, *The Clinincal Neuropsychologist*, 2: 198–212.

Maimaris, C., Barnes, M.R. and Allen, M.J. (1988) Whiplash injuries of the neck: a retrospective study, *Injury*, 19: 393–396.

Malt, U.F. and Olafsen, O.M. (1992) Psychological appraisal and emotional response to physical injury: a clinical phenomenological study of 109 adults, *Psychiatric Medicine*, 10 (3): 117–134.

—— Karlchagen, S., Hoff, H., Herstromer, U., Hildingson, K., Tibell, E. and Leymann, H. (1993) The effect of major railway accidents on the psychological health of train drivers–I: acute psychological responses to accidents, *Journal of Psychosomatic Research*, 37 (8): 793–805.

Matthews, P. and Foreman, J. (1993) *Jervis on the Office and Duties of Coroners* (11th edn), London: Sweet and Maxwell.

Maycock, G., Lockwood, C.R. and Lester, J.F. (1991) The Accident Liability of Car Drivers, Transport and Road Research Laboratory Research Report 315, Crowthorne, Berkshire, England.

Mayou, R.A. (1992) Psychiatric aspects of road traffic accidents, *International Review of Psychiatry*, 4: 45–54.

—— (1995) Medico-legal aspects of road traffic accidents, *Journal of Psychosomatic Research*, 39: 789–798.

—— (1996) Accident neurosis revisited, *British Journal of Psychiatry*, 168: 399–403.

—— and Bryant, B.M. (1994) Effects of road traffic accidents on travel, *Injury*, 25: 457–460.

—— —— and Duthie, R. (1993) Psychiatric consequences of road traffic accidents, *British Medical Journal*, 307: 647–651.

—— —— (1995) Alcohol and road traffic accidents, *Alcohol and Alcoholism*, 30: 709–711.

—— and Radanov, B.P. (1996) Whiplash neck injury, *Journal of Psychosomatic Research* 40: 461–474.

—— and Sharpe, M. (1995) Psychiatric illnesses associated with physical disease, *Balliere's Clinical Psychiatry*, 1: 2.

—— Simkin, S. and Thelfall, J. (1991) Effects of road traffic accidents on driving behaviour, *Injury*, 22: 365–368.

Meichenbaum, D. (1974) *Cognitive behavior modification*, Morristown, NJ: General Learning Press.

—— (1977) *Cognitive Behavior Modification: An Integrative Approach*, New York: Plenum Press.

Miller, H. (1961) Accident neurosis, *British Medical Journal*, 1: 919.

—— (1966) Mental sequelae of head injury, *Proceedings of the Royal Society of Medicine*, 59: 257–261.

—— and Cartlidge, N. (1972) Simulation and malingering after injuries to the brain and spinal cord, *Lancet*, 1: 445–452.

Millis, S.R. (1992) Recognition memory test in the detection of malingered and exaggerated memory deficits, *The Clinical Neuropsychologist*, 6: 406–414.

Milner, B. (1971) Interhemispheric differences in the localization of psychological processes in man, *British Medical Bulletin*, 27: 272–277.

Misch, P., Phillips, M., Evans, P. and Berelowitz, M. (1993) Trauma in pre-school children: a clinical account, in G. Forrest (ed.), *Trauma and Crisis Management*.

Mitchell, J.T. (1983) When disaster strikes: the critical incident debriefing process, *Journal of the Emergency Medical Services*, 8: 36–39.

—— (1985) Healing the helper, in B. Green (ed.), *Role Stressors and Supports for Emergency Workers*, Washington, DC: Center for Mental Health Studies of Emergencies, US Department of Health and Human Services.

—— and Bray, G.P. (1990) *Emergency Services Stress*, Englewood Cliffs, NJ: Prentice Hall.

Mitchell, M. (1991a) Lay and professional perceptions of 'delayed' recovery, paper delivered at the British Association for the Advancement of Science Annual Conference, Swansea.

—— (1991b) Putting it to rest: individuals and organisations cope with disaster, *Disaster Management*, 3 (4): 183–186.

—— (1992) Lay perceptions of post-traumatic stress disorder, *Proceedings of the International Society of Traumatic Stress Studies* Conference, Amsterdam.

—— (1993) The role of the general practitioner in the aftermath of the Lockerbie Disaster, in T. Newburn (ed.), *Working with Disaster: Social Welfare Interventions During and After Tragedy*, London: Longman.

—— (1995) Facing violence: assessing the training and support requirements for police constables in Scotland, unpublished report, Edinburgh: Scottish Office.

—— McLay, D., Boddy, J. and Cecchi, L. (1991) The police response to the Lockerbie Disaster, *Disaster Management*, 3 (4): 198–205.

—— Munro, A. and Thomson, D. (1996a) *Exposing Police Probationers to Incidents of Sudden Death*, London: Police Research Group, Home Office.

—— Carroll, L., Cowan, M. and Morrison, S. (1996b) *The Investigative Image: The Work of the Scenes of Crime Officer*, Glasgow: Glasgow Caledonian University, Police Research Unit.

Mittenberg, W., DiGiulio, D.V., Perrin, S. and Bass, A.E. (1992) Symptoms following mild head injury: expectation as aetiology, *Journal of Neurology, Neurosurgery, and Psychiatry*, 55: 200–204.

Moore, T. (1991) *Cry of the Damaged Man: A Personal Journey of Recovery*, Sydney: Picador.

Mortimer, R.G. (1984) Evaluation of the motorcycle rider course, *Accident Analysis and Prevention*, 16: 63–71.

—— (1988) A further evaluation of the motorcycle rider course, *Journal of Safety Research*, 19: 187–196.

Mowrer, O.H. (1947) On the dual nature of learning: the reinterpretation of 'conditioning' and 'problem solving', *Harvard Educational Review*, 17: 102–148.

Munjack, D.J. (1984) The onset of driving phobias, *Behavior Therapy and Experimental Psychiatry*, 15: 305–308.

Murray-Parkes, C. (1990) Planning for the aftermath of disasters. Paper presented in a symposium on Psychiatric Aspects of Disaster, Royal Society of Medicine, Psychiatry Section, London, UK.

Napier, M. and Wheat, K. (1995) *Recovering Damages for Psychiatric Injury*, London: Blackstone Press.

National Highway Traffic Safety Administration (1992) *Traffic Safety Facts*, Washington, DC: US Department of Transportation.

Nelson, G.D. and Moffit, P.B. (1988) Safety belt promotion: theory and practice, *Accident Analysis and Prevention*, 20: 27–38.

Newton, R. (1989) *The Incidents of Stress Reactions in Individual Operational Police Officers to Line of Duty Crisis*, London: HMSO.

Norris, F.H. (1992) Epidemiology of trauma: frequency and impact of different potentially traumatic events on different demographic groups, *Journal of Consulting and Clinical Psychology*, 60 (3): 409–418.

Norris, S.H. and Watt, I. (1983) The prognosis of neck injuries resulting from rear-end vehicle collisons, *Journal of Bone and Joint Surgery*, 65B: 608–611.

Novack, T.A., Daniel, M.S., and Long, C.J. (1984) Factors relating to emotional adjustment following head injury, *International Journal of Clinical Neuropsychology*, 6: 139–142.

O'Brien, L.S. and Hughes, S.J. (1991) Symptoms of post-traumatic stress disorder in Falklands veterans five years after the conflict, *British Journal of Psychiatry*, 159: 135–141.

Ollendick, T.H., Yule, W. and Ollier, K. (1991) Fears in British children and their relationship to manifest anxiety and depression, *Journal of Child Psychiatry and Psychology*, 32: 321–331.

O'Neill, D., Neubauer, K., Boyle, M., Gerrard, J., Surmon, D. and Wilcock, G.K. (1992) Dementia and driving, *Journal of the Royal Society of Medicine*, 85: 199–202.

Orner, R.J., Lynch, T. and Seed, P. (1993) Long-term traumatic stress reactions in British Falklands war veterans, *British Journal of Clinical Psychology*, 32 (4): 457–459.

Oswald, W.D. and Roth, E. (1987) *Der Zahlenverbindungstest (ZVY)*, Göttingen: Dr C.J. Hogrefe.

Parker, D., Manstead, A.S.R., Stradling, S.G. and Reason, J.T. (1992a) Determinants of intention to commit driving violations, *Accident Analysis and Prevention*, 24: 117–131.

————— ————— ————— (1992b) Intention to commit driving violations: an application of the Theory of Planned Behavior, *Journal of Applied Psychology*, 77: 94–101.

Parry, G. (1990) *Coping with crisis*, London: Routledge.

Paton, D. (1989) Disaster and helpers: psychological dynamics and implications for counselling, *Counselling Psychology Quarterly*, 2: 303–321.

Pearson, Lord (Chairman) (1978) *Report of the Royal Commission on Civil Liability and Compensation for Personal Injury*, (3 vols), Cmnd. 7054, London: HMSO.

Peck, C. (1985) *Controlling Chronic Pain*, London: Collins/Fontana.

Peterson, K.C., Prout, M. and Schwarz, R.A. (1991) *Post-Traumatic Stress Disorder: A Clinician's Guide*, London: Plenum Press.

Petty, R.E. and Cacioppo, J.T. (1986a) *Communication and Persuasion: Central and Peripheral Routes to Attitude Change*, New York: Springer Verlag.

————— ————— (1986b) The elaboration likelihood model of persuasion, in L. Berkowitz (ed.), *Advances in Experimental Social Psychology*, vol. 19, San Diego: Academic Press, 123–205.

Pilowsky, I. (1985) Cryptotrauma and 'accident neurosis', *British Journal of Psychiatry*, 147: 310–311.

Pless, I.B., Peckham, C.S. and Power, C. (1989) Predicting traffic injuries in childhood: a cohort analysis, *Journal of Paediatrics*, 115: 932–938.

Povlishock, J.T. and Coburn, T.H. (1989) Morphopathological change associated with mild head injury, in H.S. Levin, H.M. Eisenberg and A.L. Benton (eds), *Mild Head Injury*, New York: Oxford University Press, 37–53.

Prior, L. (1985) The good, the bad and the unnatural: a study of coroner's decisions in Northern Ireland, *The Sociological Review*, 33 (1): 64–90.

Putnam, S.H. and Millis, S.R. (1994) The Recognition Memory Test in the assessment of memory impairment after financially compensable mild head injury: a replication, *Peripheral and Motor Skills*, 79 (2): 384–386.

Pynoos, R.S. and Eth, S. (1986) Witness to violence: the child interview, *Journal of the American Academy of Child Psychiatry*, 25: 306–319.

—— and Nader, K. (1988) Psychological first aid and treatment approach for children exposed to community violence: research implications, *Journal of Traumatic Stress*, 1: 243–267.

—— —— (1993) Issues in the treatment of posttraumatic stress in children and adolescents, in J.P. Wilson and B. Raphael (eds.), *International Handbook of Traumatic Stress Syndromes*, New York: Plenum Press, 535–549.

—— Frederick, C., Nader, K., Arroyo, W., Steinberg, A., Eth, S., Nunez, F. and Fairbanks, L. (1987) Life threat and posttraumatic stress in school-age children, *Archives of General Psychiatry*, 44: 1057–1063.

Radanov, B.P., Di Stefano, G., Schnidrig, A. and Ballinari, P. (1991) Role of psychosocial stress in recovery from common whiplash, *The Lancet*, 338: 712–715.

—— —— —— and Sturzenegger, M. (1993a) Cognitive functioning after common whiplash: a controlled follow-up study, *Archives of Neurology*, 50: 87–91.

—— —— —— —— and Aljinovic, M. (1993b) Factors influencing recovery from headache after common whiplash, *British Medical Journal*, 307: 652–655.

—— —— —— —— (1994a) Common whiplash – psychosomatic or somato-psychic? *Journal of Neurology, Neurosurgery, and Psychiatry*, 57: 486–490.

—— —— —— —— (1994b) Relationship between early somatic, radiological, cognitive and psychosocial findings and outcome during a one-year follow-up in 117 common whiplash patients, *British Journal of Rheumatology*, 33: 442–448.

—— —— and Sturzenegger, M. (1995) Long-term outcome after whiplash injury: a 2-year follow-up considering features of accident mechanism, somatic, radiological and psychosocial findings, *Medicine*, 74: 281–297.

Raphael, B. (1986) *When Disaster Strikes: A Handbook for Caring Professions*, London: Hutchinson Education.

—— Singh, B., Bradbury, L. and Lambert, F. (1984) Who helps the helpers? The effects of a disaster on the rescue workers, *Omega*, 14: 9–20.

—— Meldrum, L. and McFarlane, A.C. (1995) Does debriefing after psychological trauma work? Time for randomised controlled trials, *British Medical Journal*, 310: 1479–1480.

Reason, J., Manstead, A., Stradling, S., Baxter, J. and Campbell, K. (1990) Errors and violations on the roads: a real distinction? *Ergonomics*, 33: 1315–1332.

Reese, J.T. (1990) Justifications for mandating critical incident aftercare, in J.T. Reese, J.M. Horne and C. Dunning (eds.), *Critical Incidents in Policing*, Washington, DC: FBI.

Reitan, R.M. (1958) Validity of the trail making test as an indication of organic brain damage, *Perceptual and Motor Skills*, 8: 251–256.

Reynolds, C.R. and Richmond, B.O. (1978) What I think and feel: a revised measure of children's manifest anxiety, *Journal of Abnormal Child Psychology*, 6: 271–280.

Robinson, R.C., and Mitchell, J.T. (1993) Evaluation of psychological debriefings. *Journal of Traumatic Stress*, 6 (3): 367–382.

Rogers, R., Harrell, E.H., and Liff, C.D. (1993) Feigning neuropsychological impairment: a critical review of methodological and clinical considerations, *Clinical Psychology Review*, 13: 255–274.

—— Sewell, K.W., and Goldstein, A.M. (1994) Explanatory models of malingering: a prototypical analysis, *Law and Human Behavior*, 18: 543–552.

Romano, J.L. (1992) Legal issues in testimony about post-concussive syndrome: a matter of proof, in L.J. Horn and N.D. Zasler (eds), *Rehabilitation of Post-Concussive Disorders*, Philadelphia: Hanely and Belfus, 193–202.

Rosen, G.M. (1995) The *Aleutian Enterprise* sinking and posttraumatic stress disorder: misdiagnosis in clinical and forensic settings, *Professional Psychology: Research and Practice*, 26: 82–87.

Rosenstock, I.M. (1966) Why people use health services, *Millbank Memorial Fund Quarterly*, 44 (suppl.): 94–127.

Ross, H. Laurence, (1980) *Settled Out of Court: The Social Process of Insurance Claims Adjustment*, Chicago: Aldine.

Russell, W.R., and Smith, A. (1961) Post-traumatic amnesia and closed head injury, *Archives of Neurology*, 5: 16–29.

Rutherford, W., Greenfield, T., Hayes, H.R.M. and Nelson, J.K. (1986) *The medical effects of seat belt legislation in the United Kingdom*, DHSS Research Report No. 13, London: HMSO.

Rutter, D.R., Quine, L. and Chesham, D.J. (1993), *Social Psychological Approaches to Health*, Hemel Hempstead: Harvester Wheatsheaf.

—— —— —— (1995) Predicting safe riding behaviour and accidents: demography, beliefs and behaviour in motorcycling safety, *Psychology and Health*.

Saylor, C.R. (ed.) (1993) *Children and Disasters*, New York: Plenum Press.

Scott J. and Stradling S. (1992) *Counselling for Post-Traumatic Stress Disorder*, London: Sage.

Scottish Police College Training Notes (1991) Tulliallan, Kirkcaldy.

Severy, D.M., Mathewson, J.H., and Bechtol, C.O. (1955) Controlled automobile rear-end collisons, an investigation of related engineering and medical phenomena, *Canadian Services Medical Journal*, 11: 727–759.

Shalev, A.Y., Schreiber, S. and Galai, T. (1993) Early psychological responses to traumatic injury, *Journal of Traumatic Stress*, 6 (4): 441–449.

Silva, M.N. (1990) The delivery of mental health services to law enforcement officers, in J. T. Reese, J.M. Horn and C. Dunning (eds), *Critical Incidents in Policing*, Washington, DC: FBI.

Simpson, H.F. (1996) *Comparison of hospital and police casualty data: a national study*, Transport and Research Laboratory Report 173, Crowthorne, Berks: Transport and Road Research Laboratory.

Singh, B. and Raphael, B. (1981) Post disaster morbidity of the beareaved: a possible role for preventitive psychiatry?, *Journal of Nervous and Mental Disease*, 189: 203–212.

Singleton, G.W. (1978) Effects of job related stress on the physical and psychological adjustment of police officers, *Journal of Police Science and Administration*, 6: 355–361.

Slapper, G. (1993) Corporate manslaughter: an examination of the determinants of prosecutorial policy, *Social and Legal Studies*, 2: 423–443.

Smith, E.M., North, C.S., McCool, R. and Shea, J. (1990) Acute post-disaster pychiatric disorders: identification of persons at risk, *American Journal of Psychiatry*, 147: 202–206.

Snow, W.G. (1992) Implications of base rates for the diagnosis of malingering, poster presented at the International Neuropsychological Society Annual Meeting, San Diego.

Solomon, R.M. (1990) The dynamics of fear in critical incidents: implications for training and treatment, in J.T. Reese, J.M. Horn and C. Dunning (eds), *Critical Incidents in Policing*, Washington, DC: FBI.

Solomon, Z., Mikulineer, M. and Hobfall, S. (1987) Objective versus subjective measurement of stress and social support: combat-related reactions, *Journal of Consulting and Clinical Psychology*, 55: 577–583.

—— —— and Flum, H. (1988) Negative life events, coping responses and combat-related psychopathology: a prospective study, *Journal of Abnormal Psychology*, 97 (3): 302–307.

Spiegel, D., Hunt, T. and Dondershine, H.E. (1988) Dissociation and hypnotizability in posttraumatic stress disorder, *American Journal of Psychiatry*, 145 (3): 301–305.

Spielberger, C.D. (1983) *The State Trait Anxiety Questionnaire: A Comprehensive Bibliography*, Palo Alto, CA: Consultant Psychologists Press.

—— Gorsuch, R.L. and Lushene, R.E. (1970) *STAI Manual for the State-Trait Anxiety Inventory*, Palo Alto, CA: Consulting Psychologists Press.

Spitzer, R.L., Williams, J.B., Gibbon, M. and First, M.B. (1990a) Structured Clinical Interview for DSM-III-R, Non-patient Edition (SCID-NP) (Version 1.0), Washington, DC: American Psychiatric Press.

—— —— —— —— (1990b) Structured Clinical Interview for DSM-III-R Personality Disorders (SCID-II) (Version 1.0), Washington, DC: American Psychiatric Press.

SPSS Inc. (1988) *SPSS-X User's Guide*, Chicago: McGraw-Hill.

Stallard, P. and Law, F. (1993) Screening and psychological debriefing of adolescent survivors of life-threatening events, *British Journal of Psychiatry*, 163, 660–665.

Stambrook, M., Moore, A.D., Peters, L.C., Zubek, E., McBeath, S. and Friesen, C. (1991) Head injury and spinal cord injury: differential effects on psychosocial functioning, *Journal of Clinical and Experimental Neuropsychology*, 13: 521–530.

Stasson, M. and Fishbein, M. (1990) The relation between perceived risk and preventive action: a within-subject analysis of perceived driving risk and intentions to wear seatbelts, *Journal of Applied Social Psychology*, 20: 1541–1557.

Stevens, A.B., Roberts, M., McKane, R., Atkinson, A.B., Bell, P.M. and Randal Hayes, J. (1989) Motor vehicle driving among diabetics taking insulin and non-diabetics, *British Medical Journal*, 299: 591–595.

Stroebe, M., Stroebe, W. and Hansson, R.O. (1993) *Handbook of Bereavement*, New York: Cambridge University Press.

Sturzenegger, M., Radanov, B.P., and Di Stefano, G. (1995) The effect of accident mechanisms and initial findings on the long-term course of whiplash injury, *Journal of Neurology*, 242: 443–449.

Stuss, D.T., Ely, P., Hugenholtz, H., Richard, M.T., LaRochelle, S., Poirier, C.A. and Bell, I. (1985) Subtle neuropsychological deficits in patients with good recovery after closed head injury, *Neurosurgery*, 17: 41–47.

Sullivan, M.A., Saylor, C.F. and Foster, K.Y. (1991) Post-hurricane adjustment of preschoolers and their families, *Advances in Behaviour Research and Therapy*, 13: 163–171.

Sutton, S. and Hallett, R. (1989) Understanding seat-belt intentions and behavior: a decision-making approach, *Journal of Applied Social Psychology*, 19: 1310–1325.

Sweeney, J.E. (1992) Nonimpact brain injury: grounds for clinical study of the neuropsychological effects of acceleration forces, *The Clinical Neuropsychologist*, 6: 443–457.

Tate, R.L., Fenelon, B., Manning, M.L. and Hunter, M. (1991) Patterns of neuropsychological impairment after severe blunt head injury, *Journal of Nervous and Mental Disease*, 179: 117–126.

Taylor, J.S., Harp, J.H. and Elliott, T. (1992) Preparing the plaintiff in the mild brain injury case, *Trial Diplomacy Journal*, 15: 65–72.

Teasdale, G. and Jennett, B. (1974) Assessment of coma and impaired consciousness: a practical scale, *Lancet*, 2: 81–84.

Tegenthoff, M. and Malin, J.P. (1991) Das sogenannte Schleudertrauma der Halswirbelsäule. Anmerkungen aus neurologischer Sicht, *Deutsche medizinische Wochenschrift*, 116: 1030–1034.

Tenenbaum, J. (1979) *Self Help Groups in Welfare: A Victorian Perspective*, Melbourne: Victorian Council of Social Service.

Transport and Road Research Laboratory, Department of Transport (1980) *Permanent Disability in Road Traffic Accident Casualties*, Transport and Research Laboratory Report 924, Crowthorne, Berks: Transport and Road Research Laboratory.

—— (1986) Long-term disability following road traffic accidents, *Digest of Research*, Report 59, Crowthorne, Berks: Transport and Road Research Laboratory.

Tsui, E., Dagwell, K. and Yule, W. (n.d.) Effect of a disaster on children's academic attainment, unpublished report.

Tunbridge, R.J., Everest, J.T., Wild, B.R. and Johnstone, R.A. (1988) An in-depth study of road accident casualties and their injury patterns, *Digest of Research*, Report 136, Crowthorne, Berks: Transport and Road Research Laboratory.

—— Murray, P.A., Kinsella, A.M. and Galasko, C.S.B. (1990) The cost of long-term disability resulting from road accidents: interim report, *Contractors report 212*, London: Department of Transport (Transport and Road Research Laboratory), HMSO.

Turnbull, G., Neal, L.A., Busuttil, W., Rollins, J. and Strike, P. (1994) Convergent validity of measures of post-traumatic stress disorder in a mixed military and civilian population, *Journal of Traumatic Stress*, 7 (3): 447–455.

van der Kolk, B.A. and McFarlane, A.C. (1996) Trauma and the challenge to society, in B. van der Kolk, A.C. McFarlane and L. Weisaeth (eds) *Traumatic Stress: The Effects of Overwhelming Experience on Mind, Body and Society*, New York: Guilford.

—— and van der Hart, O. (1989) Pierre Janet and the breakdown of adaptation in psychological trauma, *American Journal of Psychiatry*, 146 (12): 1530–1540.

van Zomeren, A.H., and Brouwer, W.H. (1990) Attentional deficits after closed head injury, in B.G. Deelman, R.J. Saan, and A.H. van Zomeren (eds), *Traumatic Brain Injury: Clinical, Social and Rehabilitational Aspects*, Amsterdam: Swets and Zeitlinger, 33–48.

Vic Roads (1995) *Road Traffic Casualties*, Melbourne: Vic Roads Information Services Department.

Victim Support Scheme (1993) *Assisting the Victims of Serious Crime*, London: National Association of Victim Support Schemes.

Volunteer Centre of Victoria Inc. (1994) Principles of volunterring, *Annual Report 1993/1994*.

von Zerssen, D. (1983) Self-rating scales in the evaluation of psychiatric treatment, in T. Helgason (ed.) *Methodology in Evaluation of Psychiatric Treatment*, Cambridge: Cambridge University Press.

Waller, N.G. (1994) Types of dissociation and dissociative types, *Proceedings of the International Society of Traumatic Stress Studies Conference*, Paris.

Watson, M.R., Fenton, G.W., McClelland, R.J., Lumsden, J., Headley, M. and

Rutherford, W.H. (1995) The post-concussional state: neurophysiological aspects, *British Journal of Psychiatry*, 167: 514–521.

Wechsler, D. 91945) A standardized memory scale for clinical use, *Journal of Psychology*, 19: 87–95.

Webb, G.R., Sanson-Fisher, R.W. and Bowman, J.A. (1988) Psychosocial factors related to parental restraint of pre-school children in motor vehicles, *Accident Analysis and Prevention*, 20: 94–97.

Wetter, M.W. and Corrigan, S.K. (1995) Providing information to clients about psychological tests: a survey of attorneys' and law students' attitudes, *Professional Psychology: Research and Practice*, 26: 474–477.

Wheatley, J. and Cass, D.T. (1989) Traumatic deaths in children: the importance of prevention, *Medical Journal of Australia*, 150: 72–78.

Wickström, J., Martinez, J. and Rodriguez, R. (1967) Cervical sprain syndrome and experimental acceleration injuries of the head and neck, in M.L. Selzer, P.W. Gikas, and D.F. Huelke (eds) *Proceedings of Prevention of Highway Accidents Symposium*, Ann Arbor: University of Michigan.

Williams, R., Joseph, S. and Yule, W. (1992) Disaster and mental health, in J. Leff and D. Bhugra (eds), *Principles of Social Psychiatry*, Oxford: Blackwell Scientific, 450–469.

Wilson, J.P. and Raphael, B. (1993) *International Handbook of Traumatic Stress Syndromes*, New York: Plenum Press.

Wilson, J.T.L., Hadley, D.M., Wiedmann, K.D. and Teasdale, G.M. (1995) Neuropsychological consequences of two patterns of brain damage disclosed by MRI in survivors of severe head injury, *Journal of Neurology, Neurosurgery, and Psychiatry*, 59: 328–331.

—— —— Scott, L.C., and Harper, A. (1996) The neuropsychological significance of contusional lesions identifed by MR imaging, in B.P. Uzzell and H.H. Stonnington (eds), *Recovery after Traumatic Brain Injury*, Hillsdale, NJ: Lawrence Erlbaum.

Wittenbraker, J., Gibbs, B.L. and Kahle, L.R. (1983) Seat belt attitudes, habits, and behaviors: an adaptive amendment to the Fishbein model, *Journal of Applied Social Psychology*, 13: 406–421.

World Health Organization (1978) *Mental Disorders: Glossary and Guide to their Classification in accordance with the 9th Revision of the International Classification of Diseases*, Geneva: World Health Organization.

—— (1992) *International Classification of Diseases: 10th Edition (ICD-10)*, Geneva: World Health Organization.

Wortman, C.B. and Silver, R.C. (1989) The myths of coping with loss, *Journal of Consulting and Clinical Psychology*, 57 (3): 349–357.

Youngjohn, J.R. (1995) Confirmed attorney coaching prior to neuropsychological evaluation, *Assessment*, 2: 279–283.

—— Burrows, L. and Erdal, K. (1995a) Brain damage or compensation neurosis? The controversial post-concussive syndrome, *The Clinical Neuropsychologist*, 9: 112–123.

—— Davis, D.A. and Wolf, I. (1995b) Effects of head injury severity and litigation on the MMPI-2, unpublished paper.

Yule, W. (1991) Work with children following disasters, in M. Herbert (ed.), *Clinical Child Psychology: Social Learning, Development and Behaviour*, Chichester: John Wiley, 349–363.

—— (1992) Post traumatic stress disorder in child survivors of shipping disasters: the sinking of the *Jupiter, Journal of Psychotherapy and Psychosomatics*, 57 (4): 200–205.

—— (1993) Technology related disasters, in C.F. Saylor (ed.), *Children and Disasters*, New York: Plenum, 105–121.

—— and Udwin, O. (1991) Screening child survivors for post-traumatic stress disorders: experiences from the *Jupiter* sinking, *British Journal of Clinical Psychology*, 30: 131–138.

—— —— and Murdoch, K. (1990) The *Jupiter* sinking: effects on children's fears, depression and anxiety, *Journal of Child Psychology and Psychiatry*, 31: 1051–1061.

Index